MEDIA
in
Church and Mission
Communicating the Gospel

Viggo Søgaard

William Carey Library

Pasadena, California

Published by
William Carey Library
P.O. box 40129
Pasadena, California 91114
(818) 798-0819

Library of Congress Cataloging-in-Publication Data

Søgaard, Viggo
    Media in church and mission : communicating the Gospel / by Viggo
Søgaard
        p.   cm.
    Includes bibliographical references and Index
    ISBN 0-87808-242-5 (pbk.)
    1. Communication—Religious aspects—Christianity. 2. Mass
media—Religious aspects—Christianity. I. Title.
    BV4319.S645 1993   93-24029
    254'.3—dc20   CIP

Printed in the United States of America

Contents

List of Figures

FOREWORD

In the early 1970s God brought an interesting group of people from around the world to the Wheaton College Graduate School. By the end of that decade, fresh thinking began to permeate the ranks of Christian communicators worldwide.

Among those pioneers was a renegade marketing professor (this writer) who decided to forsake the safe havens of Ohio State University to apply the analytical rigor of his profession to the work of God's Kingdom. Another who appeared on the scene was a Danish media missionary to Thailand, a man who was thinking in most unconventional ways (the author of this book).

That was the beginning of a lifelong partnership between Viggo Søgaard and myself. While there was a student/professor relationship at the beginning, there was an immediate "iron sharpening iron" professional synergism which continues to this day.

From the outset the two of us were motivated by the apparent lack of results in world evangelization, in spite of enormous investments in Christian communication efforts. As the author puts it in his first chapter, "... ill-conceived assumptions and outdated approaches have resulted in ineffective outreach and in inconsistent and sporadic applications of communication strategy." That fact was especially evident in Christian use of mass media, and this condition continues even to this day.

There now is a large and growing rank of Christian communication professionals who have and continue to challenge these "ill-conceived assumptions" from a variety of theological, theoretical, and strategic perspectives. Viggo Søgaard has played a major role as a practitioner, trainer, and consultant in helping to stimulate a wave of fresh thinking which now is permeating the grassroots worldwide.

In this short manual, Søgaard offers a highly readable and practical synthesis of what has been learned through this new wave of thinking over the years. His thesis is a simple one—*we cannot communicate effectively and create understanding unless we take the audience seriously.* If this is not done, well-intended Christian communication will be avoided, misunderstood, or ignored. If there still are skeptics regarding this foundational premise, this book should dispel all doubt about what has come to be known as "receptor-oriented communication."

Søgaard begins with the solid theological premise that God is a communicator and shows systematically what this means in concept, strategy, and practice. While he demonstrates excellent grasp of contemporary theory and communication strategy in the secular world, the author has skillfully avoided what I am calling the *marketing pitfall*.

Too many today are borrowing uncritically from the world of secular marketing and seem to be blithely unaware that the gospel is not a consumer product to be sold persuasively to a waiting world. There is a great temptation to be so focused on felt needs that the gospel ceases being the narrow way and becomes, instead, a broad way to human fulfillment. Unless real caution is exercised, masses are attracted and churches become filled with those to whom Christianity is only a veneer over an otherwise secular life.

Søgaard succeeds in driving home the sometimes forgotten point that strategies, no matter how skillfully they are conceived, are destined to failure unless it is fully recognized that the Holy Spirit is the ultimate persuader. There is, in short, a mysterious interworking between strategies and the ministry of the Holy Spirit. An imbalance on either side of this equation is untenable.

The majority of the chapters offer practical insights into how such media as audio cassettes, radio, film, and television can, if properly used, play an important role in conversion and spiritual growth. But the author never loses sight of the fact that the single most important medium is face-to-face communication in the context of the local Christian fellowship.

Therefore, Søgaard has little tolerance for media barrages which are not integrated with the efforts of the local church. He drives home from both a theological and strategic perspective the foundational truth that the Great Commission quickly can be reduced to the "great commotion," a barren advertising campaign, if we lose sight of this foundational principle.

Another major premise of this book is that communication effectiveness never can be assumed, no matter how much we pray—it must be documented through a conscious and continuing emphasis on research. While he can at times sound very secular in the practical counsel which is provided, this is nothing more than good old-fashioned stewardship.

Unfortunately the two of us still find far too much wishful thinking on this dimension of communication stewardship. If we were to combine the annual claims about the numbers who have been "reached" in a given year, the total would probably exceed the total population of the world. No one who takes this book seriously will fall into this indefensible and often heretical thinking.

As you may notice from footnotes, the author often honors me by citing my earlier writing, some of which are now out-of-print. Many have urged me to update these sources, and there are times when I feel guilty for not having done so. Now my guilt is ended. Viggo Søgaard has ably met that need, and it is with great joy that I adopt this book for my own use around the world and recommend it wholeheartedly to others. It is my hope that it will quickly make its way onto the book shelf and, more importantly, into the ministry of all who take world evangelization seriously.

James F. Engel
August 31, 1992

James F. Engel is Director of the Center for Organizational Excellence at Eastern College, St. Davids, Pennsylvania, USA. He also serves as Distinguished Professor of Marketing in its graduate programs in economic development and holistic ministry.

ACKNOWLEDGMENTS

A book such as this one contains a mosaic of ideas, experiences, and principles learned through years of experience and through interaction with books, teachers, and students. Some ideas may be original to me, but others have germinated in other minds, then shaped and reworked, tested and proven, and here presented in a way that fits with the principles and purposes of this book. A set of acknowledgments will therefore never be complete. Nevertheless, there are some who deserve special thanks and must be mentioned.

First, I would like to express my gratitude to the two mentors I have had in my graduate studies, Dr. James F. Engel and Dr. Charles H. Kraft. They have influenced my thinking and helped shape the content of this book. Both of them have been colleagues in the ministry around the world, and both are close friends.

Next, I would like to express thanks to my son, Kim, who has spent many hours preparing illustrations for this book. His careful attention to detail and his creative care with the drawing pen has helped to make illustrations communicate the intended message.

Thanks also to the many colleagues and students I have had the privilege of interacting with through the Asian Institute of Christian Communication, in Thailand as well as around Asia and other parts of the world. This has been study, lab, practice, consultation, and evaluation all brought together to develop new ways of communicating the gospel.

Similarly, faculty and students at Fuller School of World Mission have helped to keep the focus on mission. The dynamics of a classroom with key church and mission leaders from all over the world has been a challenge to be constantly on the cutting edge.

I am grateful to colleagues in the United Bible Societies who during the last few years have joined together to find new ways of communicating the Good News to all people, including the many who have not had the privilege of learning to read.

To the many friends and fellow servants of our Lord who have in some way contributed to this book, I give my sincere thanks. To those who should have been acknowledged in the text or in footnotes, but have been omitted due to error or lack of information on my behalf, I give my apologies. My primary purpose for writing this book has been to provide a tool that will assist Christian workers in achieving more effective communication.

Viggo Søgaard

xiv

INTRODUCTION

It was a day of joy when Leung Kaew and his teenage daughter were baptized. The small church in Bannoi village had not seen many new believers during recent years. Adding to that, Lung Kaew was well after a serious illness. Actually, it was his sickness that had started it all. The villagers had brought him to the Christian hospital, almost giving up hope for his recovery. While Lung Kaew was in hospital, he listened daily to a radio program over the hospital loudspeakers. Somehow these programs appealed to him with a sense of peace and joy.

One day he decided to speak to one of the nurses about his interest in the programs. She readily answered his questions, and also mentioned that the hospital evangelist had some cassettes he could borrow. He gladly accepted this offer, and for days he listened to cassettes with Bible teaching, Christian songs, questions and answers. Discussions with the evangelist helped him further. When the day came for his return to the village, he invited the evangelist to come and visit.

The evangelist brought a few other Christians along, as well as a Christian film, and during one such visit Leung Kaew and his daughter pledged their allegiance to Jesus and received new life from him. The local church did not have a pastor, but Leung Kaew was helped by a correspondence course and more teaching cassettes as well as fellowship in the church. And now, a public witness through baptism was followed by a festive time of praise and eating together. The gospel of Jesus Christ had been communicated faithfully, using a variety of media and methods, and Leung Kaew and his daughter had understood and received Christ.

Communication—Evangelism—Media

These words hang together in Christian ministry. Evangelism is the activity involved in bringing the gospel of Jesus Christ to people who have not yet heard or do not yet follow Christ. Evangelism involves communication. Indeed it could be argued that evangelism is communication. The Christian religion itself is a religion of communication with a communicator God who has utilized a wide variety of media. The Bible is a narrative of this communication of God to mankind: through creation, through the prophets, through "His mighty acts," through his Son Jesus Christ, through the Holy Spirit and through his people, the Church. The message of Christ should be communicated to all people in the world, and the media can play important roles as instruments of this ministry.

During my years of involvement in Christian ministry my main responsibility has been one of communication. As much of the time was spent in Thailand, it has been a constant challenge to be effective in communication among a people with a drastically different worldview. It is a country with a small and weak church, made up of less than 1% of the population, a people with low cognitive awareness of the Christian gospel and where misunderstandings are easy to come by. The challenge of communicating the basics of the Christian gospel to the people of Thailand led me into the use of media in ministry, concentrating mainly on two media: radio and audio cassettes. As we struggled to use these media effectively, we were "forced" into a serious study of communication theory and strategy. Through further studies, research projects, consultations and seminars this interest has been sharpened, and so has my belief in the potential of the "tools" we have available for Christian communication.

During my years as a missionary, using modern communications media, I was often astonished by the fact that so little help could be obtained from written materials. As we experimented with new ideas, we had to learn our own lessons. Around the world this lack of good textbooks has resulted in much Christian media work that seem to function without any clear understanding of the process of communication, without relevant media understanding, and without effective research and information systems.

Later, as a consultant, it has been my experience that Christian workers need much help in making media-based ministries effective. We know from examples and experiments, and from a considerable body of research material, that media can be used effectively in the cause of mission and that help can be provided to those engaged in such ministries. And also to pastors and church leaders who want their churches to grow and to communicate effectively in the communities where they are placed.

Our God, the Communicator

Help is also needed in the area of biblical theology. Christianity presupposes that God exists and that he has created this world. He is the One who revealed his name as *Yahweh, I Am*, to Moses (Exod. 3:14). As Christians we believe in him, and that he has revealed himself to us in the person of Jesus Christ (John 3:16). From present day analysis in Western countries we know that many people state that they believe in "God,"[1] but further in-depth research indicates that this belief is to a large extent not in a personal, living God, but in some cosmic power. Communicators need to learn how to communicate the concept of one living God to people in a confused world. Consequently, we need to emphasize the "Christian" aspect of our communication, and coupled with that, the authority of the Bible as the Word of God. The Bible contains the message we are to proclaim as well as methods and guidance on how to communicate that message.

The one eternal God, Creator and Lord of the world, is also the God who loves all people, and he has consistently been calling people to himself. Familiar Scripture texts speak of this: "For God so loved the world that he gave his only son ..." (John 3:16), and he "demonstrated this love by letting Christ die for us while we were yet sinners" (Rom. 5:8). We could also quote the first of the well-known four spiritual laws used by Campus Crusade for Christ: "God loves you and has a wonderful plan for your life."

There is a potential greatness in all human beings. We may often be blinded by the evil we see exhibited through the media, but we should not forget that God said, "Let us make man in our image, after our likeness" (Gen. 1:26). A person who is created in the image of God has dignity and a tremendous potential for greatness, irrespective of his or her race, color, culture, or class. The Bible refers to human beings with terms such as "heirs of the kingdom," "priests," and "kings" (1 Pet. 2:9-10). This potential of human beings is achieved through fellowship with Christ, and is made possible through the indwelling Spirit.

The Church, the Communicators

Christ commissioned the church to carry his mission to the ends of the earth (Matt. 28:18-20; Acts 1:8). This is primarily a communication task and the resulting mission aims at enhancing or restoring communication between human persons and God. But, the church has often failed to understand and practice such communication.

Through the years, there have been very few church documents or statements on communication, but during the last few years various attempts have been made and an increasing number of documents are being published.[2] In our attempt to discover what the church says about communication, we should not forget, though, that what is *said* is not half as important as what the church *does* about communication. The most profound statement on communication will have little influence if we fail in our communication practice.

As we look at the effectiveness of mission, we are often stunned by the fact that in spite of enormous resources committed to the task, there seem to be but meagre results. Ill-conceived assumptions and outdated approaches have resulted in ineffective outreach and in inconsistent and sporadic applications of communication strategy. In no area is this more evident than in the use of media. There are, to be true, outstanding examples of effective media applications, but often we meet striking examples of ineffectiveness and consequently a waste of resources.

Even though Christian use of media is big business, the research situation is bleak. Hundreds of millions of dollars are used, but there has been very little in-depth study of the effects, and controlled experiments are rarely carried out. This is in sharp contrast to secular use of media, where huge sums of money are used on research, and where a significant body of material is available. Million-dollar Christian organizations still operate without adequate research support, and the available statistics regarding their operations are often totally erratic or misleading in relation to audience and effects. For example, potential audience size is quoted rather than actual audience size. One television program will claim millions of viewers, when secular ratings will indicate that much less than one million of the potential audience actually view the program. A radio organization will state that they have 200,000 listeners because they receive 200 letters a month. Or, a literature organization claims a potential readership of 125 million for their books. They don't mention that about 85% of that "potential" readership cannot read.

There is, however, no lack of criticism of Christian communication. For example, Virginia Stem Owens, in her book *The Total Image*, lashes out at one aspect—the so-called Electronic Church in the United States. She contends that due to accommodation, the results have often been "ridiculous, absurd, and sometimes heretical." Quoting Marshall McLuhan she adds, "it is not time to suggest strategies, when the threat has not even been acknowledged to exist."[3] The distinguished journalist, producer and television personality Malcolm Muggeridge states that "It's very nearly impossible to tell the truth in television. ..."[4] He further contends that Jesus would have rejected an offer for free time on television, treating it as a fourth temptation.[5] Though there is some truth in such pessimistic proclamations, I believe such an attitude is unacceptable as our final conclusion in a time when media use is increasingly critical and desperately needed. The fact that prestigious critics hold such pessimistic opinions should, however, challenge us to carefully evaluate the effectiveness of media in Christian communication, and to seriously engage in research and development of effective methods of media utilization.

It is important that the urgency of the problem be understood by both church and parachurch groups who are committed to the use of media. One of the problems is that the lack of a proper understanding of the communication process on the part of Christian communicators has often resulted in a "program orientation" with little concern for the needs of the receptor. An inadequate media understanding, furthermore, results in "media orientation." And the lack of understanding of cooperation in a total, integrated strategy has led to piece-meal applications. There is a need for serious thinking, experimentation and cooperation leading to more effective applications of media.

It is estimated that there still are 3,000,000,000 people who have not yet heard the gospel in a meaningful way, so the communication challenge facing the church is an enormous task and the problems may seem insurmountable. But at the same time, we have today—at our disposal—more resources to accomplish the task than ever before. As James F. Engel and Wilbert H. Norton have observed, "There is no absence of harvesting equipment or potential workers."[6] How, then, should the church announce the Good News to the poor in this era of communication?

There is a Way for Communicators

If effectiveness is to be achieved, we are forced to ask ourselves some hard questions. How can media be used by a local church or a mission agency to reach people with the Good News and to build them in the faith? Is it possible to harness the mass media to effective evangelism? Can guidelines be worked out that will assist mission leaders, as they are confronted with the task of world evangelization? Can we really reach the vast non-reading groups? A thorough investigation and treatment of the subject is needed.

As Christian communicators we have to overcome a suspicion of words like theory and strategy. The insights of such disciplines can help us overcome the naive position that if we send the gospel out on the airwaves or print a book or tract, God will make people listen or read and understand. Such a perspective has often resulted in arbitrary programming and production policies and ineffective distribution campaigns.

During the last few years, writers have, from an anthropological point of view, done significant studies in communication theory and its importance to world mission.[7] Others have attacked the problem from behavioral and sociological perspectives.[8] Many have been written from a church growth perspective. A new understanding of the Christian communication process has resulted and such insights are available for us today.

We have, among other things, learned that communication is a process, not just an event. Or, we could say, it is a process of events. Each event will add a new part to the picture. In order to be effective in communication, we must conceptualize the process and develop strategies that are geared to that same process. For the church, such insights challenge our strategies, and force us to develop new strategies in cooperation with other organizations working in the same area and among the same people. There is, fortunately, also in some quarters a new interest in and understanding of research. As new data is available, new lessons are learned concerning media applications.

So the possibilities for applied communication theory can be utilized if we bring the practitioners and the theorists together as the two must meet in applied communication. This is already happening through such programs as those offered by Wheaton Graduate School, Daystar University College in Nairobi, Asian Institute of Christian Communication (AICC), and Fuller Seminary School of World Mission in California. Significant changes in ministries have been seen as students—practitioners—are given tools of theory and strategy. In recognition of these facts, groups such as the Lausanne Committee for World Evangelization have recently set themselves to both increase the understanding of Christian groups who use media and to encourage mutual concern between the churches and Christian communicators. The formation of the International Christian Media Commission[9] (ICMC) is also a positive step in this direction. We have examples of situations where communications media have been integrated into wholistic ministries, and the effects have often been striking.[10]

Media resources are available and must be widely used by the church in effective mission. The following chapters are written for those who want to make it happen.

FOOTNOTES

1 Research conducted by the British and Foreign Bible Society in the city of Swindon is a good example of such research.

2 "Media Development." *Journal of the World Association of Christian Communication.* London: WACC. 1984.

3 Virginia Stem Owens, *The Total Image, or Selling Jesus in the Modern Age.* Grand Rapids: Eerdmans. 1980.

4 Malcolm Muggeridge, *Christ and the Media.* London: Hodder and Stoughton. 1977:106.

5 Ibid., p.23ff.

6 James F. Engel, and Wilbert H. Norton, *What's Gone Wrong With the Harvest?* Grand Rapids: Zondervan. 1975:14.

7 Such as Eugene A. Nida, Marvin K. Mayers, Paul Hiebert and Charles Kraft.

8 Like James F. Engel and Em Griffin.

9 The ICMC was formed as a result of the International Christian Media Conference in Holland in 1987. It has an evangelical statement of faith as its theological base.

10 An example is the cassette project of World Vision India where significant results are seen for both development and evangelism.

SECTION I

FOUNDATIONAL PRINCIPLES FOR
USE OF MEDIA IN CHURCH AND MISSION

Introduction to Section I

The term communication has been understood differently by people, depending on their background and experience. For some, communication is fundraising, and for others it is publicity. For many, the word communication equals "media people." But even for the media people, the term is used differently. We therefore need to keep our perspective and involvement clear, and we can define four aspects of Christian communication involvement as it relates to media:

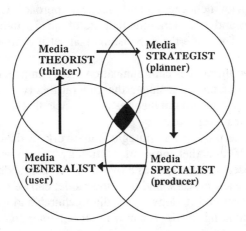

Figure 1.1. Dimensions of Christian Communication

All Christian media people must deal with these aspects of theory, strategic planning, production of good materials and programs, and the practice or use of communication materials.

Such a perspective requires both a wide cooperation and a wide variety of people with special areas of interest and gifts. There must be (1) the media theorists who study the theological, missiological, and theoretical basis for Christian use of the media. (2) We need the media strategists who can define and plan the use of a medium in the total context of a local church or some mission enterprise. (3) Then we need the artists and media specialists who can produce creative programs for the media, and (4) we need the media users or generalists who distribute and use the programs for a given audience. So, we must include among the media people the thinkers, the planners, the makers, and the users.

If we think of media people in these four categories, it will help us to appreciate one another and to utilize each others' skills and insights in the total program. In the following chapters we shall look at these different aspects, but we can from the very beginning see that Christian communication is a broad concern that overlaps the interests of many different kinds of people. To be effective in any one of the areas or categories, we need to have a working knowledge of the other areas. The producers and the broadcasters must, for example, also have a relevant and good understanding and appreciation of theory and principles if they are to be effective. And a local church pastor must have a basic understanding of communication and media, if he or she is to integrate or incorporate effective communication and media use into the work of the local church.

The following chapters will deal with aspects of communication that can provide us with a conceptual and practical approach. Chapter one deals with dimensions and considerations that are of special interest to Christian communication. These are the dimensions that set it apart from other areas of communication.

Chapter two introduces communication theory in general. As Christian communicators our theory includes the general theory of communication, and we need to understand the theories and models that help us conceptualize the communication process.

Chapter three provides a strategic framework. It deals with the topic of strategy itself, and then presents a strategy development model. The chapter also presents and discusses a two-dimensional model for illustrating the spiritual decision process, and how the model can be used in the development of an integrated strategy for media in church and mission.

Strategic thinking needs research input. Chapter four gives an introduction to the field of communication research and the methods and methodologies available to us for collecting the necessary information on the effective use of media in mission.

Finally, a summarizing chapter serves as an overview of the dimensions of effective Christian communication. It is based on the topics discussed in earlier chapters, and it can serve as an evaluation grid.

CHAPTER 1

Special Considerations for Christian Communication and Media Use

"What is Christian about Christian communication?" a friend asked recently. Another person, working as a journalist in the general media, suggested that there is no "Christian" communication as he contended that "communication is communication." If we are to be effective in the use of media in the Christian ministry, we need to come to grips with such issues and develop an adequate theoretical foundation for our work.

Christian communication has a number of special dimensions and is influenced by certain constant and variable factors that not only set it apart, but also make it superior to any other kind of communication.[1] This is primarily due to the fact that God is the God who communicates with mankind.[2] Communication is deeply rooted in God's nature, and it is this nature he imparted to humanity when he created us in his own image.[3] Communication is therefore not something accidental or supplementary for human beings, but it is the only way to be fully human. Furthermore, God has given us a mandate to communicate a message to others (Mt. 28:18-20).

Many problems encountered in the evangelistic and missionary enterprise of the church arise from the failure to distinguish between constant and variable factors. Constants are the basic, fundamental aspects that should always be kept in mind. Constant factors that never change include the commission to communicate, the opposing evil forces, and the work of the Spirit. Variables are factors that do change. They provide the environment of our communication and influence the form and the content that are relevant in any given time and situation.

The tendency is to confuse the constant and variable factors. Variables are often made constants and constants are often made variables. Our ministry is based on constants, but the methods of communication are primarily influenced by variable factors.

As most people feel uncertain about change, variable factors tend to constantly challenge our communication efforts, tempting us to make specific alternatives constants. But having the constant factors clear in our minds should relieve us of such temptations and help us make full use of the numerous alternatives provided by the variable factors.

1.1.   GOD IS A COMMUNICATOR

God is by nature a communicator. He "expressed" himself at the time of creation. He spoke, and things happened. He sought company with Adam, Abraham, Moses, and David. He let his Son live in a social context, and he leads his people into a warm community of believers. When looking at the way in which he communicates, we can learn significant lessons about Christian communication.

1.1.1.   God Makes Himself Known.

From the creation of the world God has been communicating (revealing) himself to humanity. Creation is one of the vehicles through which God speaks, and the Bible is the record of that communication. The Church is the living voice through which he continues to speak to the world.[4] In the Old Testament we see God communicating through acts and words, through the universe he created and through history as well as through special revelation. Israel knew God through their history.

> *Ever since God created the world, his invisible qualities, both his eternal power and his divine nature, have been clearly seen; they are perceived in the things that God has made (Rom. 1:20).*

> *The heavens are telling the glory of God; and the firmament proclaims his handiwork. Day to day pours forth speech, and night to night declares knowledge. There is no speech, nor are there words; their voice is not heard; yet their voice goes out through all the earth, and their words to the end of the world (Ps. 19:1-4).*

Sinai and the Red Sea are such acts of communication, where God sought to achieve communion with humans who, in turn, are also created with a capacity to hear and to comprehend his word.

In the New Testament, God reveals himself fully through his Son. In him God is present, incarnated.

> *The Word became a human being and, full of grace and truth, lived among us. We saw his glory, the glory which he received as the Father's only Son (John 1:14).*

In the past, God spoke to our ancestors many times and in many ways through the prophets, but in these last days he has spoken to us through his Son. He is the one through whom God created the universe, the one whom God has chosen to possess all things at the end. He reflects the brightness of God's glory and is the exact likeness of God's own being (Heb. 1:1-3a).

God has revealed himself to us through the Spirit. For the Spirit searches everything, even the depths of God (1 Cor. 2:10).

The incarnation of Jesus sets the stage for perfect communication between God and us. It is the climax of God's communication with us. As one translation puts it, "The Son is the radiance of God's glory and the exact representation of his being" (Heb. 1:3) and "the image of the invisible God" (Col. 1:15). When the disciples wanted to see the Father, Jesus said, in effect, "Look at me" (John 14:8ff). Jesus spoke the words the Father sent him to speak (John 3:34), and he carried out the work of the Father (John 10:37-38). The lesson for the Christian communicator is to be completely identified with the message preached.[5]

1.1.2. God Wants to be Understood.

God wants to be understood correctly so that the appropriate response can be obtained. He therefore uses communication symbols that are understood by us within our specific cultural contexts. He uses language, culture, and human form.[6] In his communication, he is not out to impress us, as we so often seem tempted to do in our sermons. In God's communication, the impressiveness is in the content of his message,[7] and not in the form or method of communication. Jesus might have been more impressive if he had spoken in Hebrew, or even in Greek, but he used Aramaic, the common language of the people so that they might understand. As an illustration we could say that he did not use a "King James Version" that would impress by its beautiful language, but a "common language translation" that was understood by the multitudes. Our Christian rituals and services may be very impressive, but do they communicate meaning to the average member of the congregation? God is teaching us that understanding must be our primary concern.

1.1.3. God Wants a Relationship.

The fall of humanity can be seen primarily as a breakdown in communication. When Adam ran away from God, he not only ran away from communion and dialogue with God, but he also caused a breakdown in other areas of communication.[8] Apart from a breakdown of communication with God, there was disruption within the person, peace was broken among people, and a breakdown of communication and relationship with the created universe (Gen. 3:8, 4:12, 6:5, 11:4, 3:17-20, 4:11,14). But God yearns to be known and this yearning makes him wrestle with Israel again and again. He yearns to be in a true relationship with each one of us.

It may be puzzling to us that God seeks relationship with us. But he does. He didn't have to look for Adam. He didn't have to choose Abraham or his descendants. He didn't have to work with David, nor did he have to call you and me. But he did. He taught us to seek relationships with those we try to reach.

1.1.4. God Wants a Response.

God does not seem to be happy with a passive response but seeks an interactive relationship. In dealing with us, he uses a variety of methods to achieve an active response. It may be a question, as with Adam. Jesus told parables where the listeners became players in a drama. An active response to God implies commitment. Kraft suggests that this commitment has at least three dimensions:[9] (a) as the head of the church, Christ commits himself to us, his body (Eph. 5:24-25) and we, in turn, are to respond by commitment to him, our head. (b) As members of a body, God desires that we commit ourselves to each other (1 Cor. 12:12ff; Eph. 5:21). (c) God intends that we share his commitment with the world at large (John 21:21). He wants us to understand that his intention is to have such a deep relationship with us.

1.1.5. The Incarnation is His Primary Method.

When we look at God's incarnation, we are looking at the center of communication[10] and the essential essence of communication theory. By this action God was bending down[11] to disclose himself through ordinary situations of human life, thus becoming completely relevant to the context of human beings. He did it at a particular time in history and through one particular culture. By studying this incarnational communication of God, we will not refute human communication, but discover the key that can redeem or restore the human communication process.[12]

The incarnation is then the ideal model of communication. It is the crowning event in which all other forms of God's communication with humanity are embodied.[13] Communication through incarnation is being involved in a context, entering into the real problems, issues, and struggles of the people. Jesus did not just speak to the Jews, but he became a Jew and identified himself with all aspects of Jewish life. He identified with the social outcasts, and participated in the social relationships of the Jewish culture. He became a true human being, even working as a carpenter. He spoke to their particular needs, rather than presenting a message of universal abstracts.

Through this example of Christ, we are challenged to go beyond mere oral proclamation and to re-enact or represent the Word in fullness to the world. This calls for new interpretations, new themes, and new actions as the Word permeates new cultures.

1.2. A COMMISSION TO COMMUNICATE

As Christian communicators we are entering into the ministry which has been God's concern through the ages: revealing himself to humanity. This commission to communicate permeates all aspects of Christian ministry, and it is the motivational force for commitment and dedication. This "communication for a purpose" is always present in Scripture. God communicated himself to the prophets and then commissioned them to be his communicators to others. He communicated himself—in fullness— through the Son and then commissioned the Son to a ministry (Heb. 1:1-3). Christ communicated with the apostles and then commissioned them as communicators (Mt. 28:18-20). Today those who have experienced his revelation are called to be his ambassadors representing and communicating him in the world (2 Cor. 5:20). How well the church has lived up to, or failed to live up to, the commission given by Christ is clearly evident in the world today. The great majority of the earth's population have yet to become followers of Jesus Christ.

1.2.1. Our Task is Communication.

Communication is implied in the words of John 20:21, "As the Father has sent me, so I send you." Christ is sending us to represent him, and to communicate him by his standards and his methods.

The Great Commission was not intended for the apostles alone, though they were "the keepers of this priority" (Acts 1:2). I believe that this missionary command was given to the whole church as well as to all its individual members (Rom. 1:5) to the end of the church age. The very essence, nature, and doctrine of the church contains this missionary mandate, but by specifically stating the command (or the commission), our Lord focused sharply on the missionary responsibility of the church.

The church has not always understood the implications and responsibilities inherent in this commission, and has often failed to communicate the message to others. The pulpit in one of the cathedrals in Denmark has inscribed in Latin—and with Gothic characters—the quote from Luke 11:28, "Blessed are those who hear the Word of God and keep it." The Latin word, which we translate "keep," is "custodiunt." This leads our thoughts to the word "custodian," a person who looks after artifacts in a museum or other buildings. The church has often treated the Word of God that way: kept it for ourselves. In the biblical understanding we "keep" the living Word of God by communicating it to others.

Central to the Christian communication process is the use of words, but just because a person listens to certain words does not guarantee that he or she understands the words the same way as the speaker and that the true meaning is achieved. Words in themselves have no magic, and they can be compared to freight cars in which we load content and words to which we associate meaning. Just because a person says that he believes in God does not necessarily mean that he believes in God, the creator of the universe and the Father of our Lord Jesus Christ. It may signify a belief in some kind of cosmic force, or even in self. The Buddhist will use many of the same terms and words as the Christian, but with drastically different meanings and connotations. The Muslim will be closer to the Christian understanding, but again different meanings are associated with the same words.

The implications for the pastor of a local church, as well as for the radio speaker, will be to study the use of words and the connotations that the congregation and listeners associate with the words. We need to choose the words that will create the right meaning in their minds. Otherwise, communication will be a wishful dream rather than a reality. And communication breakdown between the church and modern men and women will hinder those people in getting to know God.[14]

1.2.2. Our Method of Communication.

God achieved his communicational goals through love. He is a true lover,[15] and he demonstrated that to be a true lover is to have as our primary concern the needs of the receptors without considering the cost to ourselves.[16] In other words, God's approach is receptor-oriented communication. Such an approach demands a high respect for the receptors (the audience), a trust in them as persons created in the image of God, and even making ourselves vulnerable in our communication. It also means entering totally into the context of the audience, using their language and frame of reference. In his incarnation, Jesus showed us the perfect example of such an approach.

Many Christians believe that preaching is God's ordained means of communicating the gospel to others. Furthermore, we often believe that the sermon is an effective method of bringing about a change in people's lives. But if this were so, then we would expect that it would be impossible for people to listen to hundreds of sermons with no apparent change in their lives. Monologue preaching is useful for certain purposes, and the intention here is not to downgrade the importance of preaching in the church. But we do have a problem with the word "preach." The most frequent biblical term translated "preaching" is the Greek word *kerusso*.[17] The word *kerusso* was used to refer to town criers or special announcements, and it was used for both monologue lectures as well as dialogues. Today, a much more appropriate and accurate word to use for translating the word *kerusso* would be simply to use the word "communicate." We would then read Mark 16:15b as, "Go throughout the whole world and communicate the Gospel. ..." For Jesus it was not just a matter of monologue preaching, but incarnation and life involvement among the people with whom he communicated. Such an approach demands commitment to the people and to their cultural environment and at the same time forces us to work for dialogue instead of monologue.

The implications of such a position are far-reaching for Christian communicators. We need to consider questions such as: Have we devoted enough time to reflection on what the gospel is for the context we are communicating to? Have we devoted all our efforts on refining the packaging without examining the product? Is it legitimate to broadcast Bible studies produced in Europe or America on radio stations all around Asia and Africa and argue that the one gospel has been faithfully communicated to all these cultures?

We could also ask, should Christian programs and literature not concentrate more on sharing what Christians do in the local contexts in obedience to Christ rather than producing abstract universal messages about what we believe? Should communication ministries be more integrally related with the witness of the church in a given country? Should those who produce programs be vitally involved in the practical ministry of the churches? Should programs themselves not reflect more of the actual ministry of the churches in their context?

1.2.3. Our Communication Message.

The essential content of all aspects of evangelism is Bible teaching, centering around Jesus Christ. The message of the Bible is addressed to all humanity, and through it the Holy Spirit still speaks today. The apostle Paul exhorted Timothy to continue in what he had learned and firmly believed, that "Scripture is inspired by God and profitable for teaching, for reproof, for correction, and for training in righteousness, that the man of God may be complete, equipped for every good work" (2 Tim. 3:14-17).

Scripture is part of the process of God's communication, or self-disclosure, and through the Bible, God has provided the church worldwide with "uniform information." We all have the same Bible, the same records of God's revelation and dealings with men and women in their physical, mental, and spiritual realms.

Jesus was bringing the *kingdom of God* and in his kingdom the atmosphere is *shalom*. Our message will aim at communicating true peace and perfect relationships. Our goal will be to restore such true peace in all our relationships: relationship with God (theology), peace and wholeness within people (psychology), peace and good relationships among men and women (sociology), and a true relationship with the created universe (ecology). As he leads us into community with his people in the church, he also restores a new kind of bond among us (ecclesiology). He makes all things perfect; his challenge to us is to follow his example, and be true peacemakers.

1.3.   THE CHANGING CONTEXT

In downtown areas of cities around the world we find churches sitting on extremely valuable real estate but without a viable congregation. The churches were built when people lived in the city or at least those who attended church lived in the city and close to the church. Today, the immediate context of the church has changed. It may now be a business area with high-rise office buildings, or it may be a low-cost housing estate or even a slum area, and many of the church-goers live in suburbs and drive in to church on Sunday morning. On this one day of the week, the atmosphere, the traditions of decades, and the many friends provide life in buildings that otherwise look as remnants of the past. The people who live in the surrounding areas are usually not seen in their "neighborhood church."

Similar observations can be made of some Christian radio programs. Program format, music selections, content, and way of presentation all seem to speak to certain sectors of the society, that is, those who are already believers and live in comfortable surroundings. Rarely do we hear programs that are geared to the needs of the poor, the homeless, or the outcasts. A purely verbal gospel does not seem to have the answers for their situation.

Changing contexts demand variety in approaches to communication, so we shall look at some variable factors that are of special interest to Christian communication. By identifying these factors, we should be able to handle them without too much uncertainty and then develop realistic and relevant approaches.

1.3.1. The Cultural Context.

A culture defines, to a large extent, a people's way of life, their institutions and structures. This should also apply to the church planted within a new culture. Its structures, patterns of leadership, of worship and church life should be congenial to its people. Unfortunately, this has not always been true, and we have churches that only faintly mirror the surrounding culture. This gives the church an almost impossible situation as far as communication and image is concerned.

This writer experienced a striking example of this in a church in a West African country. The whole service, the liturgy, the hymns, and the sermon could as well have been taken out of a European church, except for two items: the offering and the walking out of the church. At these two points in the program, an African choir with African drums led the singing and dancing up the aisle to place the offering at the altar, and at the end of the service they led the whole congregation in a similar procession out of the church. Actually, these two items took as much time as all the rest of the service. Why could it not all be African? This church service reminded me of a beautiful, European gift presented in African wrappings.

The cultural issue was faced by the apostle Paul in his time and ministry. For a considerable period he battled the efforts of a Judaizing sect within the church to require non-Jews to observe Jewish cultural norms and forms. Paul resisted this because of his respect for cultural diversity and because he realized that in order to communicate effectively with all people, he had to become all things to all people (1 Cor. 9:22).

From our study of Scripture and cultural anthropology we must conclude that it is the communicator who must change his or her patterns to fit the cultural context of the receptor audience. The communicator must, therefore, study the culture of the audience to see how the gospel of Christ can be communicated within that frame of reference. When Christ comes into our lives, we are not given new bodies or a new color, but new life.

1.3.2. The Society in which We Live.

In contemporary society we tend to forget that society is a variable factor that constantly changes. Our understanding of society varies and the words that describe social and political factors change in meaning. This is partly due to our upbringing and to the specific society in which we live. A Social Democrat from Denmark may, for example, view social issues as much more crucial to biblical Christianity than a Republican or Democrat American does. Much of what is seen to be "Christian" or not to be "Christian" is strongly influenced by our society and its norms. A society will also prescribe its own use of media channels and media content, providing different media situations from country to country.

Time factors influence both culture and society. Cultures and societies change from one period of time to another. The tendency is to assume that activities, forms, and methods that were relevant in a past era are equally relevant everywhere and for all times. Such false assumptions turn variable factors into constants. Examples would be hymns, or particular versions of the Bible.

1.3.3. The Spiritual Position of the Receptor.

People are not all at the same stage in their intellectual or spiritual understanding and development. Some individuals are like "fields ripe for harvest," other "fields" need to be cleared of weeds and thistles, even before "Gospel-sowing" can take place. Eddie Gibbs reminds us that the hard ground of the path, as described in the Parable of the Sower, represents ground made hard by other people's feet.[18] Such hard ground may of itself be good soil, but it is made unreceptive by a variety of influences that need to be understood.

In chapter three we shall be dealing with this issue of spiritual process in much more depth, so at this time we need only to remind ourselves that as the spiritual position and background of the receptor changes, so will the need arise to select and adapt one's communication content and approach. This is one of the primary reasons for emphasizing audience-based (or receptor-oriented) media selection and use. The implications for the communicator are many. For example, we should seriously examine and test so-called canned products and procedures that are produced for a specific need among a specific audience before using them among "our" people. Such an analysis turns our attention from a mere media-oriented ministry to a person-based approach.

1.3.4. The Personality and Gifts of the Communicator.

Christ has prepared all of us for ministry. He has done so through a unique and creative process (1 Pet. 1:2) which includes our social context and education and the training we have received. Furthermore, he has prepared us by giving spiritual gifts (1 Cor. 12:4ff). The purpose has been to prepare us for ministry. The apostle Paul was given extensive "equipment" for his ministry: natural talents, upbringing and education, life experience and specific spiritual gifts. C. Peter Wagner, among others, has drawn our attention to the many and diverse spiritual gifts mentioned in the New Testament.[19]

As Christians are diverse in temperament and background, their manner and methods of communication will likewise be varied. We should accept this diversity as a blessing, knowing that God can both bless and use all of us. Change in methods and media is necessary if we are to use our gifts to the fullest, and turn our attention from the medium to the person. A method-bound movement cannot become an effective world movement, but it will soon be relegated to the outdated and the outworn. Unfortunately, the world of Christian ministry is swamped by "copyrighted" methods and products that often do not fit the personality and gifts of the communicator who attempts to use them.

1.4. THE OPPOSING FORCES

As long as we live in this age, our task of communicating the Word of God will meet with hostility and obstruction from the powers of evil. The apostle Paul gave clear teaching on this:

> *The god of this age has blinded the minds of unbelievers, so that they cannot see the light of the gospel of the glory of Christ, who is the image of God (2 Cor. 4:4).*

> *For he has rescued us from the dominion of darkness and brought us into the kingdom of the Son he loves (Col. 1:13).*

These powers of evil that have blinded the minds of those who do not believe can also directly stop or obstruct the Christian mission. Paul experienced this in his ministry:

> *For we wanted to come to you—certainly I, Paul, did, again and again—but Satan stopped us (1 Thess. 2:18).*

Yet, Paul found that there are ways to "circumvent" such evil powers. Christ is stronger, and he gives his servants wisdom, power, and endurance:

> *So when we could stand it no longer, we thought it best to be left by ourselves in Athens. We sent Timothy, who is our brother and God's fellow worker ... (1 Thess. 3:1f).*

The Christian communicator may find the ministry hindered by seemingly unnecessary roadblocks. We may tend to call such obstruction communication failures, but they may also be caused by the powers of darkness. We may experience such road blocks as obstructions when we apply for a visa or try to obtain permission to broadcast a Christian message. Or the attacks may come in the form of temptations aimed at destroying Christian leaders. As long as nothing happens, we are not dangerous, but when effective ministry is experienced, then we also see the problems and obstacles caused by the evil one.

Another obstacle to communication is the fallen nature of the human race which is in rebellion against God (Rom. 1:18); people do not seek God and are not interested in understanding God. Some may even suppress and pervert the truth. As the apostle Paul writes,

> *There is no one righteous, not even one; there is no one who understands, no one who seeks God (Rom. 3:10-11).*

> *... the godlessness and wickedness of men who suppress the truth by their wickedness, since what may be known about God is plain to them, because God has made it plain to them. For since the creation of the world God's invisible qualities—his eternal power and divine nature—have been clearly seen, being understood from what has been made, so that men are without excuse (Rom. 1:18-20).*

So, the individuals to whom we are seeking to communicate the Good News are alienated and separated from God, causing a breakdown in the communication process. The primary purpose of communication is to achieve understanding, but we cannot expect the unsaved person in his rebellious state to comprehend the things of God without the help of someone in whom the Spirit of Christ abides (1 Cor. 2:14). Christians may not fully comprehend the gospel, and they are not always able to articulate the gospel clearly and persuasively to others, yet God uses this communication process with all its limitations to bring people to Christ. Response is accomplished by the work of the Holy Spirit (John 15:26; 16:8-11), a fact that both encourages and humbles the Christian communicator.

1.5.   THE WORK OF THE SPIRIT

Christian communication is a spiritual work, and ultimately all results will depend on the Holy Spirit. In the task of proclaiming the gospel, the Spirit utilizes the church as his agent, but the task of bringing a person from darkness into the light of Christ is the exclusive role of the Holy Spirit (John 6:44; Titus 3:5-7). The communicator is a witness and a channel, not the power.

It is the Spirit who truly controls the whole process of gospel communication. We are told in 1 Corinthians 2:1-16 that the Spirit enables us to "know," "speak," "interpret," and "judge" or "appraise" spiritual truths. Thus the constant power source is the Holy Spirit. The "communication link" is prayer (Eph. 6:18-20). The implication for the Christian communicator is to commit himself or herself through prayer to the guidance of the Spirit and then anticipate the mighty work of the Spirit in conviction and healing and in the creation of true wholeness.

This involvement by the Spirit is not a "cooperative effort" by God and human beings, as if there are areas and capacities of our lives outside his control. It is not a question of God and me each making a contribution, but rather, it is a question of the indwelling Christ working through his body, the Church, and its individual members. It is an incarnational concept, Christ in us working through us (Col. 1:27). It should be an obvious foundational, constant factor permeating all our understanding.

We sometimes see references made to the "part" played by the Holy Spirit. This would seem to imply that we are "using" the Spirit, rather than the Spirit using us. Christ is not only using us and speaking through us as his ambassadors (2 Cor. 5:20), but he is also working through the mental capacities he has given us to develop plans and carry out communicational activities. In the language of communication Christ is encoded in our lives, making it essential that we, the communicators, are part of the message we communicate.

In his dialogue with Nicodemus, Jesus compared the Spirit with the wind: "The wind blows where it wills ..." (John 3). A good illustration of this work of the Spirit and our dependence on him has been given by Bishop Haakon Andersen.[20] He distinguishes a sail boat from a motor boat: the wind blows where it will but a motor works as I will. Our lives should exemplify the sailing boat, dependent on the wind to give power and speed.

Faith relates to the work of the Spirit. Christianity is a religion of faith, and Christian communication must be carried out in faith (Heb. 11). It is through the eyes of faith that we see God; and without faith, no spiritual work can be carried out. Salvation is received by faith, and the Christian life is lived in and by faith. For the Christian communicator "faith" is more than dreams or wishful thinking. It is a conviction based on the calling of Christ. It is the "confident assurance that something we want is going to happen." And it is "the certainty that what we hope for is waiting for us, even though we cannot see it up ahead" (Heb. 11:1 Living Bible). The communicator will, therefore, often continue ministry in spite of what seem to be impossibilities. Faith gives hope. In chapter three we will be dealing with strategy and goal setting, but let us remind ourselves at this point that any goal setting in Christian ministry is, to use Ed Dayton's terminology, "statements of faith."[21] In prayer we seek the mind of the Lord, depending on his Spirit for guidance. Then in his power we go forth.

1.6.   THE EFFECTS OF COMMUNICATION

Our Lord did not set a time-frame for our fulfilling the commission. The task of making disciples of all nations, tribes and people will be a constant as long as this age lasts.

> *And Jesus came and said to them, All authority in heaven and on earth has been given to me. Go therefore and make disciples of all nations, baptizing them in the name of the Father and of the Son and of the Holy Spirit, teaching them to observe all that I have commanded you (Mt. 28:18-20).*

Jesus would not give such a commission if the goal was not obtainable. Christian communicators will, therefore, always work towards this goal and they will not be content with just "participatory" communication or dialogue. A Christian will communicate for impact or for the purpose of achieving certain effects. As Jesus was not engaged in dialogue just for the sake of dialogue, we will, like him, through such encounters aim at opening the other person's eyes to new understandings concerning the kingdom of God and eventually to spiritual and behavioral change.

In measuring the effects of Christian communication, we often encounter so-called spiritual and theological objections. Some Christian groups will object to the use of research on the basis of a conviction that it is unnecessary for the Christian—who relies on the Holy Spirit—to ask questions concerning effectiveness.[22] Others will contend that research and evaluation are necessary tools of a ministry that desires to be accountable to Christ and his church. We cannot take communication effects for granted.

Effects are often defined in terms of cognitive belief, emotional affect, and behavioral intent. These can all be measured, and this may be all that is possible just after a certain "communication event," but we should not be satisfied unless we also measure long-term actual effects of cognitive improvements, affective changes, and behavioral steps. Our research methods are too limited to give a full picture of spiritual effects, "as only God knows the heart of men," so from these measures we have to infer the effectiveness of our ministry.

We may, of course, be at the mercy of the effects we choose to observe. If our perspective is single-cause effects and causes, then we may be seriously diverted by the observed effects. For example, if we have a radio-ministry among a people where only young people write letters, but our "target audience" is the adult population, we may be totally misguided if we judge our results by letters received. It may cause us to produce programs for youth only in order to get letters.

Effectiveness of Christian communication needs to be defined from at least three perspectives: (1) the perspective of God, (2) the perspective of the Christian (the communicator), and (3) from the perspective of the receptor (the audience).

(1) For God, effectiveness will be seen from the *perspective of eternity*. God, as seen through his revelation, is concerned about shalom, the presence of the kingdom of God. We find that all God's revelation and redemptive work is directed towards establishing this goal of harmonious relationships. God seems more concerned with obedience and faithfulness than with mere "evangelistic results."

(2) From the perspective of the *Christian communicator*, effectiveness will be seen in the light of *response* to the commission given by Christ: "go and make disciples of all nations" (Mt. 28:18-20). The commission also speaks of baptism and the incorporation into the life of the local congregation. It speaks of nurture and the instruction in all things pertaining to the kingdom of God. Since this is a complex mandate and since the Lord has provided a variety of spiritual gifts to carry out this comprehensive ministry, it follows that no one person will participate in all its varied dimensions. Some will plant, others water, and yet others will harvest (1 Cor. 3:5-9). We are called to be witnesses by life and by deed, as well as by vocal testimony.

(3) The effectiveness of Christian communication will from the perspective of the *receptor* be judged in relation to how he or she experiences *needs met*, and how a new joy and fullness of life in fellowship with God and with other human beings is experienced. As a result of God's intervention in his or her life, changes should be evident in such areas as values and self-esteem.

SUMMARY

The insights provided in this chapter are aimed at setting the stage and providing a basis for discussing principles and theories of Christian communication.

Basic to our understanding of Christian communication is the fact that God is a communicator who makes himself known to us, and seeks a relationship with us that will result in our response to him through praise and worship and by involvement in his mission. The primary model he has provided for us is the incarnation.

His commission to us not only permeates Scripture but must also be a central focus in all our ministry. Our task is one of communication, making Christ known and understood. Our methods must take their starting point in the methods used by God, and our message is Jesus and his kingdom. In the kingdom of God the atmosphere is shalom, that is, true peace and perfect relationships, and our task is to facilitate such true healing for all people.

Permeating all our ministry are certain constant factors which set Christian communication apart. It is on this basis we propose our strategy, and as such it is not necessary for us to make constant references to the work of the Holy spirit. It is taken for granted.

Some of the constant factors treated in this chapter are (1) the presence and activity of the powers of darkness, (2) the fallen nature of human beings, (3) the revelation of God, (4) the work of the Spirit, (5) faith, (6) the Word of God, and (7) the goal of disciple-making. These are the constants that give Christian communication its special nature.

For the application of media in our communication strategies, we also need to understand the variables that give context and direction to our communication. In this chapter we have looked at (1) the cultural context, (2) the society, (3) the spiritual position of the receptor, and (4) the personality and gifts of the communicator. Many communication problems are due to a mix-up of constant and variable factors. This is particularly true of Christian use of communication media.

The next chapter will provide a summary of communication theory that should help us understand the various dimensions of our communication task. This section will also include chapters on strategy and research, all leading to a summary chapter that sets out the dimensions of approach to Christian communication.

QUESTION FOR DISCUSSION AND APPLICATION

Discuss with your colleagues how the topics raised in this chapter do or should influence the way in which you work. Are there any changes needed?

FOOTNOTES

1 Knud Jørgensen, "The Role and Function of the Media in the Mission of the Church." Unpublished Ph.D. dissertation presented to Fuller Theological Seminary, School of World Mission, Pasadena. 1981.

2 Robert E. Webber, *God Still Speaks. A Biblical View of Christian Communication.* Nashville: Thomas Nelson Publishers. 1980:71.

3 Johannes Henrici, "Towards an Anthropological Philosophy of Communication" in *Communication Resource*, March 1983. London: WACC 1983:1.

4 Ibid. p.16.

5 Charles Kraft, *Communication Theory for Christian Witness*. Rev. ed. Maryknoll: Orbis Books. 1991:17.

6 Ibid., p.13.

7 Ibid., p.14.

8 Robert E. Webber, *God Still Speaks. A Biblical View of Christian Communication.* Nashville: Thomas Nelson Publishers. 1980:115ff.

9 Charles Kraft, *Communication Theory for Christian Witness*. Rev. ed. Maryknoll: Orbis Books. 1991:12–13.

10 Knud Jørgensen, "The Role and Function of the Media in the Mission of the Church" 1981:27. Unpublished Ph.D. dissertation presented to Fuller Theological Seminary, School of World Mission, Pasadena.

11 Charles Kraft, *Christianity in Culture*. Maryknoll, N.Y.: Orbis Books. 1979a:210.

12 Knud Jørgensen, "The Role and Function of the Media in the Mission of the Church" 1981:27. Unpublished Ph.D. dissertation presented to Fuller Theological Seminary, School of World Mission, Pasadena.

13 Robert E. Webber, *God Still Speaks. A Biblical View of Christian Communication.* Nashville: Thomas Nelson Publishers. 1980:97.

14 Gavin Reid, *The Gagging of God*. London: Hodder and Stoughton. 1969:17.

15 Em Griffin, *The Mind Changers*. Wheaton, Ill.: Tyndale House. 1976.

16 Charles Kraft, *Communication Theory for Christian Witness*. Revised edition, Maryknoll: Orbis Books. 1991:15.

17 Kraft, 1991:27.

18 Eddie Gibbs, *The God Who Communicates*. London: Hodder and Stoughton. 1985:39.

19 C. Peter Wagner, *Your Spiritual Gifts Can Help Your Church Grow*. Glendale: Regal Books. 1979.

20 Bishop Haakon Andersen is a Norwegian, and he provided the illustration at a Lausanne Committee meeting in Copenhagen in 1988.

21 Ed Dayton and David A. Fraser, *Planning Strategies for World Evangelization*. Monrovia, CA: MARC. 1990 (second ed.).

22 James F. Engel, *How Can I Get Them to Listen* Grand Rapids: Zondervan. 1977:13.

CHAPTER 2

Communication Principles That Make Us Understand

Jesus spent much of his time with his small group of disciples but a significant amount of time was also spent communicating with the multitudes or, we could say, with mass audiences and large crowds. His "program" then included plenty of stories (which we call parables), stories they could understand and in which they saw themselves as actors in a drama. He demonstrated his power to them by healing the sick and casting out demons. He fed the thousands who had nothing to eat and he confronted the power structures with prophetic announcements, in many ways the kind of things on which we build our media programs and popular sermons. But when Jesus was alone with his disciples, he taught them "theory." He explained the meanings of things and how the various items fitted together in a conceptual framework. Likewise, those of us who are engaged in the ministry as pastors of churches, as missiologists, or media practitioners need to step back and understand what we are doing. We need to utilize the created ability to conceptualize and theorize, work with symbols and signs, and to arrange concepts into theories that help us understand and visualize processes. In other words, we need to be concerned about the theories and principles on which our ministry is based.

For some people, the word "theory" may sound dry and uninspiring, but it can also be an exciting adventure into the world of ideas and concepts. An inadequate understanding of communication theory may well inhibit the effective use of media in Christian communication. As in other areas of life, a science without a theory is blind because it lacks that element which alone is able to organize facts. Theory and facts must be closely related to each other.

The special dimensions of Christian communication have been treated in the previous chapter, and we enter our treatment of communication theory on that basis.

2.1. COMMUNICATION DEFINED

Communication is not something accidental and supplementary for human beings. We communicate because we, from our beginnings, are communicators by nature. The average person spends most of his or her active time communicating: listening, speaking, reading, writing, watching television and video. The interest in communication is also increasing, and almost every discipline concerned with human society and human behavior has during the last few years concerned itself with communication. A widening interest is also evident in Christian ministry where, for example, Eugene Nida has paved the way for applying communication to Bible translation,[1] and Myron Chartier has treated preaching as communication.[2]

But communication is a complex subject where definition is difficult. This is further complicated by the different backgrounds and persuasions evident among writers on the subject. So, in spite of the fact that the communication process is utterly fundamental to all our psychological and social processes, our understanding of the communication process is limited. We often feel uncertain as to the accuracy of our conclusions and the wide variety of definitions that have been suggested.

The word communication has, like a number of other familiar words, developed from the Latin word *communis* which means to share, to have in common. Present-day English derivatives still retain this concept of commonality.[3]

Communication	– **sharing information and ideas**
Commune	– **living in a property—sharing relationship**
Community	– **having geography or interests in common**
Communion	– **showing deep friendship and also intimate sharing.**

These words point to relationships. It is thus impossible to separate the word communication from implications of mutual involvement and relationship, the development of commonality between peoples. We can also notice that God seems to work primarily among and through communities. Without constantly engaging in acts of communication with other human beings, none of us could develop the mental processes and social nature that distinguishes us from other forms of life, and without important communications systems, such as language, we could not carry out group activities or lead independent lives. Consequently, community should be demonstrated, within Christian programs and among the people who produce the programs.[4]

Actually, the attempt to understand the process of communication and how to communicate more effectively started a very long time ago. Kegemni, the oldest son of Pharaoh Huni, is reported to have received an essay on effective speaking in c. 3,000 B.C.[5] But the documented history of rhetorical communication began in Syracuse, Sicily, in the fifth century B.C., where Corax developed an "art of rhetoric" for ordinary people to use, when proving their claims in court.[6] In a review of the science of communication our attention would also be drawn to people like Aristotle, Cicero and Quintilian. These ancients thought of communication as an art, its theory being termed "rhetoric" and its practice being called "oratory." Aristotle defined rhetoric as the art of discovering in every case the "available means of persuasion." The persuader was successful to the degree to which he actually brought the audience to "right" belief and action.[7] His *Rhetoric*, published approximately 330 B.C., was one of the most in-fluential works on communication ever conceived. Aristotle viewed communication in relationship to three points of reference: the speaker, the speech, and the audience. His model has been the basis for many models of communication theory ever since. But despite such ancient beginnings, it has only been during the last four decades that the field of communication has exploded with numerous publications.

The word communication will be used here in a very broad sense to include all the procedures by which one mind may affect another. This, of course, involves not only written and oral speech, but also music, the pictorial arts, the theater, and in fact all human behavior. As we analyze available definitions, we find that each one has its own strength and its own usefulness, but it is probably impossible to arrive at one single, covering definition. We can say that communication has successfully taken place when a message has been transmitted and the intended point is grasped by another. Any adequate definition of communication must also recognize both the transfer and the impact of communication messages and that communication is a process. As a definition of communication is so difficult and a definition can actually be rather misleading, it may be far more fruitful to describe communication rather than trying to arrive at a single definition.

2.2.   COMMUNICATION IS A PROCESS OF EVENTS

Looking at communication as a process has sometimes been termed a Western perspective, while non-Western cultures are supposed to be event oriented. Communication is both process and event. That communication, like all of life, is a process is foundational to our understanding of communication. It is, furthermore, a consecutive, interrelated number of communication processes, some of short-term duration, others involving years, which are going on at the same time. But this process consists of individual segments or events that in themselves may not overtly relate to a process. To illustrate this we could compare a "moving picture" with a "still photo." As a film is made up of a long sequence of individual pictures, so the communication process is made up of a sequential process of communication events.

It is also important to look at communication as a process from the perspective of the receptor who moves through a life process. Our communication messages must be designed as a process that correspond to the needs of a receptor at his or her present position or stage in life and the needs and problems faced at that time. A person's relationship with God can be seen as a spiritual journey and if we know a person's position in this journey, we can design communication events that will be relevant at this time. We shall look closer at this dimension in the next chapter.

Essentially the communication process consists of information-processing organized around a shared orientation or topic. Ordinarily this process is portrayed as occurring between poles designated as interpersonal and mass communication, but it can also take place within the thought processes of the individual. There can be numerous kinds of situations, including the following seven illustrations.

2.2.1. Intrapersonal Communication: Communication Within a Person.

This is when we "talk with ourselves," wrestling with new ideas and trying to arrive at convictions and personal opinions. We can also meditate on the word of God or some other issue, arriving at our own meaning of ideas. No media are involved in this process, but sometimes stimuli will be received from outside one's own thought process. For example, the organ may play during private meditation, or we may listen to a musical masterpiece. We may also be out in a beautiful natural setting, meditating on God's handiwork. The psalmist David saw the moon and the stars and wondered about God who cares for the individual (Psalm 8).

Figure 2.1. Intrapersonal Communication

2.2.2. Interpersonal Communication: Face-to-Face Communication.

This is the most "basic" communication situation where two people are communicating with each other. This can be a meeting of two friends, or it can be the sharing of a personal testimony with another person. Maybe only non-verbal signals are utilized, that is, body language or touch, but usually language is involved, while non-verbal signals provide the interpretation. It is an exchange situation where active listening is important. All the basic signal systems will be used as much as possible, and the media will include the body itself, the use of hands and facial expressions, clothes, perfume, and make-up. All add dimensions to the interpersonal exchange. The exchange may be supported by printed materials, pictures, or a tape.

Figure 2.2. Interpersonal Communication, Face-to-Face

2.2.3. Interpersonal Communication: Point-to-Point Communication.

Here two people are communicating over a distance. It can be (1) live, for example a telephone call. It could be a counseling service related to a television or radio program. When speaking on the telephone, the primary signal system used is the human voice, but intonations and other sounds may give depth to the exchange. There may also be further helps through printed materials. (2) It can be remote in time. This can be an exchange of letters from one person to another. Visuals in the form of drawings or pictures may be included with the letter. The letter may be from a friend, or it may be related to business or work.

Figure 2.3. Interpersonal Communication, Point-to-Point

2.2.4. Small Group Communication: Face-to-Face.

A variety of situations are possible, for example: a board meeting, a group Bible study, or a strategy meeting of a pastoral team or a group of missionaries. In addition to verbal exchanges, a group meeting will employ

Figure 2.4. Small Group Communication, Face-to-Face

interpersonal communication signals, non-verbal communication, and levels of tension and atmosphere created in the room. Other media being used may include papers and plans, posters and maps, an overhead projector, a video player or a tape recorder.

2.2.5. Small Group Communication: Point-to-Point.

This can be one group of people where the individuals are at different locations, and they communicate live by means of a telephone, a so-called conference call, possibly supported by papers sent by mail or fax. It could also be two different groups interacting with each other by means of video or a video conference. A further example of small group point-to-point communication would be exchanges through the mail. A typical example would be memos and postal ballots by a board or committee.

Figure 2.5. Small Group Communication, Point-to-Point

2.2.6. Communication with Large Groups.

Again, a variety of situations are possible, from personal to impersonal. (1) One person to many people: such a situation can be experienced at public meetings where one person is speaking, perhaps with the help of a public address system. Any group size is possible, including tens of thousands at a Billy Graham Crusade. A church service is similar in many respects though the media utilized are much more extensive, including symbols of the faith like crosses and candles, organ music, and the general atmosphere in the church. (2) A large group may be watching a drama or stage performance with live actors. There will be no eye contact here as the audience and the actors and actresses on stage are acting out a drama, creating an illusion of another time and another situation. (3) A film show where individuals are seated in a large group, usually in a darkened theater, interacting with the story being projected on the screen. Video parlors in certain countries are close to this situation, but due to the lighted room and local group dynamics, this would often be more like a group situation.

Figure 2.6. Communication with Large Groups

2.2.7. Mass Communication: Communication with Multiple Audiences.

The primary difference between interpersonal and mass communication is that the latter involves multiple audiences. Each audience may in effect be only one person as is the case of the reader of a newspaper, or the lone radio listener in his or her car on the freeway. In this category we also have printed matter, either addressed to individuals or distributed to all. Primary among the mass media of today are, of course, radio and television. Programs may be fiction or drama, or they may be live performances that communicate with audiences in real time. We may also include videos that are rented and played in multiple homes across the country at the same time. Each of these different kinds of situation and use of media

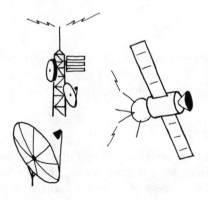

Figure 2.7. Mass Communication

is relevant to Christian communication. Each demands a different approach and provides its own unique opportunities.

As stated above, the communication process builds on relationships, but this relationship does not necessarily have to be face-to-face. Messages can be conveyed through space and preserved in time. Mass media make communication possible over great distances as well as over great spans of time. Messages of the past still communicate, as we experience with a book, a cathedral, or a symphony. Two-way communication hardly seems possible here, but that is not easy with the local newspaper, either. Yet, given the right situation, such distant communications may have very powerful results. One striking example is the Bible itself. But whatever kind of communication we talk about, whether face-to-face or mediated, whether immediate or removed in time or space, the communication relationships will include a communicator, a message, and one or more receivers. The basic "tools" used to facilitate this process and to form messages are the so-called signal systems.

2.3. SIGNALS THAT FORM MESSAGES

Signal systems, sometimes referred to as basic media, are the signals or symbols used by human beings to communicate. Again, there are problems with definitions, but the following list, proposed by Donald K. Smith, is most helpful in analyzing human communication.[8] Other signals could possibly be added to the list. Each of these signal systems is like a language with its own specific vocabulary. Rarely are they used in isolation, but usually in a combination with other signals. The twelve suggested signal systems are,

a. Verbal.

The use of spoken words. This can be through public speaking or a sermon, the reading of poetry, or just talking with somebody. It can be used by all people and many pay great attention to right formulations.

b. Written.

A written system expresses words and ideas without the limits of time or space. Most religions have written books. The big limitation on written communication is the problem of illiteracy and the increasing numbers of non-readers.

c. Numeric.

Numbers by themselves can be used to transfer information, formally in mathematics and less formally as symbols. These all are associated with situations and interpretations. Numbers such as 3, 7, and 666 have special meanings for Christians.

d. Pictorial.

Pictures convey information but the same picture may convey different information to audiences of different cultures. We can use simple line drawings, elaborate paintings, photographs, or cartoons. Also, the use of color communicates ideas. A picture in a news story becomes part of the story. In an art exhibition the picture is the story.

e. Audio.

The use of sound. Audio signals such as bells, whistles, laughter, tone and intonations of the voice communicate as well as affect the interpretation of other signals. A different intonation may completely change the meaning of a message. Music is a systematic use of sound.

f. Kinetics.

Body movements and gestures. These tell much about the messenger and the message, and may even contradict the spoken words and will then usually have greater impact than the words. The pointing of a finger, shaking one's head, or nodding while listening are examples of this. Traditional dance-drama primarily use such communication signals.

g. Artifactual.

Objects communicate, as people consciously and unconsciously use those objects in decorations, clothing styles, possessions displayed, even in architectural styles. It may be a wedding ring or designer clothes. It may also be a cross on a golden chain.

h. Tactile.

We communicate by touch and body contact, such as holding hands, shaking hands, a hug, or a kiss. Like all of these symbols, communication through touch is culture bound.

i. Temporal.

Our concern for time will indicate much about us, and our attitude toward other people or the event we are attending. Lateness is not defined the same way in every culture. For some, to be on time is important. Others communicate status by being late.

j. Spatial.

The personal and private physical space immediately surrounding a person varies between peoples; how that space is used communicates, as does the use of space in homes, offices and even in villages and cities. The distance of the pulpit from the congregation may create a barrier to communication, as does a large desk in an office.

k. Olfactory.

Smell and taste, as in perfumes or food, tell much of attitude and intention. We try to communicate who we are, or want to be, through the selection of perfumes and deodorants.

l. Silence.

We could actually place this under "audio." It is the pauses, the "waiting" time, or in print media, the blank space. Silence often communicates a desire for dialogue, acceptance and concern as opposed to one-way, manipulative speech.

Our mastery of the signal systems within a given cultural context will greatly influence the results of our communication. For the mass media communicators they provide a tremendous challenge as a variety of audiences will be exposed to the same signals. In Japan, for example, it is a sign of maturity to be able to read another's need without the use of words. The signs used are unobtrusive, like in a tea ceremony. The 6000-year-old Japanese culture will often look at Western manners as crude and uneducated.

The Bible itself speaks of non-verbal symbols in the early church. And the many Old Testament ceremonies and the New Testament communion service are good examples of such depth of communication.

2.4. THE MEDIA OF COMMUNICATION

Each individual media channel has its own possibilities and limitations and such possibilities change if it functions alone or in conjunction with other media. Discussion of the advantages and disadvantages of the various media, or the relative strengths of one method as compared to another, is often carried on without any clear frame of reference and with each user intent on proving that his or her particular medium or method is best.

Actually, to ask the question "which medium is best?" is not a very professional question, as it all depends on the situation.[9] The more relevant question is one of media mix, or rather, of using the right medium at the right time. Is it used according to the inherent and obvious advantages of that particular medium or method in that particular situation? A realistic view of a medium's capabilities will, therefore, need an intercultural analysis and an appreciation of external factors influencing the use and application in a given context. Each society has ascribed roles to each medium, so it is helpful to work out a general list of advantages and disadvantages of the individual media.

It is easier to describe the media than to define media. In popular usage "The Media" refers to the whole complex of broadcasting, particularly television, and its many uses. In McLuhan terminology, media are extensions of the human body, and the basic human communication symbols.[10] It is often helpful to see the media this way. The microphone becomes an extension of the voice, the pencil an extension of the hand, and the camera an extension of the eye. In Christian communication we are channels through which the gospel of Jesus Christ is extended to others, and we use media to extend ourselves and our message to others.

The different media channels utilize the basic signal systems, but each medium does it differently from the others. Usually a combination of signals is used. A good audio cassette program will, for example, use most of the signals, as we attempt to create pictures in the minds of the listeners. Within the context of his or her own imagination and experience the listener will create the scene and "see" the action. To achieve this the audio media utilizes the voice and its intonations, a wide variety of sounds and music, microphone distance (sound perspective), silence, etc. to give the listener a real experience of the action. Microphone distance is, then, not just a matter of "inches" to obtain a good level or technical balance, but it is very much a question of how to communicate feelings, closeness, and concern.

One way of classifying media would be to look at its use. We can then differentiate between personal media, group media and mass media. Personal media are the media used by a single person. Print becomes a personal medium when a person decides to read and use it. A stronger example would be a personal letter written by one person to another. A cassette player used by a single person is personal, and it could be argued that a mass medium like radio could equally well be used as a personal medium, or we could say that it is a mass medium from the perspective of the sender and a personal medium from the perspective of the receiver.

Group media signify media that are used to enhance or stimulate interaction with or among a group of people. This could include a cassette tape with the latest information from a mission field.

Mass media are understood as media that aim at communicating with multiple audiences at the same time. A given audience may be small, in fact, it may consist of just one person and the receptor may not necessarily understand or feel a "mass" situation. The typical mass media are radio and television, but we also have posters and out-door advertising.

2.5.   THE USE OF COMMUNICATION MODELS

Due to the complexity of theories and classifications, it is helpful to utilize conceptual models when describing communication theory and media use. In a sense, this is like the apostle Paul describing the church as a body with many members, or the pastor including an illustration in the sermon.

Conceptual models are imaginative mental constructs invented to illustrate certain activities or situations. They are not literal pictures of the world but illustrations used to develop or describe a theory which in some sense explains the situation.

The model is, therefore, an attempt at explaining how the mind of the model-constructor understands reality. But for most people theories are easier to understand when explained on conceptual models. But as they are only pictures of reality as reality is understood at this time, they need to be dynamic in nature.[11] New knowledge may help us understand reality better and consequently force the adaptation or change of models.

We should not automatically assume that models can be used freely in cross-cultural situations. Somebody else, with a different world view, may understand it differently and a certain model may therefore be inadequate in explaining reality in such situations. The same principles may have to be described and applied differently in different cultures, so a careful evaluation must take place for their cross-cultural potential.[12]

The actual process of communication is more complicated than any picture we are able to construct, and no one model is sufficient to explain and illustrate all aspects of the communication process. Some models will help us understand the processes of communication; others will help us to understand how humans interact and actually communicate with one another. Together they provide us with frames of reference within which we can discuss communication processes, variables and effects.

It seems quite obvious that much Christian communication practice is based on a one-way concept, which is partly due to a lack of information about the audience. This has left us with message-oriented theories of communication, where emphasis is placed on the design of the message rather than on the intended listener. The audience is viewed as a target, and "ideas and feelings are prepackaged in a mental and physical syringe and then forced under pressure in a straight line into the receiver."[13]

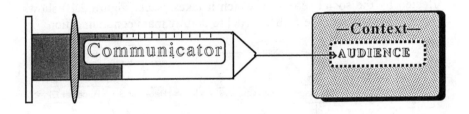

Figure 2.8. Communication as Action Model

A variety of models have been suggested by different workers. They may differ in certain details, but most agree on the fundamental elements. For our purpose, the one proposed by Engel will be sufficient for the analysis of the elements of a communication process.

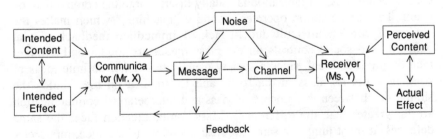

Figure 2.9. Interpersonal Communication Model (Engel 1979:39)

Engel explains the model this way:

> *Mr. X has something he wants to say to Ms. Y. Certain words are selected that then are arranged in a pattern or sequence to be*

communicated. The technical word for this is "encoding." This encoded message has both an intended content and an intended effect. It is next transmitted through a channel of some type, probably the spoken word. Now, the hope is that Ms. Y will attend to the message and attempt to decode it. The actual effect of the whole process, however, is determined by her perception of what is said, not by its intended content (Engel 1979:39).

This model can be adapted for use in conceptualizing mass media communication. Here we have many different audiences, who may or may not be in contact with each other. Mass communication is profoundly affected by the social setting in which it takes place. Figure 2.10 shows Engel's adaptation of the earlier model to portray mass communication:

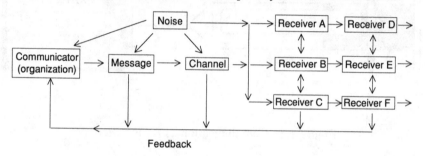

Figure 2.10. Mass Communication Model (Engel 1979:42)

Mass communication is more complicated than interpersonal communication. An organization is usually inserted into the communication chain. This organization operates around a "machine," which makes the choice of content difficult due to lack of immediate feedback. Social demands and social controls on the mass media are louder and stronger than on the individual, since a society usually has rather definite ideas of what it wants its mass media to be and to do. But on the whole "the similarities between the process of mass and interpersonal communication are far greater than the differences. Mass communication faces the same defences. It must jump the same hurdles: attention, acceptance, interpretation, and disposition"[14]

In 1960, Joseph T. Klapper raised serious questions about the effects of mass media, suggesting that mass communication does not ordinarily serve as a sufficient cause of audience effects, but rather reinforces existing conditions.[15] This generalization was premature, as Klapper himself pointed out in his introduction, but subsequent research has often supported this position. On the other hand we have also seen striking examples of effective mass media programs that have caused great changes. The enormous resources devoted to television clearly underline the possible effects.

It has been recognized that the social context is an integral part of the communication process, rather than just the location or setting where communication takes place. In order to wrestle with this issue of context and commonality, a number of different models have been proposed. The one proposed by Wilbur Schramm in Figure 2.11 simplifies the problems:

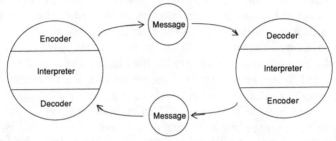

Figure 2.11. Model of Social Interaction (Schramm 1971:24)

Schramm is indicating that communication is a circular process, where both sender and receiver decode and encode. As Jorgensen observes, there is no clear distinction between them,

> *both of them are sender and receiver in the circular flow of communication where feedback is the factor that makes the clock tick. Thus response is seen as central to communication: notice further the inclusion of an 'interpreter,' hinting at the problem of meaning.*[16]

A few other terms need to be discussed, including the concept of encoding/decoding. Encoding the message for the medium refers to the process needed to change or shape a concept into a message or program that can be transmitted by the selected media channel. The channel may be the human body, or it may be the spoken word. The message must be coded or shaped a certain way to fit the "language" of the chosen medium. If the medium is radio, the message must be verbalized; if it is television, the message must be visualized. If the medium is music-radio, the length of a message must be short, from several seconds to one minute. For television, many messages must be delivered in thirty-second or one-minute capsules. A message that is to be transmitted by media which, by the cultural and social structures, have been given an entertainment function must meet the criteria for drama or some kind of enjoyment.

Decoding refers to the process of receiving the message from the media and translating it into the receptor's frame of reference. It is the receptor who gives meaning to the message. It involves perceiving the message as encoded by the source by means of the mind and body senses and the interpretation of the message by the receptor.

During the reception of a message, a selective filtering takes place in the mind of the listener. The filter can be illustrated in different ways, but it will include at least the following four stages: (1) *Exposure*: that is, a person is exposed to the message, listening to the radio when the program is on or sitting in the pew during the sermon. (2) *Attention*: we must go beyond exposure. The attention must be there while listening to the sermon, and a person must pay attention to the radio, as well as the sign at the roadside. (3) *Comprehension*: it is important that the message is understood correctly so that information processing can take place. (4) *Retention*: a message must be remembered if action is to take place.

All of these stages in the filtering process are selective, that is, it is the receiver who controls the filter, deciding to open or close. An important aspect of communication research is, then, to discover how the filter operates. The central controlling factor is the evaluative criteria, in terms of which a person evaluates an incoming signal and influences the filter. The evaluative criteria is, again, strongly influenced by a person's previous information and experience with the subject or person in question. If

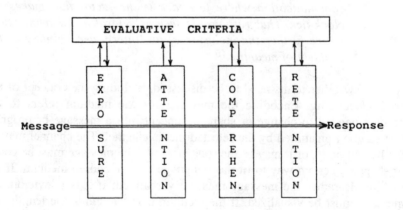

Figure 2.12. Selective Filtering of the Message

experience with the church is negative, a negative evaluative criterion will be the result, and this has serious consequences for the messages communicated.

This communicational activity on behalf of the receptor is of utmost importance in designing communication strategies, but the response may also take place within the thought-processes of a person (intrapersonal communication), as in the case of Bible reading. It could be argued that the link here is between God and the person and that feedback is to God. Feedback to mass media messages does not necessarily have to be to the broadcasting station or publishing house.

Another model, a so-called verbal model, presented by Marvin Mayers, has proved to be most helpful to this writer.[17] As all persuasive communication has to be built on mutual trust, Mayers suggests that the basic question is that of *Acceptance of Person*. Mutual respect and acceptance is the foundation of trust. The model includes four sub-models described by Mayers as follows:

> *1. The Prior Question of Trust (PQT) is the question asked before all other questions: "Is what I am doing, thinking, or saying building or undermining trust?"*
>
> *2. The Acceptance of Self permits the person to accept himself as he is at any given moment. He accepts himself as he is at that moment. Acceptance of self allows understanding of what is known and familiar to the person, thus preparing him to accept others (especially God whom he knows less).*
>
> *3. The Acceptance of the Other is the extending of our self-acceptance to others so that we can interact and accept them as fully responsible members of their own life-way.*
>
> *4. Mutual Respect involves balanced reciprocity interpersonal relations leaving both persons intact and valid.*

Figure 2.13. The Prior Question of Trust

It is on this bridge of trust that communication messages can flow. An attempt has been made to illustrate the model in Figure 2.14. The goal is to establish a "commonness" with someone else so that communication can take place.

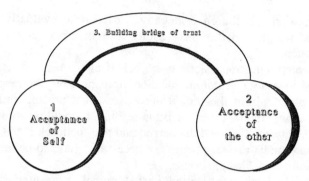

Figure 2.14. Mayers' Model Illustrated

Some writers have tried to illustrate the differences between messages and meaning. Let us just remind ourselves here that meanings are in message-users rather than in messages: that is, meaning arises in the minds of the receivers when exposed to communication messages. Media communicators should therefore be less concerned with the "correctness" of the message than with the meaning assigned to it by an audience. That is, the most important question is not what you said, but what the listener heard, or rather, believes he or she heard you say. The meaning and effect as perceived by the audience can deviate substantially from the intended meaning.

Back in 1948 Harold D. Lasswell[18] proposed a formula for analyzing the effects of communication. He suggested that communication effects depend on,

> **Who Says**
> **What**
> **In Which Channel**
> **To Whom**
> **With What Effect?**

Figure 2.15. Lasswell's Model

In this sentence Lasswell points to the key elements in the communication process. These lead us into asking serious questions concerning the source of the communication and how the source is perceived by the receptor. The formula also asks questions concerning the content and the medium through which the message is transmitted. There are questions of credibility, of availability, of cost and of relevancy. Lasswell also raises questions concerning the audience. Who is he/she? Where is he/she? What does he/she need? And finally, what did he/she do with the communication received?

The long-term effects of communication are difficult to measure, especially the effects of mass communication. Most studies tend to measure only individual aspects or short term effects. What effect, for example, will long hours of television watching have on tastes and behavior? Our attempt to analyze such effects is greatly hampered by the fact that we cannot isolate the ingredients one at a time for analysis.

The field of communication research is still a new field. There is an enormous need for basic communication research that will help Christian communicators to better understand their task and be more effective in communicating the message of Christ through media. The special considerations that put Christian communication in a category by itself demand that we do not base our understanding of communication theory exclusively on insights gained from secular research.

2.6. A COMPREHENSIVE MODEL OF THE COMMUNICATION PROCESS

The following development of a comprehensive model is based on the insights discussed so far. It is presented as a step-by-step approach to identification of the dimensions involved and their application in effective communication. It could be argued that this is not a communication model but a strategy of approach.

2.6.1. Source/Sender: The Communicator.

In dealing with Christian communication, we have a message "to proclaim to the nations." Our primary concern is that all people everywhere may hear the gospel of Jesus Christ in ways that are relevant and understandable. So we need to begin with ourselves, our purpose, our assumptions and our limitations. We are people chosen by God to engage in persuasive communication.

2.6.2. The Receiver: The Audience.

Basic to effective communication is a good understanding of the audience. Who is the person or group we are trying to reach? What are their needs? Which topics are of interest? Are we dealing with young people or the older generation, Christian or non-Christian, educated or uneducated?

2.6.3. The Context of the Audience.

It is not only a question of who is in the audience, but also where they are when receiving the message. Is my radio listener having breakfast, driving a car on a busy freeway, or watching buffaloes in a field? Is my reader among Christians or is he or she in a hostile environment? Similarly, the context of the sender influences the way in which he or she communicates. There may be serious limitations on media use, and there may be hostile forces trying to hinder our communication.

Figure 2.16. The Sender, the Receiver and the Context of the Receiver

2.6.4. Research: Getting the Information.

This is the activity needed to get the information mentioned in steps 2 and 3. Research can be both formal and informal, but our primary concern is to gain significant information about our audience so that our messages can be received in understandable terms. No one has earned the right to engage in media production without a clear understanding of the audience and their needs. We need to get such information before engaging in actual production.

2.6.5. Selection of Content.

As far as biblical content is concerned, a helpful approach to the selection of basic content for a program or a message is to follow these steps: (1) What is the general teaching in the Word of God about this need or topic? (2) Where do I find Bible passages that deal with this topic? (3) Which passages would be most helpful in meeting the needs of my audience? Then it will indeed be "Good News To Needs."

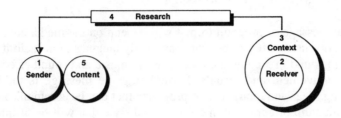

Figure 2.17. Gather Information and Select Content for Communication
Messages

2.6.6. Identifying the Channel.

Which communication approach or medium would be best suited for
my communication with the chosen audience? How could I best communicate the selected content so that the needs of the receptors will be met?
Would the situation call for a mass medium like television? Or, would an
audio cassette be better? Maybe a church service should be utilized or a
visit by a friend? Each approach will give new dimensions and possibilities.

2.6.7. Reception.

Here we are concerned with exposure to the message, captivating the
attention of the audience, gaining understanding, and commitment to retention and action. During the reception of a message numerous variables are
at work, some hindering reception, some trying to block the communication. Define such variables as clearly as possible prior to the development
of program format.

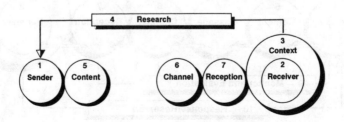

Figure 2.18. Reception of Messages

2.6.8. Formulating the Message.

The message or program format will depend on the media chosen. In a personal discussion, it will be words and body language. On radio it will be limited to sound in a combination of speech, music and sound effects. Film can use movement and visuals. Formulating the message is the task of translating ideas and thoughts into programs that can be communicated by a certain medium or approach in a format and style that will be of interest to the chosen audience.

2.6.9. Monitoring and Evaluation.

In secular communication advertisers could not imagine spending huge sums of money on commercials without careful evaluation of programs and relevant monitoring of all aspects in the process, in particular the reception. Who listened to my program? Who read the tract? Did they understand my sermon? Are they taking action? For Christian communication, we must have such monitoring facilities if we are to claim stewardship and honesty in the use of resources.

2.6.10. Response and Research.

As Christian mass communicators we cannot be satisfied with meager feedback obtained by mail. It is important to have response mechanisms, including mail, telephone, etc., but our response systems must be appropriate to all in the audience, including the non-literate. It is also important to have effective research designs that will measure the actual results.

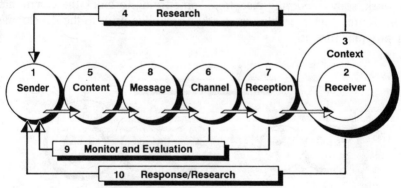

Figure 2.19. Develop Program, Monitor and Evaluate Feedback
and Effects

2.6.11. Noise.

Noise is a technical term that describes anything that hinders good communication. Unfortunately, it affects all aspects of the communication process. Noise in the sender may give cause to biased programs, and noise in the receptor may change the meaning. Noise in the channel may give poor reception, and noise in the reception context may distract the listener or viewer. We must do all we can to reduce noise to an acceptable level so that the messages can come through as clearly as possible.

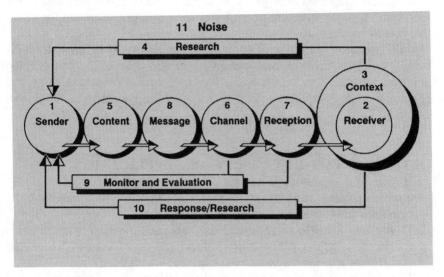

Figure 2.20. The Influence of Noise in Communication

SUMMARY

God has created in us human beings a capacity to conceptualize and theorize. It is through the study of theory and concepts that we find direction for our work and provide the basic foundations on which good planning can take place. In no other area is this more important than when we are dealing with the use of media. Every person involved in Christian media should be expected to master the field of Christian communication theory and to use it in their daily work.

The word communication is derived from the Latin word *communis*, and it includes the concept of relationships. So called one-way communication can therefore not really be defined as communication. This goes for both the local church pastor and for the media speaker. The audience must be drawn into the communication process.

Many different types of communication situations can be envisioned, ranging from intrapersonal and interpersonal communication to mass media use. In each kind of situation new dimensions are added. But in order to understand these complexities, different writers have developed communication models that aim at explaining the relationships. In this chapter, we have presented the development of a composite model, indicating the important and different aspects of the communication process. The model utilizes insights gained from different writers and earlier models.

Special emphasis was given to the interaction between sender and receiver. The basic question of trust was seen as a prior demand for effective communication.

By mastering the topic of communication theory, the Christian media person will have a conceptual framework in which he or she can develop good ministries. From such a basis, we can proceed towards strategy and development of comprehensive plans for reaching people with the Gospel of Jesus Christ.

QUESTIONS FOR DISCUSSION AND APPLICATION

1. **If you are a pastor:** What would be the implications of carefully analyzing your church services and sermons on the basis of the communication models?

2. **If you are a radio producer:** How can you use the communication model to help you gain a better understanding of your audience and consequently achieve a better communication with them?

3. **If you are a writer and publisher:** What does communication theory teach you about the production of literature and distribution channels available to you?

4. **If you are a Bible translator:** How can you develop translations that not only give an accurate translation of the Word of God, but also communicate with people who may be functionally illiterate?

5. **If you are a cassette producer:** What questions does communication theory require you to answer before producing a cassette program?

6. **If you are an evangelist:** What are the implications of communication theory for crusade meetings and their long-term effects?

FOOTNOTES

1 Nida, Eugene A. *Message and Mission, The Communication of the Christian Faith.* New York: Harper and Row. 1960.

2 Chartier, Myron R. *Preaching as Communication*. Manila: Communication Foundation for Asia. 1981.

3 Smith, Donald K. Study paper prepared for the Lausanne Strategy Conference at Pattaya, Thailand. 1979:5.

4 Frank Gray, "Radio in Mission" published as Lausanne Occasional Paper, 1989.

5 McCroskey, James C. *An Introduction to Rhetorical Communication: The Theory and Practice of Public Speaking*. Englewood Cliffs, N.J., USA: Prentice-Hall. 1968:3ff.

6 Slate, Carl Philip, *Communication Theory and Evangelization*. D.Miss dissertation Fuller Seminary, Pasadena, USA. 1976:17-18.

7 Schramm, Wilbur, "The Nature of Communication between Humans" in *The Process and Effects of Mass Communication*, Urbana, IL: University of Illinois Press. 1971:22.

8 Smith, Donald K. "Using Communications in The Kingdom of God." Study paper for Consultation on World Evangelization at Pattaya. 1979:12. See also Donald K. Smith, *Creating Understand*, Grand Rapids: Zondervan Publishing House, 1992, pp. 144ff.

9 Fuglesang, Andreas. *Applied Communications in Developing Countries*. Uppsala, Sweden: Dag Hammarskjold Foundation. 1973:117.

10 McLuhan, Marshall, *Understanding Media: The Extensions of Man*, New York: McGraw-Hill. 1964.

11 Kraft, Charles, *Christianity in Culture*, Maryknoll, NY: Orbis Books. 1979.

12 Ibid.

13 Jorgensen, Knud. *The Role and Function of the Media in the Mission of the Church*. Unpublished Ph.D. dissertation presented to School of World Mission, Fuller Theological Seminary, Pasadena. 1981.

14 Schramm, Wilbur, "The Nature of Communication between Humans" in *The Process and Effects of Mass Communication*, Urbana, IL: University of Illinois Press. 1971:49–51.

15 Klapper, Joseph T. *The Effects of Mass Communication*. Glencoe, IL: Zondervan Publishing House. 1974.

16 Jorgensen, Knud. *The Role and Function of the Media in the Mission of the Church*. Unpublished Ph.D. dissertation presented to School of World Mission, Fuller Theological Seminary, Pasadena. 1981: 7–8.

17 Mayers, Marvin. *Christianity Confronts Culture*. Grand Rapids: Zondervan Publishing House. 1974:30

18 Lasswell, Harold D., "The Structure and Function of Communication in Society," in Wilbur Schramm and Donald F. Roberts, eds., *The Process and Effects of Mass Communication*. Urbana, IL: University of Illinois Press. 1971:84.

CHAPTER 3

Strategic Plans that Guide Us

Christ's commission and mandate to evangelize the world has still to see its fulfillment, but during the last few years a renewed interest and concern for world evangelization has been evident. The Lausanne movement has been a prime example of this concern with conference slogans such as "Let the Earth Hear His Voice" and "The Whole Church to Take the Whole Gospel to the Whole World." There has also been a renewed interest in adapting the evangelization process to the various cultural settings in which mission is carried out.[1]

Unfortunately, the discussions by many Christian groups on strategy issues are often foggy and carried out without a common frame of reference. This may be experienced when discussing the relative strengths of one method, as compared to another. One person may say she can win more people for Christ in one week by personal evangelism than a radio station can do in a whole year. On the other hand, the broadcaster talks about the millions he is reaching. Both may be partly right, but they are wrong in their assumptions as to what reaching people for Christ implies.

In the previous chapters we have seen that evangelization demands communication, but the effective application of communication theory to media selection and use will only be possible within the clear framework of a research-based strategy. In this chapter we shall therefore analyze some of the insights that strategists can provide to Christian media planners and users.

3.1. STRATEGY AND CHRISTIAN COMMUNICATION

The term "strategy" was originally used as a military term and as such reminds some people of strategies of war. But for most, the term is merely a convenient word for describing any kind of plan. And, it is the conviction of this writer that strategy has deep roots in Scripture and that it is of central importance for Christian communication.

James F. Engel and Wilbert H. Norton raised the obvious and bold question about results.[2] They looked at the church, its many programs and projects, and their conclusion was the sad realization that most of the work lacked results. They then provided both a defense of and a call for the use of applied principles of communication strategy to the evangelistic task of the church, and they called for a research-based strategy that is also a Spirit-guided strategy. They find in the book of Proverbs God-given principles and wisdom concerning our strategy.[3]

> *King Solomon observed that "any enterprise is built by wise planning, becomes strong through common sense, and profits wonderfully by keeping abreast of the facts" (Prov. 23:3-4). In more detail: (1) Analyze the environment; test opinions by fact. "It is dangerous and sinful to rush into the unknown" (Prov. 19:3). "A sensible man watches for problems ahead and prepares to meet them" (Prov. 27:12). (2) Make plans based on this information. "We should make plans—counting on God to direct us" (Prov. 16:9). (3) Measure effectiveness. "Anyone willing to be corrected is on the pathway of life" (Prov. 10:17). "A man who refuses to admit his mistakes can never be successful" (Prov. 28:13). (4) Analyze results and change plans where necessary. "It is pleasant to see plans develop. That is why fools refuse to give up even when they are wrong" (Prov. 13:19).[4]*

God seems to be working within a strategy framework. He called Abraham, a specific person, so that he might bless all nations through him (Gen. 12:3; Gal. 3:8). He called a specific nation, Israel, at specific times for specific purposes (or you could say, he created Israel for specific purposes). He sent his Son at a specific time in history for a specific purpose (Eph. 1:9-10). Jesus, in turn, used a similar strategy, selecting a small and specific group of people (Mt. 3:13-19), training them and sending them out with a specific commission (Mt. 28:18-20). It was a strategy that was to begin at Jerusalem, then Judea and Samaria, and then the ends of the world (Acts 1:8). The Holy Spirit selected certain people at specific times for specific goals, like Paul to go to the Gentiles (Acts 9:15). Paul was well prepared and equipped for this cross-cultural ministry, and he could approach people and work within frames of reference that were different from his own culture, attitudes, and religion (1 Cor. 9:19ff). Consider also this Old Testament illustration. Among the thousands of men who came to David at Hebron were the strategists from Issachar, "Of Issachar men who had understanding of the times, to know what Israel ought to do, two hundred chiefs," (1 Chron. 12:32). In the mission of the church today, we also need strategists who understand the times and can give guidance concerning what we need to do.

Engel and Norton also presented the concept of the effectiveness cycle.[5] Effectiveness is measured in relation to stated objectives. If the goal is to win people for Christ, then the effects will have to be measured on that basis. They observed that organizations and churches seem to go through a cycle of effectiveness, where results decline over a period of time. An "effectiveness crisis" is evident in an organization that does not see any results as measured against their purpose and objectives. There may still be plenty of activity, but activity and effectiveness are not the same.

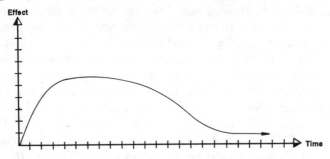

Figure 3.1. The Effectiveness Cycle

There may be many surface causes for an effectiveness crisis, but the root factor is a communication breakdown,[6] usually caused by one-way communication and program orientation. Jesus lived by an "audience orientation" and an adaptive strategy,[7] and if we are to see results from our ministry, our approach must follow his lead.

The apostle Paul adapted his approach and content to his immediate audience and context. In the synagogue his message was designed for the Jews; but when he was speaking in Athens to intellectuals and at Lystra to local pagans, his message was designed for the Gentiles (Acts 17:22-31; 14:15-17).

3.1.1. Strategy defined.

As a general definition of the term strategy, we can say that a strategy is an overall approach, plan, or way of describing how we will go about reaching our goal or solving our problem.[8] Strategy is a way to reach an objective, a kind of map of the territory to be covered in order to "reach from here to there."

Strategy is a conceptual way of anticipating the future, guiding us in major decisions concerning alternative approaches and decisive action. In this way strategy helps us by providing a sense of direction and cohesiveness, focusing on the central issues of our task and philosophy of ministry. It provides us with a frame of reference in which different aspects of theory can be seen in relationship and in their relative and interrelated application to the communication process.

We could also say that Christian communication strategy is the process of planning with an aim to align our plans with God's plans, seeking his will for us and our ministry. Edward R. Dayton and David A. Fraser aptly call it a statement of faith:

> *As Christians, a strategy forces us to seek the mind and will of God. Strategy is an attempt to anticipate the future God wants to bring about. It is a statement of faith as to what we believe that future to be and how we can go about bringing it into existence.*[9]

The development of such a strategy will involve the study of Scriptures, prayer, and relying on the work of the Holy Spirit. But it is the conviction of this writer that it will also need data collection, research and analysis. This conviction is based on personal experience with communication research and on the significant amount of research experience gained by colleagues.

Strategy development demands goal-setting. As such, strategy makes it possible for us to measure effectiveness and helps us to visualize steps leading to the ultimate goals. A strategy, then, helps us develop effectiveness measurements, both for the ultimate goals as well as for intermediate goals. Such measurements also serve to keep us from becoming discouraged to the point of giving up when the ultimate goal seems unattainable. A failure to set realistic goals will almost certainly guarantee failure in ministry. When "you fail to plan, you plan to fail."[10]

Strategy development also includes decisions on media development or "media mix." This means that the theoretical framework leads to practical decisions concerning which media should be used, and when, and for what purpose a particular medium should be selected, or which kind of program is needed at a particular time or phase of the communication process.

Strategy based on a receptor-oriented communication theory is also needed to guide us in intercultural applications. A lack of such strategic understanding may otherwise leave us with canned approaches that in reality are merely the application of monocultural methods. A genuine attitude of dialogue and a high regard for the other person is required as we approach intercultural strategy development.

3.1.2. Strategy Planning Model.

When applying strategic thinking to the work of churches and mission, it has been found extremely helpful to use a circular strategy development model. The model follows basic strategy models developed by other writers.[11]

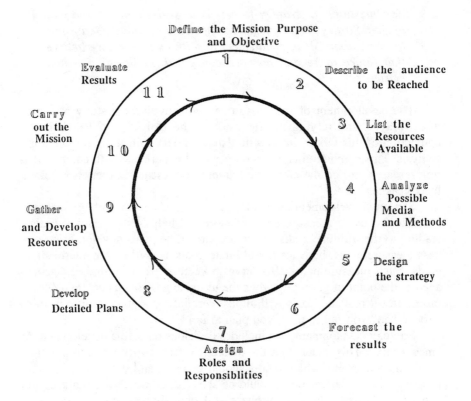

Figure 3.2. Circular Planning Model

The work of Edward R. Dayton, in association with the Lausanne Strategy Working Group, has provided significant input for our understanding and application of strategy to evangelism and Christian mission. They have helped us think strategically, and the production of helpful workbooks and audio-visual material has helped to make the insights of strategy available and acceptable to missionaries and church pastors as well as to students in various training institutions. A helpful, practical manual has also been prepared by John Robb.[12]

The application of the strategy and planning model will be demonstrated in more detail in the last section of this book, but brief introductions to the various points are needed here.

Step 1. Define the Mission Purpose and Objectives:

The first step in any planning process is to clearly define the purpose of the mission. Precisely what is it that we are trying to do? And why are we doing it? Our mission agency or church does not exist for our own sake but in order to fulfill certain specific purposes. Unfortunately, a major problem facing Christian organizations and churches is that their purpose and objectives have been described in such broad terms that they are almost impossible to evaluate. A mission statement must both include the mission distinctives and be precise enough to guide in the development of the strategy and verify the results.

Step 2. Describe the Audience to be Reached:

Who is my listener/reader/viewer? It will make a big difference in our planning if the person is a new Christian or a church leader or maybe a person from another religion with hardly any awareness of the Christian gospel at all. Does he or she have grave misunderstandings about the gospel, or is maybe even hostile? We must know as much as possible about our audience in order to reach them effectively. This calls for extensive research and constant involvement with the audience.

Step 3. List the Resources Available:

Each mission will need resources. What is available for our present task? Who are the people we can draw on to help us? Where can we get financial resources? Who are the cooperating organizations that can assist us with necessary skills? Where can we get the necessary media products? It is important to be a "possibility thinker" in this regard. We should never limit our vision to the resources that are immediately available to us.

Step 4. Analyze Possible Media and Methods:

Here again, we need extensive brainstorming. List all the possible media and methods that could be used to help us achieve our mission purpose among our chosen audience and with the potential resources listed above. Analyze each possibility for its advantages and disadvantages. Which media could be utilized effectively in this project?

Step 5. Design the Strategy:

Here we are making a sketch of what the actual strategy will look like. We will choose the media and the methods that should be used to reach our specific objectives, based on resources available. We will also make decisions on which media not to use. We cannot do everything, so a careful selection must take place.

Step 6. Forecast Results:

Here we ask the tough question: If we follow this strategy, what can we realistically expect as results? If these are not satisfactory in relation to our objectives, we need to go back to step number one and work through the process once again in order to arrive at a strategy that we expect will give the desired results. We also need to consider the next steps. For example, if a new church has been formed, who will be the shepherd?

Step 7. Assign Roles and Responsibilities:

This is critical in Christian communication. How much are we depending on ourselves and how much do we depend on others? Our own skills and resources are limited. A careful listing of roles and responsibilities will not only help us in planning but will also safeguard us from running into serious complications in management and cooperation later on.

Step 8. Develop Detailed Plans:

This is the point where the "blueprint" is developed. As Jesus reminded us, we need to plan before building the house. We need to have the details put in order so that those involved in the mission can follow them. If many people are involved, a written plan can help to keep the focus on the real objectives.

Step 9. Gather and Develop Resources:

Most likely the resources are not readily available. On the financial side we may need to start a fundraising drive. Tracts, radio programs, or films may have to be produced. Staff and volunteers may need to be trained. The primary purpose is to develop our resources so that they are ready for the mission to be carried out.

Step 10. Carry out the Mission:

Without this step the whole planning process will be futile. Here we put our faith and plans into action. Often this will demand great courage and faith on behalf of all involved. During this period good management will ensure that people, money, time, and programs are used in the right order and for the planned purposes.

Step 11. Evaluate Results:

What has God been doing through us and as a result of our engagement in this ministry? Did we see results that correspond with the mission purpose and objectives? How can we learn from the results and redefine our objectives and redesign our strategy? What lessons have been learned that can assist us in becoming more effective in the future?

This particular model has been found to be extremely useful in joint planning sessions. It may look "innocent," but it will force us into serious planning and into asking the right questions. Actually, asking the right questions may be more important for us than searching for the right answers.

3.2. DEVELOPMENT OF A CONCEPTUAL STRATEGY MODEL

The Great Commission demands a strategy that covers the total commission and provides a comprehensive strategic framework in which media applications can be discussed and evaluated. Due to the lack of such a comprehensive strategy, a large proportion of Christian work and use of media has centered around very limited areas of the total program, and, on the other hand, other tasks remain undone. Much Christian media work focusses on conversion, and few concentrate on the "sowing" or initial phases of the spiritual decision process. Evangelistic material produced in the West is often far too narrow in scope to reach the intended audience.

3.2.1. The Principles Of A Total Program.

The need for some clear frame of reference in terms of which one can explain the integration of various media and guide the development of new projects led this writer to start experimenting with new conceptual models. The need called for an overall conceptual model by which we can design and explain the various parts of a total program needed to fulfill the Great

Commission. The commission is to preach the gospel to all people, make disciples from all nations, and then build up by Bible teaching. This gives us three general areas to which we shall designate the more popular terms of sowing, reaping and refining. The basic segmentation model makes this task visible.[13]

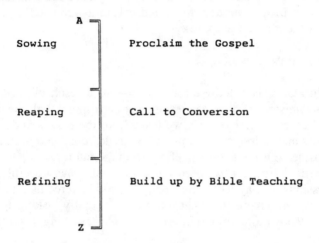

Figure 3.3. Total Program Principle[14]

On this early version, different stages were envisioned, that is, the stages a person passes through on the spiritual journey towards Christ and on to full maturity in Christ. It should be noted that the model indicates stages, which themselves are processes. Reaping is also indicated as a process. The "decision point" could be at any point on the "scale," but experience indicates that conversions which are genuine and lasting usually take place after a person has understood the basic characteristics of the gospel. Conversions would, therefore, usually take place in the area indicated as reaping.

Even though this early version was a strictly cognitive model, a biblical basis was given. For example, the parable of the sower seems to teach this same principle. It was the person who understood and received that in turn bore much fruit, while the person who was like the seed falling on the road did not understand the message received. A conversion requires at least some knowledge of the basic characteristics of the gospel. "But how can they call to him for help if they have not believed? And how can they believe if they have not heard the message?" (Rom. 10:14; Mt. 13:19-23).

If we are to lead a person from his or her present position and on towards spiritual maturity, it is important for us to know the present position of the person or intended audience, as a message designed for one audience segment will generally not be effective for another segment. This particular model has been used in studies to evaluate the effectiveness of specific ministries as well as to analyze target audiences. One of these research studies was an analysis of the listening audience to the Voice of Peace radio programs in Thailand.[15] The questionnaire was based on eighteen topics of biblical understanding, and the research data were then applied to the segmentation model. The result was a clear picture of the present position of the audience and their awareness of the gospel.

A primary purpose of the model was to be used as a tool to measure and illustrate the effectiveness of various programs and methods, as well as that of different communication media. This particular model stimulated the design of similar models by other writers, and it can be found in numerous editions and forms as people have tried to adapt it to their particular situation or their way of thinking. It was realized at the time of publishing the model that it was incomplete, as it only dealt with the cognitive dimension of the spiritual decision process. Other dimensions had to be added. A decision is not only based on understanding, since feelings may play a significant part. The model also depicted progress as a downward trend.

3.2.2. The Spiritual Decision Process.

The version developed by James F. Engel has become well-known around the world.[16] Engel has done much to coordinate the thinking and research of secular behavioral science with theological perspectives. To a large extend, he follows the paradigm of a linear approach to decision making: Knowledge-Belief-Attitude-Intention-Behavior.[17] In *Contemporary Christian Communications* Engel gives a very full description of the model, and he aptly applies the implications to the church and to the mission of the church.

As pointed out above, there was a need for a two-dimensional model that would allow for more accurate descriptions and strategy development. There also had to be room for changes in the sequence of elements in the decision process, as well as allowing decisions at different stages in the process.[18] The knowledge-persuasion-decision sequence may actually be culture bound and in some socio-cultural settings different sequences may occur, at least for some innovations. It is clear that there is a process, but the elements may not always be in the same order or they may be simultaneous processes.

For some people their spiritual journey begins with information and knowledge, but others will begin their spiritual journey as a result of a power encounter which has caused attitude change. For most people, there will probably be concurrent processes of cognitive and affective changes and these will continue after the decision or change in allegiance has been made.

3.3. A TWO-DIMENSIONAL STRATEGY AND DECISION MODEL

The two-dimensional model provides a grid on which "mapping" can take place. The two dimensions used here are the cognitive dimension, that is, knowledge, and the affective dimension which consists of attitudes or feelings.[19]

3.3.1. Knowledge and Feelings.

The vertical axis is the cognitive dimension. The main differences from the earlier model presented above are that it is turned around so that increased cognitive understanding will be illustrated as an upward move and the increase in cognitive understanding is indicated as an ongoing process. There is no fixed conversion point, as decision for Christ can theoretically take place at any stage of the cognitive process. Ideally, decisions should take place on the basis of a good cognitive foundation, but in practice we often see people accepting Christ at a very low level of biblical knowledge. Such a situation will then demand heavy emphasis on cognitive input in the form of Bible teaching to safeguard and nurture further growth and permanent results.

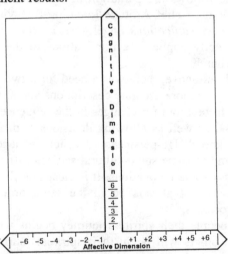

Figure 3.4. Two-Dimensional Model with both Cognitive
and Affective Dimensions

Based on the conviction that conversion is not an entirely cognitive process, the affective dimension has been added to make the model more useful. The affective dimension will primarily be a person's feelings towards the gospel, towards the church, and towards Christ. The actual decision is to a large extent an affective change, or change of allegiance. The result is a matrix on which strategy can be developed. Through research we are able to discover a person's or a people group's position on the "chart."

3.3.2. Journey Towards Maturity.

The journey towards spiritual maturity becomes a journey from one's present position towards "the upper right hand corner" of the model, as illustrated on figure 3.5. Most likely, this will not be a straight line as on this illustration, but it will fluctuate between cognitive and affective changes. Or both may take place at the same time. As already mentioned, conversion is to a large extent the crossing of the affective line from negative to positive, and it can occur at multiple places. Most conversions will probably take place in the area indicated on figure 3.5. The line between negative and positive attitudes should possibly be broadened to allow for an area of non-commitment or neutrality.

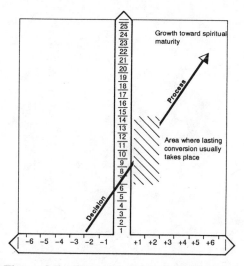

Figure 3.5. Concept of Spiritual Progress

In the previous chapter, we concluded that an acceptable Christian communication theory must be process-oriented and that it must correspond to the decision process of the audience. This process can be illustrated on the model. Each step in the spiritual decision process caused by our ministry can then be seen as an evangelistic effect.

The development of a comprehensive, integrated strategy is like planning a "highway" from the present position of our audience and on to spiritual maturity. Some examples will be provided later to illustrate that such a "highway" will consist of different methods, approaches and media applications. Each ministry or program becomes a section of the "highway" and must therefore be closely integrated. This will require clear sub-goals and strategies for each ministry involved. We cannot cause a person to walk on this highway, but we can make it possible.

3.3.3. Illustrations of Previous Journeys.

In order to understand our audience, it is helpful to analyze an individual's or people group's movements up to this present time. In other words, we can map the "journey" which they have already taken. It is important for applied strategy (programming) to know where "they" have been, so that we can understand the knowledge and belief structures that form the basis for their present attitudes. A few illustrations of such possible journeys are given in the following figures. For each one, a strategy can be worked out and necessary ministries planned.

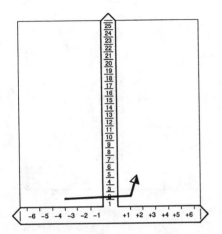

Fig. 3.6. A tribal group that has just burned their idols and want to become Christians. They have experienced change in attitude, but have very little biblical understanding.

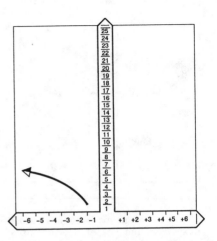

Fig. 3.7. The effects of Western schools on children. As they are taught by teachers who are atheists, their attitude to the gospel has become negative.

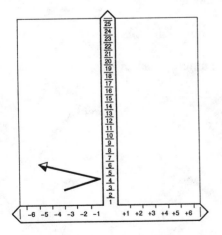

Fig. 3.8. A person who "accepted" but did not understand, and then turned negative. He is like the seed that fell on the road.

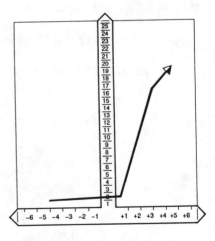

Fig. 3.9. A person won through a power-encounter, then well-trained.

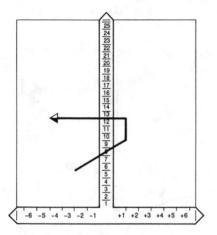

Fig. 3.10. Someone who has turned away from the gospel. His cognitive knowledge has not diminished.

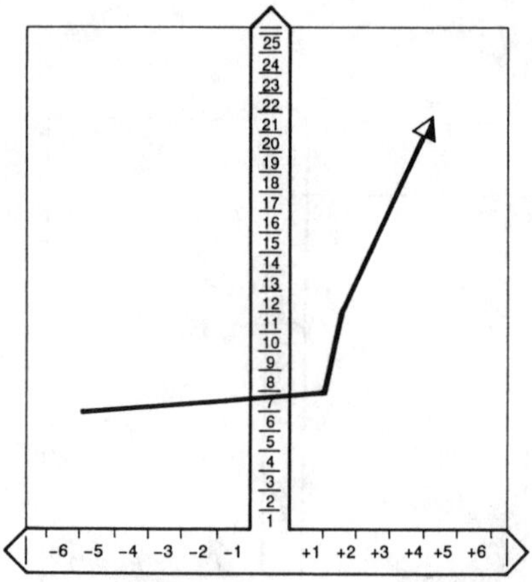

Fig. 3.11. A church-leader who was converted after being a rebellious, negative, Western youth.

If we are to approach these audiences, we will have to develop different strategies and approaches for each one. The starting point will be to plot the positions of our audiences on the model. Media selection will need to be based on the local context and possibilities.

3.3.4. Identifying the Position of our Audience(s).

The following illustration shows six different audiences.

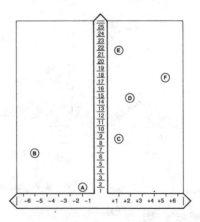

Figure 3.12. Illustration of Various Audience Positions

3.3.5. Analyzing our Present Reach.

We may have many good strategies that are independently effective, but due to the fact that they are not integrated but disconnected and isolated steps, ultimate results are not seen. Much Western-produced evangelistic material is very limited in scope and does not reach much beyond the area of reaping. Development programs carried out by Christian agencies may cause significant changes in attitudes, but due to lack of integration permanent spiritual results are lacking.

The emphasis by missions and local churches on the "middle area" of conversion is probably due to the lack of a comprehensive strategy, but it is also due to the limitations of our research measurements. Usually, we have only measured conversions, baptisms or church membership, and such indicators relate to the middle section of our model. Consequently, our desire to measure effectiveness and show results has forced us to concentrate strategy development on areas that can be measured. But any movement toward spiritual maturity should be seen as a measure of effectiveness.

3.3.6. Openness to Change.

For any development of effective strategy and programs, we need to discover people's receptivity and openness to change. At any position on the model, there will be a certain latitude of openness. The analysis of a group's position will not guarantee any changes or responses, but will help us to discover how to communicate with the person.

Some groups in a society are always more open to change than others, and at certain times in life we are more receptive to new ideas and to change than at other periods. Church growth advocates have focused on receptive fields. But even though this is a very important topic to consider, we have to be extremely careful in our analysis. People may be closed to my approach rather than to the gospel, or my approach may actually be hindering a change.

This will lead us into a discovery of felt needs. If we focus our attention on such needs, we may be able to uncover deeper needs and in turn provide answers to such needs. By discovering the latitude of acceptance/ rejection of our audience, we will also discover their receptivity.

Our communication strategy must take its starting point here. Some may be open to the study of Scriptures as long as it is done outside a church. Others will attend a social event at the church, but not a church service. Some will listen to a Christian radio program in the privacy of their own homes. The skillful communicator will use such events to expand the latitude of acceptance, so that change can take place. The following examples illustrate this point.

3.3.7. Examples of Actual Use of the Two-Dimensional Model.

The model was used to illustrate the ministry of an organization in South India that has been producing evangelistic programs in the form of traditional Indian dances. The cognitive content of the dances was limited, but they affected change of attitudes. The Hindu audience was basically negative towards the gospel, but by presenting the gospel in Indian dress through Indian dances the gospel was seen as Indian. The organization also produced radio programs that provided biblical content and further understanding. The actual contact ministry was based on local church outreach, and in order to assist the churches in this ministry they produced a number of cassette tapes. The actual nurture of new Christians is the responsibility of the churches.

As seen in figure 3.13, where the total ministry of the organization has been plotted, the audience has a very limited understanding of the gospel, and at the same time is quite negative. On the model their position would be at approximately -4 on the affective scale and 2 on the cognitive scale. Dance-drama aimed at affective changes, moving the audience from -4 towards -1 or even to a neutral position. Cognitive change was the goal of radio programs that aimed at giving foundational Christian teaching. The bridge to the church, or we could say the actual "reaping" ministry, was provided by church members using cassette tapes as part of their personal witness.

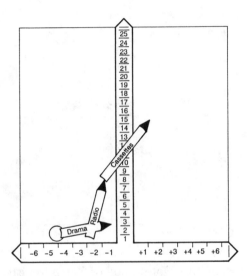

Figure 3.13. An Integrated Ministry in South India.

Another example can be taken from the ministry to a group of young people in Denmark. The group is located at approximately 7 on the cognitive dimension and -5 on the affective dimension. A church has established a youth club as a contact ministry. There is no preaching, but as the leaders spend time with the youth who come there a testimony is given, and a trust-relationship is established. This should provide a basis for affective changes from -5 and towards a neutral position. The leader of the club conducts a Bible study in his home and interested youth are invited to attend. Here basic Bible teaching is given to provide growth in knowledge. The nearby church has occasional youth rallies, and interested young people from the club can be brought along. Such evangelistic rallies will provide a definite challenge to accept Christ. Those who are converted will then be channeled into the discipling programs of the church.

The planning of such an integrated ministry was enhanced by the use of our two-dimensional model. It helped the church to understand the need for a long-term strategy, and that they should not expect results in the form of conversions at the beginning of the ministry.

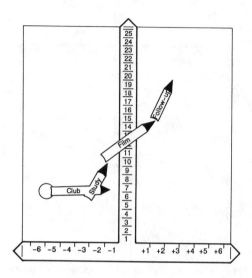

Figure 3.14. Integration of Youth Ministry

A two-dimensional model was also used for the development of a comprehensive strategy for a large Asian city.[21] This is a project aimed at evangelizing a whole city of four million people, a comprehensive program for church planting and growth. The aim was to confront every person in the city with Jesus Christ as a living option. This would include awareness of who Jesus is as well as further cognitive understanding of the message. They would also seek to penetrate the culture of the city with the gospel in order to present Jesus Christ as a culturally acceptable option. For this purpose, it was necessary to use all available media for a comprehensive program. The specific objectives were described as follows:

> *(1) Climatizing the City: building awareness and positive atti-tudes towards Christianity. This part would be based on mass media strategy: television, radio, newspapers, and news events.*

> *(2) Confronting the Interested: creating responsiveness by pub-lic presentations of the gospel. This part would also be mass media strategy, but using such media as films, concerts, and drama.*

(3) Contacting the Responsive: calling for commitment by those who are responsive. Here the strategy would be totally decentralized, based on outreach by local churches. They will use a wide variety of media.

(4) Churching the Committed: incorporating new converts into churches, discipling them, etc. This is also a decentralized strategy, and the churches will use relevant media, including cassettes, print, correspondence courses, seminars, etc.

(5) Catalyzing the Church. In order to carry out such a campaign of comprehensive church planting, it is of crucial importance that the church members be trained to play their significant roles in this strategy. So, this fifth point becomes, chronologically speaking, point one.

The total program can be illustrated as follows:

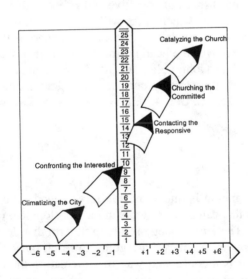

Figure 3.15. All Media Penetration Project for a Large City

As many different ministries and organizations are involved in such a project, illustrations like the one above are almost mandatory for understanding and coordination. Each particular ministry or program can see where they fit in, even though they may be working without any administrative links to each other. The present hostile environment in many countries of the world will call for such integrated strategies or partnerships with administratively separated ministries and approaches.

3.3.8. An Incomplete Model.

Any model or scale of the spiritual decision process will be incomplete. Even if we could construct multidimensional scaling, they would still be insufficient in depicting the spiritual life of human beings. We may therefore not always be in disagreement as to which dimensions should be depicted on a model, but, on the other hand, we can often be helped by a variety of complementary models. Some are good for educational purposes, others are excellent for actual strategy planning.

In an earlier chapter we dealt with the topic of constants and variables of Christian communication. The work of the Spirit is the unseen dimension that is basic to all our ministry. It cannot be depicted on graphs or scales, as the Spirit, like the wind, blows where he wills. We know that all spiritual growth depends on the inner working of the Holy Spirit. Educational theorists speak of cognitive and affective dimensions as well as the psychomotor effect, which is the will or drive to move ahead. The psychomotor effect on our model, i.e. the will to change, is that caused by the Holy Spirit as he moves the hearts of people in their process toward Christ and new life in him (John 6:44; Tit. 3:5-7). We cannot cause that movement to happen, but we can by our concern, witness, and challenge make the move more likely (2 Cor. 4:2). It is Christ who deals with the will of a person.

SUMMARY

Strategy planning is important to effective media work, and there are helpful models that can serve as tools in the development of good and relevant strategies. The term strategy is a helpful term that describes an overall plan or approach as to how we are going to reach our objectives or solve our problems. It is a conceptual way of anticipating the future. As Christians, statements relating to our strategy objectives and goals are statements of faith.

An eleven-step circular strategy development model was introduced as a useful tool that will help us ask the right questions and lead us through an orderly process of strategy development.

In order to provide a "framework," we have in this chapter presented a spiritual decision model. The purpose is to present a strategic framework for the development of strategies and for communicating the use of media to others. The model is built on two dimensions: knowledge and attitudes. It is not the intention that models should illustrate or answer all questions relating to spiritual decision processes. The models developed so far are still in the process of development, changing as we learn more and understand better. They are not saying, that this is the way it is, but rather, this is the way we try to illustrate what we understand, based on our present insights.

It is the view of this writer that the relationship between our work and the work of the Spirit should not be explained as a partnership. It is necessary to describe the relationship from an incarnational perspective, Christ in us and working through us.

QUESTIONS FOR DISCUSSION AND APPLICATION

Take a careful look at the ministry you have been involved in recently. Then, try to put it on the two-dimensional model and see where it fits, whom it reaches, and how it integrates with other ministries. Then decide what you need to do in order to have a comprehensive plan for your ministry.

FOOTNOTES

1 Hesselgrave, David J. *Communicating Christ Cross-Culturally*, Grand Rapids: Zondervan. 1980; Kraft, Charles, *Christianity in Culture*. Maryknoll, NY: Orbis Books. 1979.

2 Engel, James F. and Norton, Wilbert H. *What's Gone Wrong With the Harvest?* 1975. Grand Rapids: Zondervan.

3 Quotes from Living Bible.

4 Engel, James F. and Norton, Wilbert H. *What's Gone Wrong With the Harvest?* Grand Rapids: Zondervan. 1975:39.

5 Engel, James F. and Norton, Wilbert H. *What's Gone Wrong With the Harvest?* Grand Rapids: Zondervan. 1975:20.

6 Ibid. p.23.

7 Ibid. p.33-39.

8 Dayton, Edward R. and Fraser, David A. *Planning Strategies for World Evangelization*. Revised Edition. Grand Rapids: William B. Eerdmans. 1900:13.

9 Ibid. p.14.

10 Schuller, Robert H. *Your Church has Real Possibilities*, Glendale: Regal Books. 1974:72.

11 Dayton, Edward R. and David A. Fraser, *Planning Strategies for World Evangelization*. Grand Rapids: William B. Eerdmans. 1990.

12 Robb, John D. *The Power of People Group Thinking*. MARC. 1989.

13 Søgaard, Viggo *Everything you need to know for a Cassette Ministry*. Minneapolis: Bethany Fellowship Publishers. 1975a:27.

14 Ibid. p.28.

15 Søgaard, Viggo. Unpublished research report on Radio Listening. 1975.

16 Engel, James F. and Wilbert H. Norton, *What's Gone Wrong With the Harvest?* Grand Rapids: Zondervan. 1975; Engel, James F. *Contemporary Christian Communications, Its Theory and Practice.* Nashville: Thomas Nelson. 1977.

17 See *Consumer Behavior* by James F. Engel and Roger D. Blackwall for a description of this perspective.

18 Søgaard, Viggo B., *Applying Christian Communications.* Ann Arbor, MI: University Microfilms. 1986:175ff.

19 See Engel, James F. *How to Communicate the Gospel Effectively*, Africa Christian Press. 1988, for another variation of the model.

20 Griffin, Em *The Mind Changers.* Wheaton, IL: Tyndale House. 1976.

21 Søgaard, Viggo *Bangkok All Media Penetration.* Bangkok: Foreign Mission Board. 1979.

CHAPTER 4

Information that Makes Us Relevant

The question of research has been raised several times during the previous chapters. But how do we get the information that is needed for relevant, intelligent and effective use of media? This present chapter will seek to introduce the necessary research methodologies and techniques that are available and their function in the service of Christian communication.

Unfortunately, research has not always been readily acceptable to Christian leaders. The term itself may be rejected due to theological reasons like, "only God can truly evaluate the effectiveness of ministry." With this we do not disagree, but it is our contention that research must be seen as a valuable and indispensable tool of effective and accountable ministries.

Actually, research is a non-threatening daily phenomenon that we all engage in, one way or another, as we seek information from or about each other and the surrounding environment. A look out the window to see if it is raining is research. Or a study of the religion followed by our audience is research. In our desire to be accountable and good stewards we should have no theological problems viewing research as a legitimate tool of communication. We all want to know if people understand our message, or even if anyone is listening.

We may often be tempted to study results focusing on single causes, as we try to prove that observed changes were caused by our ministry or program. We need to support such claims by reliable research. In reality, there may be a combination of reasons, so if we focus on only one or two, our attention may be diverted from the real causes. The public crusade meeting may be able to count the decisions but the real cause may be the constant, faithful witness by local churches in a community.

Likewise, the effects of communication can also be hindered by a variety of causes. For example, in a Muslim context the choice of message may create barriers. Topics such as pork eating, freedom of women, music, or Christian names are all problematic and may cause resistance or even hostility. We may wrongly interpret this as resistance to the gospel.

Christian communicators need a good information system that will provide us with reliable data. In this chapter we shall first look at the functions of research in strategy development and media use. We will then try

77

to get a grasp of the field of communication research, and finally we will focus on actual media testing and research methodologies. Chapter 16 will provide practical guidelines on evaluation and pretesting procedures.

4.1.   THE FUNCTIONS OF COMMUNICATION RESEARCH IN STRATEGY DEVELOPMENT FOR CHURCH AND MEDIA

The circular planning model presented in the previous chapter has proved to be a very useful tool, both for strategy development and for the illustration of research needs. Research in one form or another can play a vital role for most of the eleven steps as we seek relevant information that will guide our decision making.

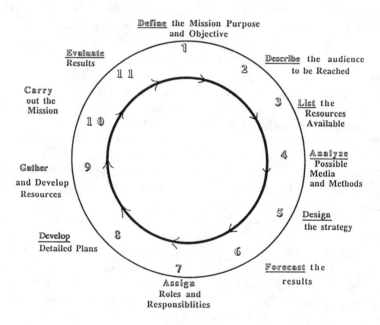

Figure 4.1. The Function of Research in the Planning Process

4.1.1.   Research Helps Us Define the Mission.

The work of the Holy Spirit is fundamental to all mission, and this cannot be planned or defined by research. On the other hand, through research we can document where the Spirit seems to be working. Visions are given by God, but mission is needed to translate vision into practical action. We often find pastors and other Christian leaders with great visions and their mission has been defined on the basis of experience and intuition. A research project can help to confirm if they are still on track, or otherwise help to redefine the mission at hand and to explore new possibilities. Likewise, many media ministries are in operation without a clear definition of their mission or their target audience. Research can help to gather the information that will help them sharpen the vision and redefine the mission.

Many churches and organizations could profitably start by an analysis of what is actually happening because of their ministry. Such an analysis can describe the people being reached now, and with what results. It is important to know where we are. An analysis of evangelistic magazine ads, for example, might aim at defining the people who actually responded.

Research data may also be used to give new visions as the needs of people are communicated to churches. An example of such research is the work carried out by Missions Advanced Research and Communication Center (MARC) for the "Lausanne movement." An extensive database has been created on Unreached Peoples and this information is communicated to churches around the world. Books like Patrick Johnstone's *Operation World* are also being used widely to inspire people for mission.[1]

4.1.2. Research Helps Us Describe the Audience.

One of the demands of an acceptable Christian communication theory is that it is receptor-oriented. We need to know who the listener or reader is if we are to meet felt needs and to effect real change. An effective communication strategy will, therefore, have as its starting point a clear description of the audience and their needs. We need to study their relationship to God and their position in the decision process. Such detailed information gathered prior to the start of a Christian media ministry will provide a basis for later evaluation of results.

A study of radio listeners may aim at describing the listening audience, their attitudes, interests and opinions, and then try to define them in terms of the spiritual decision model. Listener needs and interests would then be able to direct the preparation of communication messages that will reach within the listeners' latitude of acceptance. Similarly, the study of a church may be conducted to obtain a clear description of its members for the purpose of developing a relevant teaching program. Through research we can describe subgroups in a population and, as such, provide the basis for an audience-based strategy.

4.1.3. Research Helps Us Describe Our Resources.

The development of sound communication strategies will always need to seriously consider the available resources. The basic resources are people (with gifts), organization, facilities and funds. Most tasks are too big and too broad for any one organization to handle, so a listing of resources available from other sources may be an important activity.

So, which resources are available for the task at hand? We often find that organizations that aim at reaching the same audience do not know the resources developed by the others. During a recent consultation in Pakistan, we discussed the needs of a specific, non-literate tribal group. Several missions are involved in reaching them, but we discovered, for example, that one group had produced a set of teaching cassettes several years ago, but only a few copies had been distributed. The other organizations were not aware of their existence.

4.1.4. Research Helps Us Analyze Media And Methods.

In some countries we have the luxury of being able to choose whatever medium we fancy, as a number of media are available and free to be used by anyone with the necessary resources. In other countries our choices may be very restricted due to the political situation. But in every case we need to make intelligent choices so that the most appropriate medium will be used. Often we need to carry out experiments or pilot programs to obtain the necessary information and experience.

Marketing organizations will collect extensive data on the usefulness of individual media channels and their effectiveness in a given context. Diffusion studies have, likewise, analyzed the effects of various methods, and how methods and media can be best integrated for reaching certain desired goals. Some church growth studies have analyzed evangelistic campaigns and media ministries, but, generally speaking, there are very few studies on the comparative effectiveness and use of media from a Christian communication perspective. Usually, available information is not comparative in nature, but focus on an individual medium. The World by 2000 advance is, for example, collecting extensive data on the use of radio in Christian ministries around the World.

Often information can be obtained from secular organizations concerning the availability of media channels, cost, listenership, readership, age-groups, and how the media are perceived by a given society. Television would, for example, need to be treated differently in the United States, Israel and republics from the former Soviet Union.[2]

In process-oriented communication, as advocated in this book, the various media will play different roles in different societies. We should, therefore, not take the easy way out and just copy programs and approaches from another country and context without considering their usefulness and financial feasibility in the society in which we work. For example, a poor church in a poor country should not select an approach based on expensive technology that is unrealistic in their situation. Actually, the simplicity forced on certain organizations due to the lack of funds or unavailability of certain media has often resulted in far more effective strategies than might have been the case if excess funds had been available.

4.1.5. Research Helps Us Design the Approach.

Designing an approach may be more a selection process than actual research. It is the use of research data, case studies, and experimentation results that will guide us in developing realistic programs. Strategists do not need to be professional researchers, but they need to know how to interpret and use research data. Without the availability of research data, it would be extremely difficult to define an effective approach to Christian communication in a given country or context. The models presented in the previous chapters are aimed at conceptualizing and understanding communication, media, and strategy, but we need information to actually use the models in applied communication.

4.1.6. Research Helps Us Forecast Results.

Throughout the chapters of this book, we are calling for a goal-oriented communication strategy. As Christians are communicating for the purpose of achieving certain goals, so our communication must have effects if it is to portray true Christian communication.

Dayton and Fraser term this point on the strategy planning model "Anticipated Outcome" which implies that we should, on the basis of research, be able to anticipate what the strategy can accomplish. The forecasting of results can be helped by a comparison of results from similar projects, as well as from the results of pretesting and pilot programs.

4.1.7. Research Helps Us Develop Plans.

During planning phases of a communications program, research can primarily help us by pretesting methods, programs and other products. As an example of such testing (or experimental research), we could mention the field testing of a cassette with Bible selections. This particular study gave directions for future productions and distribution of audio-based Scriptures.[3] Internal evaluation and critique will help us remove many of the problems prior to testing with the intended audience, and, at the same time, help us to work as a team.

Pretesting can help us avoid serious mistakes in layout as we test a magazine cover or an ad prior to publication. Field testing can provide guidance before large sums of money are committed to expensive productions. A later chapter will be devoted to this important aspect of pretesting and the development of effective media programs.

4.1.8. Research Helps Us Evaluate.

Evaluation should be seen as an element of good stewardship. As the church entrusts resources to communication ministries, such ministries must be accountable for effective use of the resources. The primary question to ask is, Did we reach our objectives? If yes, what did we do right? If no, what did we do wrong? There is nothing wrong in failing as long as we learn from our mistakes!

A radio survey can be aimed at studying the effects of radio programs, as well as providing information on cost effectiveness of media selection. How many did actually listen, and what changes did the programs cause in their lives?

Let us hope that the refined research methodologies and techniques that are available for Christian communication will increasingly be used to enhance the ministry and evaluate our effectiveness.

> **In summary, research can be used to:**
> — **sharpen the vision**
> — **provide information on the audience**
> — **make receptor-oriented communication possible**
> — **help evaluate media products and programs**
> — **assist in strategy development**
> — **direct in goal-setting**
> — **guide in planning**
> — **test the effectiveness of ministry**
> — **reveal the necessity of seeking the direction of God**

4.2. THE FIELD OF COMMUNICATION RESEARCH

We could also look at communication research from the perspective provided by Lasswell in his famous sentence on the effects of communication: "Who Says What To Whom In Which Channel With What Effect."[4] Each of these five elements can be researched, so we need an information system that will gather information on the communicator, the content, the media, the audience, and the impact.

Our information system will usually draw on the insights and methodologies obtained from various academic disciplines. Consequently, communication research can be seen as an applied science that draws on other fields of study and research: anthropological, sociological, marketing, as well as media research. The methodologies are similar, yet influenced by the specific interests and demands of the particular academic discipline. In the following, we shall look briefly at some of these disciplines and their usefulness for communication research.

4.2.1. Marketing Research.

As the marketing concept is adopted by more and more organizations, including service and nonprofit organizations, the understanding of the nature and role of marketing research has expanded. Marketing research has developed extensive methodologies and techniques for the actual collection of data, and it is primarily from marketing research that we obtain the necessary tools for survey research, which is a primary methodology used by communication researchers.

Prior to any survey research, an analysis of *secondary data sources* will be conducted. Secondary data is information already gathered by others. The primary advantage of secondary data is that it saves cost and time. Among the disadvantages of using secondary sources is the fact that the data has been collected for other purposes, so categories may not fit the need of our present decision-problems.

Survey research will begin by clearly identifying the purpose of the research project. This is a question for both the researcher and the management/leadership. Following the development of research objectives, the next question concerns the information needed. A listing of specific information needs is designed to guide the development of the questionnaire and other aspects of the study and it will help in the interpretation of the collected data. Careful preparation of objectives and information needs will save time and money later, and it will avoid the collection of unnecessary data.

The research design will serve as the basic plan and framework for data collection. Included in the design will be a sampling plan. Usually, a questionnaire must also be constructed.

A questionnaire is a formalized way of collecting data from respondents, but, due to possible measurement errors, the help of a skilled researcher is needed to design the questionnaire. There are no series of steps, principles, or guidelines which guarantee an effective and efficient questionnaire. It is both an art and a scientific undertaking. During personal experiences with research projects, the "checklist" presented in figure 4.2 has been compiled. Each of these questions should be asked concerning each question on a questionnaire.

---

1. Is the question necessary?
2. Are several questions needed instead of just one?
3. Does the respondent have the information?
4. Does the respondent have any experience with the subject?
5. Does the respondent remember the necessary information?
6. Is the respondent willing to give the required information?
7. Does the question look reasonable to the respondent?
8. Is the question ambiguous?
9. Is the question biased?
10. Is the question clear?
11. Is the question too broad?
12. Are you able to answer yes or no?
13. Do you need a graded answer?
14. Will the question(s) obtain the needed information?
15. Does the question embarrass the respondent?
16. Does the question frighten the respondent?
17. Are the questions in a logical order on the questionnaire?
18. Does any question influence the following questions?
19. Is the first question interesting to the respondent?
20. Does the questionnaire look interesting?
21. Is the questionnaire easy to use?
22. Have the questionnaire and the questions been pretested?

Figure 4.2. Checklist for Questionnaire Design

After data collection and tabulation, the final stage of writing a research report can begin. Such a report is designed to communicate the information to the decision makers in such a way that they can actually apply the findings to the ministry. A research report is of no use if the findings are not used to solve problems or phased into a communication strategy.

We could summarize and say that survey research helps us to recognize and define a decision problem, help to identify possible courses of action, and then help us select the course of action to take.

4.2.2. The Process of a Research Project.

The question often arises, Who should do the research? Research is a technical task, requiring certain skills, but both management and producers must be involved in the process if you are to safeguard relevant data collection and actual use of the information. The management must be involved in planning the research and the establishment of research objectives and then later be involved in the interpretation and application of the data. The actual collection procedures in a survey research project involving questionnaires are the task of the researcher.

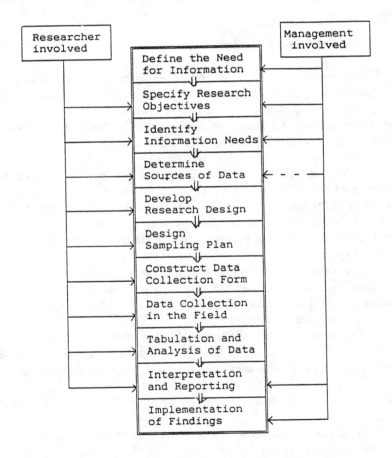

Figure 4.3. The Research Process

But, there are many kinds of research we all can take part in. Any producer can spend time with representatives of the audience, asking questions and getting to know them. We all need a research perspective so that the information gathering can be a joint effort. If it is just left to the researcher, the result may be reports sitting on shelves without being used.

The perspective of this writer is a marketing research perspective where research facilitates good decision-making in particular by management and producers of communication programs and products. The concept implies a deeply involved role for research in the management decision-making process.

Such a perspective suggests that we only gather the information we need according to stated objectives. This may be the development of a strategy or the selection of relevant biblical texts for a program or printed booklet.

4.2.3. Anthropological Research.

Survey research is important for gathering certain kinds of information that can be quantified, but for other areas of communication research and for the purpose of analyzing a people's worldview, we need to learn from the principles of anthropological research. Anthropological research distinguishes between the following methods of study,

a. Participant Observation. Here the researcher will take up residence in the community, and detailed data are obtained by observations. Producers of Christian radio programs can follow the same approach as they try to understand their listeners, possibly living in a community for a period. A friend of this writer once became a shepherd for a week to prepare himself for making programs for shepherds and their families.

b. Key-Informant Interviewing. The researcher will use "key informants" as sources of information about their own cultures. Similarly, Christian communicators can conduct regular in-depth interviews with selected people representing the group they are trying to communicate with. This may even be a neighbor.

c. Collection of Life Histories. Such stories can often serve the researcher in his or her study of how past events have an effect on present beliefs and values. Testimonies of individuals, mapping their life-history, can help us understand the background to their present attitudes and understanding, as well as help us design strategies for reaching others like them.

d. Structured Interviews. In this much more structured phase of a research project, a representative sample is studied to provide quantification. This is similar to survey research, but will often be done with a much smaller sample of respondents.

e. Projective Techniques. A number of different techniques can be used, for example sentence-completion techniques. A person is asked to complete a sentence like, "I would consider becoming a Christian, if ..." Such a procedure will often give clues as to their real felt needs and attitudes.

f. Unobtrusive Measures. This refers to situations where the people studied are not aware that an analysis is going on. It may be analyzing responses to a ministry on the basis of follow-up cards, or just to listen as they tune their radios to the music they like.

Through such methodologies and techniques anthropological research can provide significant data on media communication and, most important, provide media programmers with significant information on how to establish communication with a particular group of people. Their felt needs, their interests and their daily concerns can be uncovered by a researcher who actually lives among the people.

4.2.4. Intercultural Research.

Intercultural research is not a methodology like marketing or anthropological research but should be understood as the applied area of adapting and using research methodologies and principles in intercultural settings.

Outside highly developed industrial countries marketing research data and studies are very few, and many approaches developed in the West may not be suitable. Anthropological researchers have, on the other hand, primarily worked in so-called developing countries, and they have usually worked with research measures other than those using probability sampling. Western-developed approaches to probability sampling are often impossible in intercultural settings, so great creativity is needed. This does not imply that such sampling cannot be carried out but that new and creative adaptations are often needed.

The question of data quality control in intercultural surveys should always be taken seriously, as errors in the data can completely distort the results of an analysis. It is our experience from studies in Asian countries that a stratified probability sample is possible and very useful. Panels with self-administered questionnaires have also proved helpful. Similarly, group interviews with individual, anonymous, self-administered questionnaires have worked well. On the other hand, non-probability samples are often more realistic, and a carefully planned quota sample may in a number of situations be more practical and representative. A researcher with proper training in research methodology should be able to work out designs that give reliable data.

4.3.　RESEARCH MEASUREMENTS

As we look at different parts of our environment and daily experiences, we need different kinds of special tools and techniques for gathering information about them. Some instruments, like a thermometer, can be used by anybody, but other instruments and techniques need training and practice if they are to be useful. For an untrained person a look into a microscope or telescope will tell him almost nothing. For others, numbers or economic data will make no sense. The novice needs to acquire a conceptual framework and gain additional experience. Likewise, the media researcher must, in addition to the basic tools and instruments of observation and measurement, have a general conceptual framework for sorting out and organizing the data received.

It is important for us to master both methodologies and techniques to obtain the reliable and valid information we need. We cannot base this on letters received from the audience, whether praising or complaining, as it is very difficult to tell how much of the audience they represent. Letters are important to many mass media programs, but the more sophisticated the mass communicators are, the more suspicious they should be of such unsystematic feedback.

Measurement is a fundamental aspect of research, and it is often stated that the best way to really understand something is to try to measure it. The measurement process involves using numbers to represent the phenomena under investigation, or we could say that measurement is concerned with developing a correspondence between the empirical system and the abstract system.[5]

The measurement task in communication research is typically more difficult than the counting of numbers, as we know from church growth studies. The problem lies in the measurement of the behavior of people and of measuring concepts believed to exist in people's minds. There are, of course, certain types of data that can be obtained relatively easy by counting, for example conversions, or the number of people listening to a sermon, but the majority of our studies will need to be based on increasingly difficult scales. The issues of faith are in the area which is very difficult to measure.

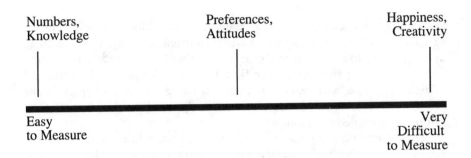

Figure 4.4. Difficulty of the Measurement Process

Most data collected through survey research involves "ordinal" measurements, that is, putting products or concepts in some kind of order. It is the measurement of attitudes, opinions, preference, and perception that frequently involve a "greater than" or "less than" judgment. Before we can study such opinions, they need to be defined precisely. We often need to develop accurate and measurable definitions of such topics as a person's loyalty to the family or to his or her church before we can gather the information.

Attitudes are important because of the assumed relationship between attitudes and behavior. Attitudinal data is used to identify audience segments and to measure openness to change. The Christian communicator needs, for example, to understand people's attitudes toward Christ and toward the church, in order to prepare programs that are relevant and that will gain a listening.

4.4. MEDIA RESEARCH

We will look at three specific areas of media research that are of special interest to our present purpose: (1) media vehicle research that deals with the medium itself and the selection of media, (2) copy testing, that is, testing media products and programs, and (3) testing effects of media programs, that is, looking at actual effects in relation to stated objectives. Each of these areas has their specific approaches which can readily be used by Christian media researchers.

4.4.1. Media Vehicle Research.

Many management decisions relate to the selection of media vehicles or channels of communication, as we have discussed earlier. We need to ask questions like, Which media channels should we choose: television, radio or newspapers? What specific television time should be selected? Which magazine will reach our intended audience? All such decisions require the availability of data related to the media vehicle itself. The information needed is as follows:

a. Distribution of the Media. This will include such items as the circulation number for a magazine or newspaper or the number of television or radio sets available to carry the message. If you are a producer of audio cassettes, you will want to know the distribution of cassette players. Distribution data are the most readily attainable and are relatively free of controversy in terms of their accuracy.

b. Exposure to the Media. This is the number of people exposed to the medium itself. Here we measure the number of readers who obtain a copy of a given issue of a magazine or newspaper or the number of viewers of television. It is a study of the potential audience size.

c. Advertising or Program Exposure. Here we are dealing with the actual number of people who are exposed to a specific advertisement or program in the media. People may be exposed to a program or article but not notice a specific advertisement. The number will probably be much less than the potential audience.

d. Program Perception. The number of people who perceived the program in question. This will include the people who actually listen to the sermon. Perception is influenced by the color and size of an ad, positioning in the medium, and the topic itself.

e. Communication Understanding. The number of people who comprehend specific things about the program and commit this to memory. The number is typically less than those perceiving the ad.

f. Behavioral Response. These are the people who take buying action as a result of the placement of the specific advertising or the people who actually take steps in their spiritual journey towards Christ. This may be indicated by a letter.

A variety of methods are used for media distribution research and many of them can be used by Christian communicators. Points *b.–f.* above are increasingly more difficult to measure, but, at the same time, they are of increasing importance for the communicator. He or she needs to know if the message is getting through to the intended audience, or, if the message or ad does not result in overt response, we need to know the reasons. Secular advertising will therefore spend considerable time and effort in pretesting an ad in controlled situations before placing it in the media so that it will be as effective as possible.

4.4.2. Copy Testing.

Copy is the technical word for the text or program itself. Usually advertisers put a great deal of time and money into copy testing, where an ad will be tested at different phases of its development from written concept to finished ad. For such pretesting procedures a variety of methods can be used,

a. Consumer Jury. Here 50-100 consumers from the target audience are interviewed either individually or in small groups. They may rank a set of ads in order of preference or some other perceived variable. We could test our listener's music tastes in a similar way.

b. Portfolio Tests. A group of target consumers are exposed to a package of both test and control ads, called a portfolio. Respondents are asked to look through the portfolio, reading whatever interests them. Book covers can be tested in a similar way, using a dummy sample.

c. Physiological Methods. These are among the more sophisticated measurement procedures. An eye camera can track the movement of the eye as it examines a picture or an ad. Galvanic skin testing is another way of measuring physiological response. The tachistoscope is a slide projector with special capabilities that allows for the presentation of ads under different levels of speed and illumination.

d. Inquiry Tests. Inquiry tests measure the effectiveness of an ad on the basis of either measured sales inquiries received as a direct result of an ad or special offer. It can be coupons returned from a magazine or newspaper.

e. On-the-Air Tests. This is a real market test where the program is placed on actual television or radio in test areas. Contacts may be established by telephone.

f. Theater Tests. Television commercials are often tested in a theater environment. Typical measures taken are for brand (or we could include denominational) preference, shifts based upon before and after exposure, and recall of copy points in the commercial.

Christian communicators can use all of these methods for testing media products. The main concern is not the number of methods used or how sophisticated the measurement techniques are but the fact that our products (radio programs, brochures, books, videos, etc.) are adequately tested before broadcasting or distribution.

4.4.3. Testing Effects of Communication.

Most companies are also interested in testing effects after a communication event, and for this purpose several post-testing procedures are available,

a. Recognition Tests. Here we try to count the number of readers who remember seeing an ad and also those who actually read some or all of it. Such an approach has been followed in the study of denominational and evangelistic magazines.

b. Recall Tests. This is a measurement of how much content is actually remembered by the respondent. This may be a specific teaching series or the main points of a sermon.

c. Sales Tests. This measures impact of the ad on the sales of the product. This often involves experimental procedures prior to actual distribution. For the Christian communicator, the "final" result is new disciples of Jesus Christ, but we need to study how communication programs affect steps leading to that decision.

SUMMARY

All Christian communication organizations need an information system to provide useful data for strategy development. Research tools and methodologies are available for gathering such information.

Communication research utilizes methodologies and techniques which have primarily been developed by sociological and marketing researchers. Several aspects of anthropological research are also valuable for certain types of research needed by Christian communicators.

As in other areas of research, we need specific measurement procedures and techniques in order to obtain reliable information. This process is not just an activity carried out by the researcher. Management must be centrally involved, and the producers should also be involved in the process of media and copy testing. Procedures for such testing are readily available for us to use.

QUESTIONS FOR DISCUSSION AND INTERACTION

Take a look at your own ministry. What function does research have? Is that satisfactory? What steps would you suggest?

FOOTNOTES

1 Johnstone, Patrick. *Operation World*. 4th edition, Gerrards Cross, England, WEC publications. 1986.

2 Tunstall, Jeremy, ed. *Media Sociology, A Reader*. Urbana, IL: University of Illinois Press. 1970.

3 The experiment was conducted by Voice of Peace in Chiangmai, Thailand under the sponsorship of United Bible Societies. Similar experiments have been carried out in other countries.

4 Lasswell, Harold D. "The Structure and Function of Communication in Society". In *The Process and Effects of Mass Communication*, 84, Wilbur Schramm, ed. Urbana, IL: University of Illinois Press. 1971.

5 Kinnear, Thomas C. and James R. Taylor, *Marketing Research. An Applied Approach*, 2nd ed. New York: McGraw-Hill Book Company. 1983:287.

CHAPTER 5

Summarizing the Dimensions of Christian Communication

An adequate Christian communication theory that will assist us in effective utilization of media in Christian ministry will build on an adequate set of principles based on communication theory, strategy, and research. This particular chapter will serve as a summary of the preceding chapters, organized in a set of seven dimensions that will provide a sound conceptual framework for applied Christian communication and use of media.

The following list is not exhaustive, but consists of those foundational principles on which our media ministry must stand. Together they form one approach. We may not be able to achieve these ideals completely, but the seven points can direct and govern our actions and provide a grid for testing our approaches to the use of media in ministry.

5.1. THE COMMISSION IS OUR MANDATE

The scriptural mandate and spiritual foundations of our media involvement must be the starting point. We are not just communicating for the sake of communication or for the purpose of highlighting a Christian perspective on a certain topic. There is a clear goal to present the gospel in such a way that people will want to listen, understand, follow, and commit themselves. Without clarity of purpose and goals, we will be working in the dark. "What am I here for?" might be a good sentence to have as a daily reminder in our calenders, as a plaque or inscription on the studio wall, and as a question to be answered during sessions of praise and intercession.

The moment we lose this perspective or forget the primary purpose of Christian communication, we will be ineffective. In his stirring article, "Who is Converting *Who*?," *(Worship Times)* Chuck Fromm calls our attention to the fact that so many Christians enter the arena of the performing arts and media to utilize the stage as a platform of ministry. But, sadly, many of them do not have the background and ongoing counsel of church leaders, so instead of using the media for evangelism, they become "converted" to the media and the demands of the media. They become "stars" and results seem then to be measured by records sold and the level of personal publicity rather than praise to God. The same general problems face the Christian media user. From being a ministry developed to facilitate Christian communication, the ministry becomes an end in itself and all our concerns become centered on keeping our particular ministry going.

The mission belongs to Christ. It is his mission and we are the agents of that mission. This also means that we through prayer and the study of his word seek his constant guidance in making plans and carrying out our tasks. The real challenge of the world is therefore the challenge of Christ who is the Lord of the mission, and with him as our model the incarnation is the method and the cross is the price. We then see the millions who do not know him and the peace of his kingdom, and we are compelled to be involved with Christ at whatever cost to ourselves.

Foundational to all Christian communication is the work of the Holy Spirit. As we have seen, this causes certain constant factors to permeate all our ministry and set Christian communication apart. In other words, Christian communication is unique, and we need to require that this uniqueness be expressed in an adequate theory of communication.

The effects of our communication will in the final analysis depend on the work of the Holy Spirit. It is the Holy Spirit that works on the will of a person, calling, challenging, and urging a response, and that same Spirit is capable of guiding us in planning and applying principles of communication for gospel proclamation. In prayer we seek the will of God and plan the ministry. Then in the power of the Holy Spirit we go forth communicating through word and deed in accordance with his will.

5.2. THE PERSON AT THE CENTER.

The final and complete communication of God to humanity was in the form of a human body: the incarnation of Jesus Christ. Similarly, the Christian communicator needs to learn how to communicate as a human being.[1]

The commission given by Jesus was a person-based commission: "You are witnesses of these things ..." (Luke 24:24), and, "when the Holy Spirit has come upon you, you shall be my witnesses ..." (Acts 1:8). People may look at the church as a collective group but they need to experience the church as individual people. Jesus gave us the example by becoming a real human being, participating in our affairs (Phil 2:7; John 1:14). In him, the message and the medium became one.

The challenge of Jesus in John 20:21, "as the Father has sent me, so I send you," has implications far beyond our human understanding. Jesus was sent on his mission by the Father to fully communicate him in a worldly context. As people looked at Jesus they saw the Father. As they listened to Jesus, they heard the Father. They could watch him at work, and they saw the work of the Father. In that same way, Jesus is sending us, his church, to communicate him, his words and his deeds to the whole world.

A sign on a truck in Ghana read, "I see the man, but I do not know his party." The truth proclaimed by this statement—we look at the man before inquiring about his party or faith—has clear implications for Christian communication. If the local church is faced with a lack of credibility, or if you are not believable, few will pay attention to what you say. Only a credible source, program and channel can expect a hearing. If the local church is associated with a foreign image, this can be changed and credibility improved through the active ministry of local Christians and by use of mass media. The local church can, for example, be given a local image by the broadcasting of personal testimonies.

Acceptance of the Person is, according to Marvin Mayers, the beginning point of change, and central to that is the question of trust: "Is what I am doing, thinking, or saying building or undermining trust?"[2]

What gives communication its character is, therefore, not only the message but the messenger. The red phone to the Kremlin did not resolve the cold war any more than magnetic recording tape condemned Richard Nixon.

This person-centeredness must be carefully guarded in media communication. Let us take the example of literature. Free and random distribution of literature has, generally speaking, not proved to be effective, especially at the beginning stages of the decision process. Credibility of a piece of literature is associated with the way it is distributed and with the person who is giving it out. In one town Christian workers distributed literature in every home six times within a year or two. No results were seen, no doors opened and no indication that any of it had been read. But good results have been experienced in situations where people have already been exposed to the gospel or taken the first steps in the process. They may have listened to a radio program, attended a film show, or been exposed to a personal witness.

The distribution and use of audio cassettes also needs to be person-centered. The most realistic use of evangelism cassettes is in the hands of a Christian. The player is merely a machine that extends a person, so we have to see the person and the player as one unit. A cassette tape does not gain acceptance by itself. It is the Christian neighbor who is accepted within the other person's limited latitude of acceptance/rejection, and he or she brings the cassette. The cassette then works from within, expanding the listener's latitude of acceptance as the gospel is communicated. The cassette is listened to because it is brought there by someone who is trusted.

Similarly, the video cassette could be an important evangelistic tool if the use is personalized. Through the openness of a personal friendship you gain acceptance, and then the video cassette works to expand that latitude and start or enhance the spiritual process towards Christ.

So, in the communication of love and truth, the Christian communicator must be a true lover of other people.[3] The communicator is one who cares more about the welfare of the other person than his or her own ego. It is a life that could be compared to a clear, crystal window through which light shines and clear vision is achieved, rather than a stained glass window that draws attention to itself and blocks the view beyond. Care for the other person will determine means and methods and will be sensitive to that person's present position in the spiritual decision process. This is receptor-oriented communication.

5.3. THE AUDIENCE (RECEPTORS) HAS PRIORITY

Even though our primary concern here is media communication, where large audiences are often involved, the term "receptor" is preferred due to its singular assumption.[4] The term audience-oriented[5] could also be used to indicate that there is usually more than one receiver. The "target audience" is usually a people group with individuals who have a certain degree of homogeneity.

Jesus is the prime example of receptor-oriented communication. In John 3 we have the memorable conversation between Jesus and Nicodemus. The receptor, Nicodemus, was a highly educated man, a philosopher, a man with status, someone who would be embarrassed if seen talking alone with Jesus. Jesus showed his acceptance and empathy by sacrificing his sleep to meet with Nicodemus on the roof when nobody would see them. The very language Jesus used shows respect for Nicodemus and an understanding of his needs. Jesus aptly entered into that frame of reference and from there led Nicodemus into new discoveries. The conversation was not just a monologue. Jesus dealt with the questions and assumptions which Nicodemus experienced.

The language used in John 3 with Nicodemus was quite different from the language used in John 4 with the Samaritan woman. Jesus was obviously very sensitive to the diverse cultural and social backgrounds of his audience. The Samaritan woman, an outcast the Jews did not even treat as a human being, was given self-confidence as Jesus bowed down and spoke with her, treating her as a person. His language was appropriate, and he quickly led her on to discover the truth. The apostle Paul also seemed to master this skill of understanding specific audiences, their needs and dominant concerns, as well as their cultural distinctives. He became all things to all.

The way Jesus used parables is another illustration. Parables were created out of the everyday life of the people who listened. In a parable, the audience become players, and as such each one discovers new truths and principles. The need is not preconceived answers, or prepackaged stories and programs, but life-involvement by the communicator with the people to whom the communication is directed.

In the light of a receptor-oriented communication theory, we need to challenge the worldwide use of "canned" evangelism. We do not seem to be following God's example of receptor orientation when translating material made for one kind of audience and then using it for a totally different kind of audience. Often they will not understand or may even misunderstand the message. Jesus was very sensitive with people who did not understand. With the crowds we see Jesus patiently building on their understanding. Little by little they understood and a cumulative effect was achieved.

In a Buddhist country people have no real concept either of God, of creation, or of a redeemer. They have experience with demon/spirit worship and manifestations, and miracle healers. They teach cycles of reincarnation and have a desire for total individual extinction into "the nothing." Suffering is understood as retribution for past evil deeds. With such a background, a receptor-oriented communication (and theology) will require a long and dedicated process of preparing their minds for understanding the signs of God's kingdom. Evangelism, therefore, will to a large extent be a teaching ministry that starts with the concept of a personal, living God who has created the world.[6]

The apostle Paul could freely use "proofs" in the synagogues (Acts 13:16; 15:12-29), but he was frustrated at Athens and had to begin with the concept of God (Acts 17:16-34). If we analyze his sermons, we find that he usually chose a part of the truth of the Gospel which was suitable to the audience. It could be love and grace for the illiterate and suffering farmers, the biblical meaning of history for the scholars, national sin of pride to the Jerusalem mob, and the full gospel to the congregation of believers. The presentation always involved an intellectual challenge to the audience.

Today we can find striking similarities between the context in which Paul worked, and the situation in many areas of the non-Christian world. It is a very different task to prepare radio programs for a people where the sovereignty of God is more or less accepted, than for a people where there is no such understanding. Many Anglo-Saxon approaches to evangelism tend to take too much for granted and their presentation presses for an immediate decision. At the same time, they often give minimal intellectual challenge to the listeners.

The sovereignty of the audience is a God-given capacity.[7] The context of the receptor, his or her life-style, needs, and spiritual background and position must, therefore, form the basis for our program form and content. An example of a clear violation of this principle is the dubbing of Western-produced television programs for airing in the Philippines. This writer experienced a Christmas show with a special Christmas appeal by a well-known American television producer broadcast in the Philippines during the month of February. Even then US telephone numbers were flashed on the screen!

During the last few years, we have, fortunately, experienced some outstanding examples of receptor-oriented communication. Prime examples are magazines like *Breakthrough* in Hong Kong, *Magalla* in the Middle East, and *Step* in Africa, where extensive research is carried out and topics chosen on the basis of needs and interests among their readers. There are also examples of relevant receptor-oriented radio programs, but in our search for receptor-oriented media applications, our attention is drawn more and more to the "small" media such as audio cassettes. In India, a wholistic audio cassette program has demonstrated the viability and effectiveness of a receptor-oriented approach. (This particular project will be treated further in the chapter on audio cassettes.)

Some years ago, the Franciscans in their downtown Los Angeles facilities produced a series of excellent television spots. During the 20-second or one-minute spots they were able to capture the attention through a pertinent, human interest topic, give a punch line that would not be forgotten, and then tie it in with the program or outreach from a local church. The Mennonites have done similar things through short programs on "drive-time" radio.

We can summarize a receptor-oriented approach by the following four questions:

1. **WHO is my listener/reader/viewer?**
2. **WHERE is my listener/reader/viewer?**
3. **WHAT are the NEEDS of my listener/reader/viewer?**
4. **HOW can I meet the needs of my listener/reader/viewer?**

These questions may sound easy and simple but they are extremely profound, and were they to shape our media communication, the message of the church through the media would be relevant to the needs of people. They require a lot of work and dedication as well as a new orientation to carry them out in practice. But there is no shortcut if we want to be relevant in our approach.

5.4. THE CHURCH IS THE OWNER

The church is God's primary agent for world evangelization. It alone has the mandate to be a servant to all people, with a priestly, missionary and evangelistic vocation.[8] It is the Church that demonstrates the reality of the incarnation.[9] The calling is to mission, and this mission can reach its highest potential as media is rightly used in the context of a local church. It is the local church that best can provide permanency and continuity to our efforts, providing permanent structures for effective communication. Therefore, church-based media use is extremely important.

But, if the church is to function as a base for our strategies, the decision-making with respect to media employment and program design cannot rest exclusively with parachurch organizations. The local church must have a sense of ownership of the media, and see the outside producing agency as a true servant in helping with its outreach and mission. Sometimes this may cause a delay in the implementation of a mass media project until such a time as the local churches are ready to fulfill their role in the ministry.

It is gratifying to note the development of close relationships with local churches in a number of countries. In Kenya Cinema Leo operates a training system for local church leaders so that when film showings are held in their community, they, the local church, are the sponsors of the program, giving the official welcome as well as counseling and following up inquirers. Local Christians can in this way utilize more advanced approaches in their local situation. Film showing will be delayed until training of the local church has taken place and they are ready to be involved.

Personal evangelism training programs have often been conducted for "individuals," whether or not the individual concerned is a member of a church. However, other recent programs have linked the individual's activity to a local church, thus making the church the center of strategy. The "Person-to-Person" program developed jointly in England by the Bible Society, Scripture Union, and Campus Crusade for Christ is a striking example of such a church-based approach to personal evangelism and evangelism training. As a strategy, it is ideally suited to the local context with its many subcultures.

Robert Schuller's Southern-California-based television approach is a well thought-out strategy by which he draws people into his church by "extending" the Sunday morning service through the television channel. The assembled congregation functions as a studio audience, while the millions of viewers around the world are the audience for which the program is designed. Others who have merely tried to broadcast a regular church-service have often failed since the "program" did not fit the medium and the audience.

The print media provides similar illustrations. Free literature does not seem effective when distributed at random, but it can be very effective if church-members are giving the material to family and friends. Literature, as well as all other media, requires a church base. While each medium is limited in scope and usefulness, the church provides the strategic framework in which media can be used effectively.

For example, television and radio may affect dramatic movement in the spiritual growth process of an individual, but they alone cannot provide the basis for development at every stage of the process. They need to be integrated with other ministries, particularly with the outreach of the local churches, if ultimate goals are to be achieved.

5.5.   A PROCESS IS INVOLVED

The communication process may be likened to a 16-mm movie. The viewer sees it as a real-life motion when in fact it is a sequence of individual "still" pictures or events. In the same way, each program, each encounter, provides a picture that together with many other "frames" is an ongoing process. The listener will also be involved in an ongoing decision-making process, beginning at the time of initial exposure and awareness and continuing through various stages leading to full acceptance of the message. During this process the needs of the audience will change and the communicator must adapt his or her methods and programs accordingly. At each stage the purpose is to elicit cognitive, affective and behavioral changes.

In the New Testament we see that the apostle Paul's initial aim was to plant new churches. Later he concentrated mainly on a ministry of encouragement and teaching. In this apostolic role Paul became a confidant and advisor to the churches. In our modern terminology we may compare this itinerant ministry to that of a process consultant. As in New Testament times, there is today a need for persons with a similar calling who work to facilitate a process of change, ministering over a long period of time and responding to the peculiar needs at different stages of the process.

A similar development is seen in secular communication strategy. Everett M. Rogers' *Diffusion of Innovations* gives us a new perspective on the role of the "change-agent."[10] It has become clear that a change-agent is needed throughout the whole change process, acting as a facilitator of change, not just being one step in the change process. The change-agent is called a "linker," but the term consultant could also be used. Such persons provide a communication link between a resource system and a client system. As "change agents" Christian missionaries and ministers facilitate the process of change.

The different media channels can be used at different stages in the process, depending on the need and the capabilities of the medium. For example, radio can be used at several stages of the decision process and it can be programmed to communicate within a person's limited latitude of acceptance/rejection. This effect is demonstrated by the many testimonies of how radio has opened doors for other kinds of evangelism—literature distribution, film showings and campaign meetings. It has created a positive climate for change. Radio is therefore ideal at the initial steps of a decision process, as it can be listened to in the privacy of the home by non-Christian listeners. On the other hand, radio seems weak at the actual reaping stage. It will create a positive climate for change but not necessarily a decision to change.

5.6.   INFORMATION IS MANDATORY.

Research is like a flashlight. It can guide us through the maze of multiple decisions and lead us through the darkness by throwing light on the path ahead of us. Research does not provide us with the answers but does provide us with the information on which decisions can be based, making receptor-oriented media communication possible. Research, in addition to sharpening the vision, also helps monitor and evaluate a ministry by providing effectiveness measures.

We cannot prepare good programs for the media without basic information about the people and their context, and such knowledge can only be obtained through formal or informal research. For any receptor-oriented approach, for the setting of goals, and for intelligent and effective planning processes, we need good information.[11]

If we do not have relevant information on the audience, we may easily be tempted to turn away from the so-called hard and unresponsive fields and target what appear to be more responsive areas. However, before making such a determination we should attempt to discover the reasons for "unresponsiveness." What are the barriers and how were they created? Have we really taken time to understand our listeners? Are we using a language they readily understand? Have we failed to "incarnate" the message in life and blood? Are we beginning the process in the appropriate place in terms of content and approach? At times, little feedback is available, as was the case for many decades in China. Response to radio programs was almost non-existent because letter-response was not possible. In due time, however, we discovered that there had been a large listening audience, but they were hindered by political conditions from responding to the broadcasters.

Breakthrough, an "evangelistic" magazine published in Hong Kong, was designed to meet the needs of teenagers in the 14-17-year age group. The plan was to sell the magazine rather than to give it away by free distribution. To accomplish this the producers needed up-to-date information on the interests of the target group, something that was constantly changing, influenced by the current trends in fashion, music, and behavior. To achieve this, they appointed a group of twelve people whose one task was to discover the topics high school students discussed during breaks. The result is a high-quality magazine that sells on the news stands and has led the organization into numerous other related ministries, including a phone counselling program for young people.

If leaders and managers, as well as the producers of media programs, understand the function of research, they can utilize the data and information in planning and relevant programming. We all need to be involved in asking questions and pretesting the materials we produce.

Though research principles and methodologies are readily available, the concept of research as relevant to ministry has not always been accepted by Christian media people. Sometimes a theological justification for such a position is given, but it is a non-threatening daily phenomenon that we all engage in as we seek information from or about each other. In the interest of accountability and good stewardship, we should have no theological problems in viewing research as a legitimate tool of communication. We need a good information system that will provide data on all steps in the communication process.

5.7. THE CULTURAL CONTEXT GOVERNS THE APPROACH.

As human beings we are totally immersed in our culture. This limits communication as well as makes it possible. Essentially, we use the same symbols of communication but such symbols may have radically different meanings. An intercultural perspective will always accept the fact that different cultural perceptions give different views of reality.

Much of our evangelism and mission takes place across cultural boundaries; therefore, the question of meaning in communication will need more attention than the specific forms of communication utilized. Consequently, we must seriously study how communication takes place when there are cultural differences. We must begin with a high view of culture, not prejudging as anti-Christian aspects which God can use or which may even be given by him. The leader of the Balinese church,

Wayan Mastra, once said: "Bali is my body, Christ is my life." The gospel must be clothed in the new culture as it penetrates that culture with the true life of Christ and then, from within that same culture, it blooms to new tunes and new instruments.

God seems to view human culture primarily as a vehicle to be used by him and his people for Christian communication purposes. God is not bound by culture, but he utilizes human cultures as communication channels. Even though the similarities that unite people are much greater than the differences that separate, it is the differences that provide the greatest challenge to Christian communicators, in particular to producers of mass media products.

Bible translation is also faced with the problem of understanding the meaning of a written communication stemming from a period thousands of years ago and passing that message on to another reader or listener in a totally different age, setting and language, hoping that the same meaning will be created in his or her mind. Only serious application of communication theory can solve such a problem.

As we study the Scriptures our cultural perspective draws us to certain sections, and we all tend to assume that those Scriptures that have greater value to the members of our culture have the same value to members of other cultures. Those portions written to people within Greek culture seems to speak more to Euro-Americans,[12] but Asians or Africans may be drawn more to other parts of Scripture.

An intercultural perspective on communication will lead us into a study of how media tools and systems function in different cultures and societies. For example, television takes on different dimensions in the United States with heavy emphasis on commercial utilization than in Sweden where there is a predominance of cultural and educational programs. Again, a different use will be experienced in countries with authoritarian leadership that seeks political control. Seen from a Christian communications perspective, all attempts should be made to produce media programs within cultural contexts, rather than imposing foreign productions on a society. Let us imitate Jesus, who became like us, spoke like us, lived like us, acted like us in order to present the message of the kingdom of God to us in a form we could understand.

An intercultural understanding will automatically lead us to investigate local and traditional media and art forms. This does not mean that we will be limited to folk media, but that such media will be included. Nor will we impose a seven-tone musical scale on a people who traditionally sing in a five-tone scale. A number of groups in Asian countries, such as India, Thailand, and Indonesia, have demonstrated the viability of using traditional forms of dance and drama in evangelization. If such ministries are well integrated with local churches, the impact is enormous as the gospel is expressed in the local cultural forms and communication symbols.

Another interesting intercultural communicational approach has been taken by the Balinese church. The church building in Denpasar has local cultural themes incorporated in its architecture. Among key themes in the culture are water, light, and wind. As you enter the church, you pass over a basin of water. Isn't the water of baptism the entry to the church? In the huge structure, with its high, steep roof, there are no windows except at the very top of the roof where a row of flat windows throws light down into the sanctuary so that you can almost see the rays of light. Isn't Christ the light of the world? There is no air-conditioning in the building, but there is an opening over the low walls with the roof almost hanging down over the walls. This architectural design has created a constant flow of air in the church. Isn't the Holy Spirit like the wind? Thus, the Christian message has been enhanced by the adoption of a culturally unique architectural design rather than the use of traditional church architecture.

SUMMARY

A summary of the elements of an adequate Christian communication theory has been treated in this chapter. Though it would be difficult to make a concise statement defining Christian communication theory, our main concern is the formulation of a conceptual foundation that can be applied for the selection and use of media. Adequate theories of communication are already available. Our primary need is, therefore, not to search for a theory but to apply the theories already developed.

A dependence on the Holy Spirit is a constant factor that permeates all Christian communication. As we submit our lives and ministries to the guidance of the Spirit, we become his "extensions" or ambassadors. Christian communication must be person-centered, and of this Jesus is the outstanding example. The Word became a human being who lived among us. Media communication must therefore be evaluated on the basis of its capacity to communicate personalness.

Receptor-orientation is mandatory for Christian communication. Christ was receptor-oriented and he spoke to the needs and context of the receptor. Process-oriented communication is a logical consequence of receptor-orientation and person-centered communication. Both source and receiver live through processes and a relevant communication strategy must follow these processes.

Christian communication must be seen in the light of an intercultural perspective. Our culture provides a grid through which we see and understand reality. We communicate and understand each other through the specific perception provided by this cultural grid.

If the seven topics provided in this chapter were to be joined into a verbal model, we might come close to an adequate set of guidelines for Christian communication. Such a verbal model can then be used as a "checklist" in the development of strategies for media selection and use in Christian communication. The statement could be constructed as follows:

The application of communication theory to Christian communication, and in particular to the selection and use of media
  — **must reflect a dependence on the Holy Spirit**
  — **must be person-centered**
  — **must be receptor-oriented**
  — **must be church-based**
  — **must be process-oriented**
  — **must be research-based**
  — **must have an intercultural perspective**

FOOTNOTES

1 See Charles H. Kraft, *Communication Theory for Christian Witness,* Revised edition, for a thorough treatment of this topic. Maryknoll, NY: Orbis Books, 1991.

2 Marvin Mayers. *Christianity Confronts Culture.* Grand Rapids: Zondervan Publishing House. 1974:30.

3 Em Griffen, *The Mind Changers.* Wheaton, IL: Tyndale House. 1976.

4 Charles H. Kraft, *Christianity in Culture*, Maryknoll, NY. Orbis Books. 1979; *Communication Theory for Christian Witness*, Revised edition. Maryknoll, NY: Orbis Books, 1991.

5 James F. Engel, *Contemporary Christian Communications*, Nashville: Thomas Nelson. 1979.

6 At the Asia Christian Communications Fellowship conference in Taipei in May 1980, the Rev. Makito Goto of Japan gave a relevant paper titled, "Soft-sell Approach or Hard-sell Approach. An Analysis of the four messages of Paul." (Goto 1980:6).

7 James F. Engel, *Contemporary Christian Communications*, Nashville: Thomas Nelson. 1979:318.

8 Emilio Castro, *Sent Free*, Geneva: World Council of Churches. 1985:70.

9 William A. Dyrness, *Let the Earth Rejoice!* Pasadena, CA: Fuller Seminary Press. 1991.

10 Everett M. Rogers, *Diffusion of Innovations*, 3rd ed. New York: The Free Press. 1983.

11 For a brief but excellent introduction to media research see James F. Engel *How Can I Get Them to Listen.* Grand Rapids: Zondervan Publishing House, 1977.

12 Charles H. Kraft, *Christianity in Culture*, Maryknoll: Orbis Books. 1979:289.

SECTION II

SELECTED MEDIA DESCRIPTIONS

Introduction to Section II

Each medium has its strengths and weaknesses, possibilities and limitations. Some of these are unique to the medium in question, but often the advantages or limitations are due to the context or the circumstances in which the medium is to be used. A good understanding of media is therefore a prerequisite for the development of good strategies.

It is impossible to be comprehensive in a book such as this one, so in this section only a number of media have been selected for special treatment. Furthermore, each chapter could easily be developed into a book, as there is so much to say, but an attempt has been made to be short and at the same time point out the importance of the medium on the basis of the principles set forth in Section I.

Television has been included due to its all pervasive influence and the extensive use of television that we see in the United States. With statistics showing that the average person spends several hours in front of the television set each day, it is important for all Christian leaders to be aware of both the possibilities of using the medium in Christian ministry, but also the possible dangers extensive exposure to television can have on church, society, and family life.

Radio has been used extensively by churches and missions around the world. Its possibilities are many for both evangelism and Christian nurture. In the chapter on radio, we have tried to evaluate the medium on the basis of the guiding principles set forth in chapter five. Such evaluation needs to be done for each medium, so the chapter serves as an illustration of that process.

The third chapter in this section deals with video. The video medium is having an enormous impact on societies around the world. it is changing entertainment patterns as well as family life, and it is impacting classroom instruction and educational methods. We could argue that video has caused a communication revolution that may be on the same level as that experienced at the invention of the printing press. Video changes us and the way we think and act. It is imperative that we learn how to use this medium effectively in church and mission.

Audio cassettes are small and unimposing, but the possibilities of this unique and versatile medium are possibly greater than any other medium available for Christian mission. It is financially within the reach of almost every church, and it can be used to extend almost every kind of ministry.

Literacy provides a threshold to a new world. It gives access to the information in books and newspapers, it gives you unlimited use of printed material, and it makes it possible for you to communicate through letters. It is quite understandable that print media have been chosen by churches and missionary organizations as their primary communication tools. But today print is increasingly being challenged by the electronic media and it is estimated that less than half of the world's population read.

A chapter has also been allocated for film even though that medium is today challenged by other media, in particular video and television. But film is a medium with unique possibilities in Christian mission, and the "low-cost film," that is audio-visuals in the from of slides and tape, still have good possibilities for use. Few media are more persuasive than film.

Music, painting, and dance-drama have been treated together in one chapter, but it is fully realized that they all deserve much more extensive treatment. We cannot envision a radio or television program without music, and it is central to church services and evangelistic approaches. The artist is important in all media work, and much more extensive use can be made in integrated strategies. Dance-drama and other folk media are today being re-discovered by many churches, and we are experiencing exciting new use of both drama and traditional music.

The computer must be treated in a media book today, but it is most likely that significant new technological achievements have been announced before this book is published. The computer can assist us in numerous ways, and the future technology of multi-media, including video and audio on compact disks, will certainly change our production processes.

In this section, each chapter has been treated differently, so that various dimensions of applied communication can be illustrated. Together these chapters should provide a good insight into the possible functions of media in our churches and missionary enterprises. Section III will then treat some practical steps to help us get started.

CHAPTER 6

Television

"We see it as it happens"

In spite of the relatively high financial outlay, television has quickly gained acceptance around the globe. In the United States it only required a decade to reach saturation point. For most people today, television is the primary time-consumer of their waking hours. In some countries the average household spends more than 7 hours a day watching it. So, apart from working and sleeping, more hours are spent in front of the tube with its heroes, villains, and news-stars than in school, in church, or at any other organized activity. Eighty-two percent of all Britons watch an average of four hours of television a day, with teenagers in some areas spending as much time in front of the TV as at school. It is obvious that the basic values communicated by television will have an effect on such an audience.[1] The primary television shows have actors that are better known by their television names than by their real names, and as programs are syndicated, the same performers become household names in countries around the world. And even though television is still "young," many can date important happenings in their lives by events that "happened on television," whether in reality or in fiction programs. It may be "the day Kennedy was assassinated" or the day "J.R." was shot. We saw astronauts on the moon, and the explosion of the Challenger happened before the eyes of millions of viewers. We followed the bombing of Bagdad from the cockpit of a military jet; and we have seen riots and looting presented live.

We follow the news as it happens, or we can switch to a news channel, or just look it up on videotext. Even in the most remote villages the television antenna speaks of the presence of television, while parabolic antennas in a city like Jakarta give status to families who can afford to receive the signals "from abroad." In Europe, a variety of satellite stations and community antenna systems give people opportunities to tune in constant sports, music videos, news, film shows, and this in French, English, German, Swedish, or any of a host of other languages. The U.S. Information Service "World Net" program is there and so is CNN and the BBC World Service. The way television was able to show how life was like in the West, with its many choices, was probably one of the major factors in creating a climate in Eastern European countries for sweeping changes and ultimate victory over totalitarian rulers.

A Brief but Amazing History

The development of television is closely linked to basic research and development in the field of electronics. Though the first television experiments were conducted towards the end of the last century, real testing did not take place until the 1920s. As experimentation continued in the 30s, experimental stations took to the air in the United States. World War II slowed progress in development, but after the war it almost exploded. By 1948, thirty-six television stations were on the air in the United States, and more than a million receivers had been sold.[2] Soon the net expanded from VHF to UHF, giving access to more channels. In the late 40s, networks appeared on the scene, making it possible to share costs for expensive and elaborate productions. New program series continued to appear, many becoming known worldwide. Color was added in the mid 50s but, due to the relatively high cost involved, the main U.S. networks did not become "full color" until 1966.

Further development of television has been related to the use of satellites, by which signals reach almost everywhere. Cable television, with its subscribers, teletext, and the wide distribution of video recorders and remote controls have followed in rapid succession, giving viewers the widest possible selection of programming as well as some control over the use of television. Presently, new advances are being made in high density picture formats.

From the beginning the United States opted for commercially-based television, and non-commercial public broadcasting has had extremely difficult times in the States. In Europe, led by such agencies as BBC in Britain, television has been financed by a license fee, paid by all owners of television sets. With the new initiatives, especially satellite-based broadcasting, the commercial model is advancing rapidly all over the world.

Television use is, then, strongly linked to the social, cultural, political, and historical circumstances which in each country surround broadcasting operations. In the United States television is primarily an entertainment medium. In countries with totalitarian regimes, it becomes a tool of political propaganda and indoctrination. Some countries primarily use it for educational, news and cultural programs. These factors influence the effectiveness of television itself as well as its potential use for religious purposes.

And across the world the development of television continues. At hotels in Manila guests can tune in to programs in Japanese, Chinese, Indonesian, Thai, and other languages apart from numerous U.S. stations and local channels. In the desert kingdom of Saudi Arabia, for example, 95% of the population is covered by television through sixty stations. During Hajj season, they broadcast twelve hours a day, including live telecasts of all Hajj rites.[3] In India, television made its appearance in 1959 with an experimental service for villages around New Delhi, providing them with a package of agricultural, educational, health and hygiene programs and with only a small component of entertainment.[4] These issues provided the rationale for the development of the expensive television medium which at that time was looked upon as a luxury. Later more entertainment programs have been included, but the state-controlled Doordarshan, as the service is called, continues to emphasize educational and development programs. A major problem is caused by the fact that while the audience is primarily rural, the electronic media are urban-based.[5] The recent satellite channels from Hong Kong-based Star-TV are making an impact in India, including Indian language broadcasts, and as such are providing a new, strong challenge to the state-run channels.

In Europe television for many years enjoyed a monopoly situation with government-owned stations having exclusive rights. In several countries this meant no commercials, giving television a much more important role in spreading information and education. During the last few years this situation has changed, mainly due to two factors. There has been a proliferation of small community television stations operated by semi-private groups such as churches. The other main development has been the advent of satellite broadcasting beamed to all of Europe, most of which also uses commercials. Consequently, national television stations have adopted a commercial format to safeguard the interests of national companies. Such changes will give new opportunities for Christian broadcasting, but they will also bring in more programming that aims at entertaining rather than informing. The European-type low-power local stations, together with the main national channels, will probably be the area where national television will continue, and where local, cultural flavor will prevail. Commercial stations and satellites will increasingly become "world" channels due to their commercial nature and need for a broad appeal to all of Europe. They also need to develop their own programs that can be sold to stations in other countries so that the financial feasibility of productions can be enhanced. Some American-based Christian television programs are already on European satellites, primarily broadcasting in English with sub-titles in German, Dutch or another language.

6.1   STRENGTHS AND WEAKNESSES OF TELEVISION

When looking at a medium's capabilities, it is often helpful to compare it with other media. If we, for example, compare television and radio, we find a number of similarities between these two broadcast media, but at the same time there are significant differences. Perhaps the most obvious difference is that people do not look at radios. They listen to radio while driving, washing dishes, working in a factory, or looking at each other and possibly interacting with the program through personal comments. In this way radio listening is conducive to community, but television, on the other hand, tends to destroy community. Even when gathered in the same room, everyone must line up and face the same direction. Each person's attention must remain focused on the television set, and they have to allocate the necessary time to watching television.[6]

6.1.1.   Strengths of Television:

(1) Television reaches a large group of people at the same time. It is a true mass medium that has an enormous appeal and impact among a wide segment of the population. It can deliver the same message to this large group at the same time, even to the whole world if the right hook-ups are in place. Many people spend up to 80% of their leisure time in front of the television set.[7] For the Christian communicator this gives the possibility of speaking to a whole nation at the same time, providing a platform for the Christian gospel and the mission activities of the church. With such possibilities it is obvious that Christians concerned about obeying the Great Commission will attempt to use television for our communicational objectives.

(2) Television is a powerful medium that combines both sight and sound, and it is capable of combining these in an unlimited variety. Most of the signal systems discussed in chapter 2 can be utilized, and it will be important for the television user to master the *combination* of such signal systems if effective programs are to be the result. Television can utilize almost any form of program presentation: lecture, dialogue, drama, dance, etc. It brings the communication directly into the living room of millions of people at one time. This gives tremendous possibilities, but it also adds its problems and influences the message, as we in the living room have a free flow of all kinds of prejudices such as color, religion, social, sexual, national, and generational prejudices. But by getting the message directly into the living rooms of people that may otherwise not be willing to listen to a Christian message, the local church has an opportunity to communicate its message and ministry to the community.

(3) Television is involving. Marshall McLuhan describes it as a "cool" medium, demanding input from the audience.[8] This is not always so, but television has a tremendous capability of drawing the audience into the action. They become emotionally involved, talking with others about the events that happened "on television," or they may take part in a television game show. But the audience can also draw television into its objectives, as we saw in the Philippine "people power" revolution. The fight was to a large extent carried out on television, and there was a fight to gain control of the stations. Similarly, the world followed the revolution in Romania as the new leaders were constantly on television, guiding events, and we experienced live the attempts by the secret police to capture the station itself. As seen in these instances, television, like so many other media, is at its best when it is involved in community and in an integrated strategy. We could say that people should be involved in television and television is involved in the lives of people. A local church could learn from this and be involved in community directly and extended through the use of television.

(4) Television gives a sense of intimacy. Such intimacy is, of course, an illusion but it does bring closeness. The examples from the revolutions mentioned above are examples of this. In nondramatic programs a variety of techniques is used to create and sustain the illusion of intimacy between speakers in the program and the audience in their living rooms. By being as casual as possible in a setting that appears appropriate for informal face-to-face social interaction, they create an atmosphere of being with the viewers. They treat each other as intimates and use first names. The sharing of off-camera experiences gives credibility to the appearance of intimacy among the performers. A studio audience helps to blur the distinction between the audience and the stage set, and a camera fixed to a roller-coaster can do more than create the visual experience of a roller-coaster ride; it can create the physiological sensations for the viewer as well. It is as though the viewers weren't really confined to their living-room chairs.[9] In this way an elderly person or someone confined to a bed may follow the church service on television and actually feel a presence with the congregation in the church.

(5) Television has a perceived immediacy. Sometimes this is a true immediacy; we see it happen as it happens, a feature that is loved by the news broadcasters. Newspapers will always be a few hours behind. But the viewer will rarely notice when this is only perceived immediacy. A program has been recorded and edited ahead of time, giving the viewer a reconstructed situation, a "make-believe" world. Even the questions from a studio newscaster may be answered by a taped response. But this possibility of immediacy can be used by the Christian humanitarian organization that wants to bring the urgent needs of an earthquake area to the attention of the viewers and elicit their financial response.

(6) Television is believed. In most countries television is ranked as the most credible medium for news.[10] This may be due to its "we see it happen" feeling. The most famous of all newscasters, Walter Cronkite was for years considered the most trusted man in America. This high acceptance of television is in stark contrast to the famous British writer and television personality, Malcolm Muggeridge, who claims that "... it is very nearly impossible to tell the truth in television."[11] The believability of television is directly associated with the credibility of the sponsoring agencies and the person seen on television. A study conducted by the University of Leister found that Indian rural people distrusted the national television programs due to the accent and dress of the urban producers.[12] In a government-controlled situation the news on television will often be disbelieved. Likewise, the believability of a Christian program will be influenced by the credibility and perceived trustworthiness of the church in the country. In the previous section it was pointed out that Christian communication must be person-centered if we are to follow the example of God's communication to us through the person of Jesus Christ. The personal life of the program presenter is important also in television.

In spite of these unique advantages, television confronts us with a number of problems and limitations. These problems may not relate so much to the medium itself but rather to the way it has been used and the way it has been manipulated.

6.1.2. Weaknesses of Television:

Actually, it is difficult to treat strengths and weaknesses of a medium in isolation. What is seen as a weakness in one situation or for one purpose may be a strength in another situation or for another purpose. The following listing will include such limitations and should be interpreted within a given context.

(1) Television is very expensive. Television costs are staggering. In some countries, a commercial—which is supposed to pay for the production—runs into thousands, or even millions, of dollars. This limits its use to those who can provide the financial backing for station operation or for program production. Television does not work well as a "democratic medium." It is controlled by the gatekeepers who are usually huge commercial companies. Consequently, we find syndicated programs produced for one society being used in totally different societies. Similarly, Western-produced programs are put on stations in the Third World without consideration of the cultural implications and the demands for an intercultural approach. In many countries churches and Christian organizations are provided with a limited amount of time on television free of charge, usually for the purpose of broadcasting a Sunday worship

service, but in most other situations, rather large organizations have to be created and funded if extensive use of television is envisioned. This will call for good cooperation among churches and Christian organizations.

(2) Television caters to the lowest common denominators. It ought not to be so but, due to the wide audience, it seems unavoidable. In commercial-based systems, a large number of viewers are needed to attract the necessary financial sponsors, and consequently the topics that attract the greatest number of viewers are chosen. Frequently this results in programs dominated by violence and sex. In such a "world" Christians have tried to live up to the demands of the medium which is primarily an entertainment medium.[13] In order to speak to a wide audience, the speakers have chosen a message that has been widely criticized as superficial or weak. And it is the same message to all, irrespective of their position in the spiritual decision process.

(3) Television tends to avoid deep issues. This is, of course, a consequence of the previous point. In many countries, they try to stay away from politics and religion, apart from reporting issues of conflicts and scandals. In most countries television seems to be used much more for entertainment than education, even though we should expect that education could be made entertaining or entertainment could be made educational. But television can be used to educate and to reinforce values, and there are examples of significant in-depth treatment of issues. We could also mention programs like the CBS-produced "60 Minutes" which aims at getting behind the headlines. Actually, mass communications research indicates that television is good at reinforcing the opinions and beliefs that viewers already hold, and thus the TV preachers who do not challenge viewers' beliefs are the most successful. They accomplish this, in part, by offering only the bare rudiments of faith, avoiding complex theological issues about which people might disagree.[14] There is a wide variety of situations around the world, and as a culture cannot be judged by one individual's action, neither can television be judged by its use in a single society.

(4) Television lacks continuity. There is no provision for a viewer to see a program again (unless he or she video tapes it). The viewer may see one program in a series, but not the next. Like radio, television therefore demands a certain amount of repetition, communicating the same point over and over again. Such a situation can be greatly helped if television is well integrated into a comprehensive strategy as we see in refined commercial use of television. For example, a commercial for a new car may not aim at selling the car but aim at getting the potential customer into the showroom. Likewise, a Christian organization could so integrate the television with "on the ground forces" that they are helped with their work of direct contact.[15] Television can be used to create a positive climate for change.

(5) Television is impersonal. There is a sense in which television personalities, including many Christian users of television, work for a para-personal relationship with the viewer. Ben Armstrong's contention is that television restores person-to-person communication, creating a continuing face-to-face relationship between the performer and the audience.[16] But such relationship is an illusion and cannot take the place of true relationships and community. Television can be an extension of such relationships, but not a substitute.

(6) Television does not allow immediate feedback. There is, to be true, often a feedback through mail, but such mail may be handled by a machine, that is by a computer. Even if such feedback is there, it is delayed in time, and it will be from a very small fraction of the audience. A telephone response system may be the best alternative, even though it does not really give feedback to the communicator, who has often been videotaped ahead of time. On the positive side, the problem of feedback should force the television producer into a close cooperation with local churches which will help provide personal follow-up and community. One organization in Brazil is, for example, planning a decentralized telephone counseling system with local churches answering telephones during and after telecasts. Such systems can also be used as ongoing counseling services for people in need. There is also a realistic possibility of using intrapersonal feedback as our goal, that is, engaging the thought-processes of the audience in a response to God.

6.2   CHRISTIAN USE OF THE MEDIUM

So, in spite of the many advantages, there are obviously serious problems associated with the medium. We may conclude that they are insurmountable, and therefore the medium should not be used for Christian purposes, but we cannot afford to take such a position. The medium is too powerful and too pervasive to be left exclusively in the hands of those who have no Christian interests and concerns. And we can notice that Christian use of television in the United States is already a billion-dollar enterprise, and smaller stations are being established in countries across Europe. One organization has specialized in the production of a "Studio in a Box," that is, a complete television station in a container that can be shipped anywhere in the world. The question is, therefore, how do we harness this medium for gospel proclamation? How do we use it to extend the kingdom of God and his concern for shalom and true wholeness in the world?

The church will first of all have to learn that TV writes its own rules. Television is not radio, and it is not like a service in the local church. It is communication in the living rooms of the audience. And here the Christian communicator will be judged on equal terms with other television producers as to skills and mastery of the medium. You cannot merely stand on a podium reading a script, as the "talking head" is often the most boring form of television. The screen has to be filled with scenery, people, motion, and visual effects. There are exceptions, and a person like Billy Graham seems to be one of them, but we must underline that those who want to produce religious television programs will have to come to grips with the nature of the medium.

In some countries, television stations have provided free time to churches, but when no cost is involved, no resources are committed, the churches have usually resorted to just broadcasting church services, and most of the viewers will be Christians. In the European context radio and television monopolies have usually made time available to mainline denominations with a more liturgical service and not to free and evangelical churches. As the conditions in Europe are changing and new broadcasting opportunities have opened up, the evangelical groups, in particular those with a Pentecostal or charismatic flavor, have become very active in this field. Their concern is evangelism and they are willing to pay the price for television, even when the cost is astronomical. They have also committed more resources to programming and production than other denominations.

The situation in the United States has been unique and we have seen the rise of the televangelists, the superstars of American religious television. As opportunities arise in other parts of the world, the U.S. approach may be imitated, at least in part by other countries and continents. Let us therefore have a closer look at this phenomenon before answering the questions regarding how we can utilize the medium.

6.2.1. The Electronic Church

This basically American phenomenon of the electronic church has given rise to many books and articles, ranging from horror stories to unreserved praise. The misbehavior of a few people has had significant influence on the perceived credibility of all television preachers, and it has caused financial difficulties for most.

Ben Armstrong, former chairman of the National Religious Broadcasters, has come out strong in praising the electronic church as a revolutionary new form of the worshipping, witnessing church that existed twenty centuries ago. His book praises the outstanding service rendered to American society by religious broadcasting. The critics who claim that religious programs keep people away from churches are rebutted, as Armstrong believes this is not the fault of the broadcast medium but of the local churches. "The electric church has launched a revolution as dramatic as the revolution that began when Martin Luther nailed his ninety-five theses to the cathedral door at Wittenberg," is Armstrong's victorious call.[17] To the question, "Would Jesus go on television," he answers, "My immediate and enthusiastic answer is Yes! In fact He is the coming attraction."[18] We could compare this with Muggeridge, who claims Jesus would decline the offer, treating it as the fourth temptation.[19]

Almost every kind of format used by secular television entertainment is being used in the electronic church today, and at least some of them are having a fair amount of success.[20] There are variety shows, news, drama, soap opera, talk shows, and game shows. For children, there are cartoons, puppet shows, and Christian versions of "Captain Kangaroo." The electronic church has learned that TV writes the rules for its use.

But most religious television, like its secular counterpart, deals largely with simple solutions to human problems. Television can't handle complicated material very well. Unless an organization can afford the luxury of time and money for imaginative illustration, they are limited to what can be said. And what is said must be said quickly and very simply or the audience won't understand. Furthermore, the audiences also want to be entertained and they want to be made to feel good. When they are made to feel bad, they turn to another channel.

The capacity of television has tempted some "electronic churches" to move beyond parasocial interaction to parapersonal communication, making the viewers financial partners in the ministry. "... if television made the electronic church, the computer has made it profitable,"[21] and that "profitability" is to a large extent based on direct mail targeted to viewing audiences. Modern sophisticated communications technology makes this possible.

This does, of course, raise some critical ethical questions concerning the use of parapersonal correspondence generated by computers. If a person has not sent in his contribution to the ministry this month, the computer will send a letter. Even prayer requests are computerized and the computer will "remember" to ask about it in the next letter. A lot more research and experimentation is needed to conclude who is right. It does seem as if the methods by which you raise your funds say much about who you are, and they have a lot to do with the evangelistic effects of the programs.

There are many critical voices and there are numerous studies showing negative effects of television, especially on children. And, unfortunately, many Christian leaders have taken a very negative position as to the possible use of television.[22] A graphic illustration of this can be seen on the cover of Steve Bruce's book *PRAY TV, Televangelism in America*. The "T" in the title is made of dollar bills.[23]

6.2.2. The Concern for the Total Image

Among the strong critics of religious television we find Virginia Stem Owens, who in her book, *The Total Image, or Selling Jesus in the Modern Age*, makes some strong accusations against the television preachers. Her questioning is hard and she does not really offer any answers. In the criticism she is joined by Muggeridge, who has come to see an ever-widening chasm between the fantasy in terms of which the media induce us to live, and the reality of our existence as made in the image of God, as sojourners in time whose true habitat is eternity.[24] Muggeridge has come to conclude that the very make-up of television makes it impossible to communicate reality, because television functions in a world of fantasy, or fiction. Quoting Simone Weil,

> *Nothing is so beautiful, nothing is so continually fresh and surprising, so full of sweet and perpetual ecstasy, as the good; no desert is so dreary, monotonous and boring as evil. But with fantasy it's the other way round. Fictional good is boring and flat, while fictional evil is varied, intriguing, attractive and full of charm.*[25]

There are times, Muggeridge concedes, when television cannot stop the communication of true life, as was the case of the television program he made with Mother Teresa of Calcutta, and in his recollection of that episode, Muggeridge may in fact have given us a significant clue as to how television can be used to effectively communicate the Christian message.

> *She told me more about our Lord, and helped me to understand more about the Christian faith, far, far more, than anything I have ever read, or thought, or heard on the subject. In the television programme that we made about her, Something Beautiful for God, the fact that she does truly live in Christ, and he in her, shines triumphantly through the camera's fraudulence. With God, all things are possible, as Jesus told the disciples. ... Yes, with God, all things are possible, even bringing the reality of Christ on to the television screen.*[26].

In his book, *Television and Religion, The Shaping of Faith, Values, and Culture*, William F. Fore also takes great objections to the electronic church. Fore seems to confuse American culture and worldview with the worldview of television, and, as such, his book is primarily aimed at American religious television. As he compares that with a Christian worldview, he arrives at a totally different perspective and consequently rules out television as a medium suitable for Christian communication.[27]

He sees the electronic church as a formidable threat to mainline churches today.[28]

> *A main reason for this threat is that the electronic church has developed an extremely accurate diagnosis of the spiritual hunger of millions of people who are reacting intuitively against the inhuman and unchristian worldview of our media culture. The TV evangelists understand that people are hurting because they feel ignored and not needed, because they are often treated like commodities by business and like dummies by politicians, because they doubt their own worth and feel they have no real say in how their world is run.[29]*

Fore contends that the mainline churches by and large have failed to identify with people, who are hurting, or even to recognize they are there. Consequently, they have failed to minister to the needs of millions who live within reach of their ministry. The mainline churches are perceived by many to be a part of the problem, and they are seen as "dry, unfriendly, cool, dead, or dying" while the electronic-church ministers are perceived as those who care because "they answer my letters."[30]

Fore then discusses why the electronic church cannot be accepted. He considers them anti-community, not good evangelism, a captive of commercial broadcasting systems, and values implicit in electronic-church programs are actually the values of the secular society they pretend to reject.[31] Seventy-seven percent of those who are heavy viewers of religious television are also church members, but at least for some people, watching religion on television is an expression of their religious feelings.

The Bible story is a struggle with reality, and the most retold stories are all built on historical events. Jesus spoke usually in parables, or stories tied to the particular context of the audience. The audience is encouraged to look deeper than the surface of the parable and discover rich illustrations of human experience. In one way or another, the parable becomes a story in which the listener finds himself deeply involved. The purpose of the parables seemed to be a singular response: repentance and new life. "If you have ears to hear, then hear" (cf. Mk.4:9). The "programs" of Jesus were not just good stories, they were about life and truth, and they were presented in a context with plenty of time to think, and not in ninety-second capsules.

6.3   SO, WHAT IS THE ANSWER?

It is relatively easy to speak of theology and communication theory—or to get lost in that discussion—but it is much more difficult to wrestle with the theological implications of applied communication theory to actual media use. On the surface, we can accept Marshall McLuhan's statement that the media are "the extension of man,"[32] and we can "extend" that and say, media are the extensions of the church. While this may be true, it does confront us with serious theological issues.

6.3.1. The Big Worship Service

Every Sunday, hundreds of church services are broadcast on television around the world. How does this affect the purpose and meaning of the liturgical service, which the Sunday worship is? Liturgy presupposes a community which liturgy on television lacks.[33] When television cameras are present in a church two different modes of communication are joined, one entirely "human directed," the other directed to both human beings as well as to something beyond human existence: God. The pastor is brought into an almost impossible position of having to communicate with such diverse audiences at the same time. A fraction of the audience or the receptors are sitting in the church, but the majority are scattered in homes across the country. Some may never have attended church, others have attended weekly for the span of a lifetime. The only realistic answer seems to be to let the "target audience" be those who are hindered in attending church. The objective would then be to draw them into the worship experience together with those in the church, and to direct their response to God.

6.3.2. The Emergency Room

One possible approach for Christian television producers is the format of the Hour of Power. Schuller calls this Sunday morning telecast "the emergency room" where he wants to communicate with non-believers. Like other heavy users of television he has adopted an approach to "Be in there and use it." Schuller, affiliated with the Reformed Church in America, is the only mainliner among the "super" broadcasters. He is using a worship service format, but the congregation is treated more like a studio audience, so the program is somewhere in between a studio-produced program and the broadcasting of a church service. He skillfully and dramatically blends psychology and religion into positive possibility thinking. He doesn't like people to refer to his television program as a church. Television, he argues, is a powerful but limited medium that can be used to point people in the right direction, not attempting to give them the full gospel.[34] To increase the TV audience, he publicizes positive and challenging topics for the telecasts in *TV Guide* and other magazines.

6.3.3. The Influence of the Medium

Television isn't just a "neutral" medium that simply duplicates a visual reality in front of the camera. There is an interference with reality, and a new "television reality" is created. Proclamation and communal celebration are the two main elements of liturgy, so if "true" liturgy is to be televised, then both proclamation and communal celebration must be present.

Johan G. Hahn illustrates the problems quite well.[35] The moment liturgy is broadcast on television, we have a totally new communication situation. There is the interference of the television director with his crew and equipment. The television director now resumes the role of a "mediator" between the minister and the viewers. This "unseen" television director decides—by manipulating the use of cameras and microphones—what the viewers are going to see and hear on their living-room television sets. The television director becomes both receiver and transmitter. He or she receives the message from the original sender (the minister), records it, and sends it through the television chain out to another set of receivers, who are separated by hundreds of miles, and are in totally different environments. The communication process involved is totally different from the one in the church itself. The only safeguard for the Christian producer or speaker is to be in full control of the script, including video treatment and camera angles, so that the decisions are not left with a director who may or may not be sympathetic to the message proclaimed.

6.3.4. Television and Communication Strategy

It is the experience of this writer that media applications must be seen in the light of Christian communication theory and strategy. That is why the previous section was devoted to the treatment of such issues. If, for example, we understand the spiritual decision process of a person, or a group of people, we will also understand that they will at different stages of that process need different types of communication. There will at certain stages be a need for significant information and Bible knowledge; at other stages, there is a strong need for fellowship. In certain non-Christian cultures the audience will need huge amounts of background information in order to understand the message, while certain Christian contexts will call for "melting," that is, softening the resistance to the Gospel.[36] If the church strategists understand the media, including the possibilities and limitations of the particular medium in question, then they should be able to utilize this media tool at the right time and for the right purpose. Arriving at the right media mix is the task of the strategist.[37]

6.3.5. Programs

Television is good for story-telling and drama, but it is probably rather poor for preaching. The Bible is full of stories—parables, travel, history—that should provide ample material for exciting programs that will help make people think and respond. Unfortunately, few have gone into that aspect of programming, and most have focused on preaching. CBN is a notable exception to this practice as they through the 700 Club aim at presenting the gospel in a news or talk show format that deals with present-day issues around the world. The format was developed and refined after extensive research was carried out. CBN is now a national network that is distributed by satellite to any cable TV system in the country that will accept it. The difference between CBN and the secular networks is that CBN does all of its programming from an explicitly Christian perspective. Another CBN production, the Superbook, has been translated into numerous languages for broadcasting on stations around the world.

6.3.6. Television Spots and Short Items

The use of short programs, lasting from a few seconds to one minute or more, has been attractive to Christian communicators for a number of reasons. The program can be inserted into breaks between programs, just like other commercials, and it is cheaper to produce and broadcast than longer programs. Groups like the Franciscans and the Mennonites have produced excellent television spots that are based on human interest appeals and provide a succinct Christian message. By repeating the spot the message is remembered. Local churches could successfully utilize this approach. In Portugal, evangelical groups have managed to produce short news items and to get them on the regular news broadcasts. In India, Mahatma Gandhi could freely quote from the Bible to his Hindu audience. Can we not do the same through television, letting the Bible speak to present-day problems?

6.3.7. Education

Feedback is very difficult in television. But television can be used in education as we have seen in such programs as the Open University in Britain, and, of course, in the popular teaching series for children such as Sesame Street. Well-prepared programs can be used in evangelism if they are geared to the initial phases of the spiritual decision process, providing information and background, that will help to open filters for the Christian gospel and for Christian ministry. For example, a film that describes the positive effects of missionary work can in some countries change a basic negative perspective. Well-developed educational programs based on Bible stories will find a welcome on many television stations.

6.3.8. A City Station

Many Christians have a sincere desire to build television stations in order to reach people, and some are succeeding. A Christian television station in a European city received permission to broadcast at the time when the national radio monopoly was breaking up, and they managed to build an impressive station with a license to broadcast 27 hours a week, using a station shared by several secular groups. Beyond that, the station can broadcast over a number of other low power, local stations with a potential total coverage of 75% of the households in the country. Telephone counseling services have been established, and the station has had quite an impact. The results of the programs are seen in increased attendance at their churches, as well as at other evangelical churches. They have made an effort to be interdenominational in approach, and they have proven that Christians with vision, dedication, and faith can develop, use and manage television. As they gain in experience and improve in quality, the credibility of the station is enhanced.

6.3.9. Local Television

In many towns, there are opportunities for low-cost television programming and for uniting television with the local church ministry. Time for such broadcasting can often be obtained from local community stations or even on a local cable system. In a real sense television can then be an extension of the local church and it can direct the viewers into a living community. The church could also be involved in television the same way as it has entered numerous other fields—like education and medicine—in its missionary work, and provide high quality social and educational programs for television stations. These may have no or little religious content, but they may help transform the media, and they will certainly be good contact points for church outreach.

6.3.10. Integrated Use of Television

The question of media mix, that is, using the media and methods in a combined approach, will be a central topic for Christian evangelists. Issues involved relate to audience reach, cost, and quality of communication.[38] For a major Asian city, television was selected as the anchor of a planned city-wide evangelism campaign. The programs were planned to focus attention on the topic, prepare the way for local church-sponsored programs and to make it easier for the personal testimony and witness of the local Christians. The programs would not call for decisions, but they would prepare the way for such decisions, communicating a positive image of the church and making the gospel seen as being relevant to the needs of the individual. A national television program can also be "localized" by having a decentralized phone response system. By making contact with local churches, training of counselors, and the provision of follow-up guidance and material, the national television program can be assured of an effective follow-up system.

6.3.11. Money

Financially, television is expensive, and creative ways of financing need to be developed. As long as the budget is to be raised by contributions from the viewers, as is the practice in America, the producers will have to pay careful attention to the wishes of the contributors, who are primarily Christians. A broadcaster in Brazil has a group of twenty Christian business men who together sponsor the ministry. Some broadcasters have sold commercials to pay for the time, others utilize church collections, and again others have obtained free time. Then there are the special approaches, like selling time to game shows. For an effective television ministry, the problem of financing should be squarely faced and solved prior to start of broadcasting.

6.3.12. Television Awareness

Perhaps the most urgent point for the churches is to educate their members on how to switch off their television set and when to switch it on. If the Christian family will let television destroy their family life, it will also destroy the church. Then the church will have little to share on television. Some Christian organizations, like the LWF office in Japan, have been conducting such Television Awareness Training,[39] so that viewers can learn to use television, rather than be used by television. Even though this may seem like a defeatist response, it is important for Christian families to seriously treat the subject and teach their children a responsible use of the box in the living room. Any church can engage in such a "television" activity and benefit from it.

SUMMARY

Television is gaining a wider and wider acceptance and coverage. It has some outstanding possibilities but at the same time serious limitations for Christian communication. Many have started to use the medium for evangelism, some with success, others seemingly only able to reach Christians. The electronic church in the States has been the object of both praise and criticism, primarily due to its size and financial involvement. In other parts of the world different approaches have been followed. There are many possibilities for the use of television, but serious planning needs to take place if effective ministry is to be the result.

QUESTIONS TO CONSIDER

1. What television possibilities exist in your country?
2. Would television be a help to the ministry of your church or organization?
3. How would you produce the programs?
4. Can you provide the financial foundation?
5. Are you ready for wide cooperation with other churches and organizations?
6. How could television be integrated into your ministry and into the ministry of others in the area covered by the television signal?
7. Where could you get the necessary training and consultancy?

FOOTNOTES

1 *LandMARC*, newsletter published by MARC Europe, Bromley, Kent BR2 9EX, U.K., New Year 1990.

2 Hiebert, et al., *Mass Media IV: An Introduction to Modern Communication*. New York and London: Longman. First ed. 1974. 1985:417.

3 *The Nation*, Bangkok, September 23, 1989.

4 *Vidura* magazine, Vol.26, No.5, Sep–Oct 1989.

5 V. S. Gupta and Indu Grover, "TV and rural folk" in *Vidura* magazine, Sep–Oct 1989.

6 Jeffrey K. Hadden and Charles E. Swann, *Prime Time Preachers*. Reading, MA: Addison-Wesley Publishing Company, Inc. 1981:17–18.

7 William F. Fore, *Television and Religion. The Shaping of Faith,Values, and Culture*. Minneapolis, MN: Augsburg Publishing House. 1987:16.

8 Marshall McLuhan, *Understanding Media: The extensions of man*. New American Library. 1964:268ff.

9 Jeffrey K. Hadden, and Charles E. Swann, *Prime Time Preachers*. Reading, MA: Addison-Wesley Publishing Company, Inc. 1981:66.

10 James F. Engel, *Contemporary Christian Communication, Theory and Practice.* Nashville: Thomas Nelson. 1979:144.

11 Malcolm Muggeridge, *Christ and the Media.* London: Hodder and Stoughton. 1977:196.

12 Paul Hartmann, B. R. Patil, et al., *The Mass Media and Village Life. An Indian Study.* Leicester: University of Leicester, Centre for Mass Communication Research. 1983.

13 James F. Engel, *Contemporary Christian Communication, Theory and Practice.* Nashville: Thomas Nelson. 1979:145ff.

14 Jeffrey K. Hadden, and Charles E. Swann, *Prime Time Preachers.* Reading, MA: Addison-Wesley Publishing Company, Inc. 1981:101.

15 Phillip Butler has treated this topic extensively in papers such as, "Strategic Evangelism Networks/Partnerships."

16 Ben Armstrong, *The Electric Church.* New York: Thomas Nelson Pub. 1979.

17 Ibid. 1979:10.

18 Ibid. 1979:16.

19 Malcolm Muggeridge, *Christ and the Media.* London: Hodder and Stoughton. 1977.

20 James F. Engel, *Contemporary Christian Communication, Theory and Practice.* Nashville: Thomas Nelson. 1979:145.

21 Jeffrey K. Hadden, and Charles E. Swann, *Prime Time Preachers.* Reading, MA: Addison-Wesley Publishing Company, Inc. 1981:13.

22 See, for example, John R. W. Stott, *Between Two Worlds: The Art of Preaching in the Twentieth Century.* Grand Rapids: William Eerdmans Publishing Co. 1987:70–76.

23 Steve Bruce, *PRAY TV: Televangelism in America.* London and New York: Routledge, 1992.

24 Malcolm Muggeridge, *Christ and the Media.* London: Hodder and Stoughton. 1977:30.

25 Ibid. 1977:46.

26 Ibid. 1977:70.

27 William F. Fore, *Television and Religion. The Shaping of Faith,Values, and Culture.* Minneapolis, MN: Augsburg Publishing House. 69ff.

28 Ibid. 101.

29 Ibid. 110.

30 Ibid. 111.

31 Ibid. 111–113.

32 Marshall McLuhan, *Understanding Media: The extensions of man.* New American Library. 1964.

33 Johan G. Hahn, "Liturgy on Television or 'Television-liturgy' in *Media Development* 3/1984, pp. 9–11. London: WACC.

34 Robert Schuller. Comments given in personal interview, 1980.

35 Johan G. Hahn, "Liturgy on Television or 'Television-Liturgy,'" *Media Development* 3/84. London: WACC, 9–11.

36 Em Griffen, *The Mind Changers.* Wheaton, IL: Tyndale House. 1976.

37 See Engel, *Contemporary Christian Communication,* or Søgaard, *Everything you need to know for a Cassette Ministry.*

38 See Engel, *Contemporary Christian Communications,* 1979:160–176, for a fine treatment of media mix.

39 George Olson, a Lutheran missionary to Japan, has been directing this program.

CHAPTER 7

Radio

"The Talking Box"

After the "onslaught" of television many predicted the doom of radio, but it has come back strongly as a medium in its own right. Anyone possessing a receiver can be reached anywhere, even while engaging in other activities. There is no screen to watch, no reading to do, no records to turn, and no other people to rely on. Radio is "theater of the mind," where listeners create mental scenes, stimulated by skillful manipulation of voices, music, and sounds. And this sound is everywhere. All you need to catch it is a box with a simple circuit and a small speaker.

7.1. RADIO AT "RETIREMENT AGE"

The first wireless transfer of the human voice took place around the turn of the century. The foundations had been laid by the scientific discoveries in the fields of electricity and magnetism, and in 1844 Samuel Morse achieved the first transmission of an electromagnetic message over wire. Radio broadcasting, as such, began around 1920 and quickly expanded. News was now available to all, and so were the sounds of music halls. The "wireless," as radio was called, was treasured and, as seen in Europe during World War II, became even more so when the occupation forces made listening to "the other side" illegal.

It was the eventual development of transistors that made radio the medium it is today. Radio can, more than any other medium, readily adapt to changing social conditions and cultural systems. It has in many cases become a personal medium, catering to specialized groups and special issues. We still have some networks, but today's radio stations are not trying to make just one program for everyone. Rather, programs are aimed at carefully identified segments of the audience and their tastes and interests, whether it be hard rock, classical music, or just news and talk shows.

It is not only Christian stations that broadcast throughout the world. We still have the World Service of BBC in London that by shortwave provides news to all corners of the globe. Then there are the more politically-oriented networks and there are nets like the Saudi Arabian that aim at spreading the teachings of the Islamic faith. We also have the national stations and the FM music stations, some with commercials and others without. And, at the opposite end of the spectrum to the "world" stations, we have the low-power community stations with a reach of barely ten miles. At the age of seventy, radio broadcasting is a mosaic of initiatives and possibilities.

7.2. THE RADIO MEDIUM AND ITS POSSIBILITIES

1. Radio requires listening only, making it possible to reach all, including the non-literate, the blind and the elderly. You can also listen while driving a car or engaging in some other activity, so radio requires less from its listeners than television does of its viewers. The listeners do not need to allocate special time to listening, and the financial cost of receiving equipment is much less. Similarly, reading takes special time, years to learn, and constant practice, but anyone can immediately follow a radio program. For the more than one billion people who cannot read at all, and the estimated one billion more who are functionally non-literate, or at least non-readers, radio has capacities not matched by any other medium.

2. Radio is sound only. This makes programming fairly inexpensive, but through a blend of speech, music, and sound effects images and pictures can be created in the minds of the listeners. On the other hand, visual treatment is impossible on radio, and gestures and facial expressions are not seen, only heard. A tape recording of a church service will never be able to capture the total visual communication and atmosphere evident during the service. Only the sound will be captured. If a church service is to be communicated through an audio medium, certain effects will have to be added to compensate for the loss of visual communication signals. As we listen to a person's voice, we also form certain attitudes towards that person, and he or she may actually communicate much more by intonations than by the words themselves. A poor use of the medium, like using the wrong voice, may turn people away: that is, they will switch off their radios. A too dramatic voice may also cause people to focus on the person rather than on the content.

3. Radio is real time. Radio is a living medium with live sounds and voices. It brings current news and information, and in times of crisis people will tune in to their radios for the latest updates. Radio news is an almost indispensable necessity for a democratic nation, as democracy demands wide participation in government by the people, and only informed people can make realistic decisions. A main limiting factor for radio is, however, that the listener cannot control the time of listening, but must tune in at the precise time when a program is aired. There is no opportunity for a replay. A newspaper, on the other hand, can be read at a convenient time and, if necessary, re-read. Likewise, a teaching cassette can be played at a time convenient to the listener, but a cassette will always be delayed in time and as such not really fit as a medium to disseminate news.

4. Radio has wide coverage. Radio is truly a mass medium, and technically we can reach most people through radio. The availability of radios varies from country to country but it has been estimated that there are 1.2 billion radio sets in use around the world.[1] On a local station the broadcaster can potentially speak to a whole town, while on international stations the audience may include all who understand the language being used, even if they are scattered over thousands of miles. Radio can reach into closed homes and across barriers of race, politics, and social status. It can be "personal" from a distance and does not require the presence of an operator as a film does. It does not need a physical delivery system as magazines and video cassettes do, and due to a variety of frequencies used, it is not limited by distance as television is. Through shortwave it spans the globe and can be received everywhere as long as people have short wave receivers. Through AM, or Medium Wave, it comes in stronger in a local or regional context, but with a much higher demand for powerful transmitters. On FM, it delivers a clear signal with low power to a receiver that can receive the signal in a straight line from the transmitting antenna.

5. Radio can bring knowledge. Radio's basic capability seems to be that of "knowledge conveyor." For this reason it is used extensively in development programs to provide the necessary incentives and information for effective accomplishment of particular projects.[2] It shares that capacity with other media, in particular print, but in comparison to print it must be more simple due to lack of repetition. On the other hand, the message can deliver knowledge and education to the non-reading population of the world. It shares that capacity with media such as audio and video cassettes.

6. Radio can focus attention on specific topics. A positive climate for change can be achieved if issues are well presented and thereby create a desire for change. Radio can influence social norms and help form new tastes. But in this area it is weaker than television due to the lack of visual treatment. On the other hand, it can better cover topics where no pictures are available. In some areas, like fashion and dress styles, a medium like film will have more possibilities for long-term changes, especially when that is combined with public billboard displays.

7. Radio is believed. Radio seems to have built-in authority and in most countries a high degree of credibility. This credibility is closely related to the perceived image of the broadcaster. A rural audience may reject the guidelines presented on radio purely because the speakers have an urban accent.[3] The speed of delivery, the communicated concern for the listener, emphasis on words, etc., can all influence credibility. But, generally speaking, radio is believed. The representative of an international broadcasting agency is reported to have been given permission for a news-paper in a certain African country but had a request to build a radio station rejected: "The newspaper would be OK because not a lot of our people read, so you couldn't do much. But people believe what they hear on the radio."4

8. *Radio is personal.* Even though the radio broadcaster is remote in space from the listener, not allowing face-to-face communication, radio does have a certain personal quality. We have to remember the listening situation, which is the actual context of the communication, and we find that most radio listeners are alone, often listening through earphones or sitting alone in the car. Others listen while working. A listener comes to feel a certain affinity for the radio speaker, even though they have never met. The speaker becomes a person, much more than a mere voice, and a sense of trust can be developed. The good broadcaster will learn to dia-logue with this person, always trying to understand him or her and the context in which listening takes place. Few people will want preaching done in their homes or cars, and preaching does not fit in the earphones either. But personal dialogue and interviews are popular on radio. A speaker may be helped by having a person sitting on the other side of the table when broadcasting to create the right atmosphere in the studio.

9. *Radio can handle a variety of program formats.* A radio program must be entertaining and easy to follow, and also simple enough to be memorized instantly. By *entertaining* we mean something that is worth my listening. The amount of content communicated in a single program is lim-ited by the fact that it is heard only once, but the formats in which the content can be communicated are numerous and only limited by the cre-ativity of the producer. Apart from the dialogue and interview formats, you can have dramatic reading and extensive dramatic plays like the "soap operas." You can teach and entertain through music or you can bring the listener on "location" in a faraway country.

10. *Radio is limited by difficulties of feedback.* The response to a radio program will be delayed in time, and only a very small fraction, if any, of the audience will actually try to get in contact with the broadcaster. This may provide the speakers with a certain temptation to think in one-way communication terms. Where telephones are readily available, phone-in programs can help to a certain degree, and so can phone counseling systems. The only realistic answer is for the broadcaster to constantly be involved in audience and program research, so that the listeners and their needs are well known by the speaker. Media such as audio and video cas-settes that are distributed personally have greater advantages here, and the use of film even more so as a person is present. Most Christian broadcast-ers ask for letter response from the listeners, but asking for letters of a non-literate person will be felt like a put-down rather than a bending down

on behalf of the broadcaster to the other person. Unfortunately, most Christian radio ministries have not developed effective feedback systems that do not require mail.

11. Radio is cost-effective. As with other points mentioned above, this statement is relative. The capital outlay of radio facilities may be high and the cost of air time is in some cases very expensive. But the cost to the listener will be minimal. He or she needs only a simple transistor radio. For the broadcaster total costs will include script writing, production, studios, tapes, salaries, follow-up material, as well as the cost of air time or transmitter operation. In comparing the cost effectiveness with that of other media a number of issues need to be considered, and they may give different answers in different situations. We need, for example, to consider the amount of information transmitted in one program and the number of people reached. A cassette can carry a much more concentrated content, as it can be listened to repeatedly, but cassettes do not have the same wide distribution as radio does.

7.3.   CHRISTIAN USE OF THE MEDIUM

The first wireless voice broadcast ever sent out to the world was an informal Christian religious program on Christmas Eve, 1906. A Canadian scientist, Reginald Fessenden, working in the United States, broadcast a program to ships at sea.[5] The program included a solo, "O Holy Night," as well as reading of the Christmas story from the Gospel of Luke. Christian radio broadcasting as such began on January 2, 1921, when a service was broadcast from a church in Pittsburgh.

The first missionary station, HCJB, "The Voice of the Andes," began in 1931. After the war, stations like Far East Broadcasting Company (FEBC), Trans World Radio (TWR), Radio ELWA, and others were founded. Today there are Christian radio stations and programs all over the world. In the United States alone there are more than 600 such stations.[6]

In the hands of Christian communicators with the knowledge, means, and courage to use it creatively, radio has proved to be a powerful and effective tool, and there is no question that Christian broadcasting has had a significant influence on American society throughout the decades that followed. Programs such as "The Lutheran Hour," "The Old Fashioned Revival Hour," "Back to the Bible," "Haven of Rest," and others have made a significant contribution to the religious life of America. It is estimated that Charles E. Fuller had twenty million listeners a week up until retirement in 1967. In 1939 The Old Fashioned Revival Hour was the highest buyer of radio time.[7] In 1988, FEBC alone received approximately 615,000 letters in total from listeners. But many difficulties and limitations have also been experienced by Christian broadcasters, often due to vaguely defined goals and purposes and the relative lack of background training by many of those who are engaged in Christian radio.

Christian radio broadcasters are today on the air in some 200 different languages. The statistics are impressive: 1,000 hours of transmitter time per week from major international broadcasters alone, not including local in-country stations, commercial time, public broadcast time, etc. But there is a vast difference in the amount of time allocated to a single language. The latest information on the percentage of time used for each language shows that a few languages are dominating:

English	34%
Spanish	22%
Mandarin	8.6%
Russian	6.4%

The remaining 190 languages and dialects total only 29%, a very disproportionate distribution favoring English.[8] Programs for India prepared by evangelical broadcasters are a good example of this. There are eleven million English speakers and a total of more than 102 hours of broadcasting each week in English, but there are 153 million Hindi speakers and only twenty-seven hours of broadcasting in Hindi. The situation is much worse for the "smaller" languages. Fifty million Marathi speakers only get three hours a week, and the thirty-three million Urdu speakers get less than four hours a week.

Some countries are completely closed to Christian programs from within the country, some allow a few programs, others unlimited use. The restrictions vary from country to country, and in at least some countries Christians can broadcast as long as they do not speak negatively of the government or the religion. By obeying such limitations the Voice of Peace, for example, achieved at one time up to 36% listening in certain areas of Thailand.[9] During the last few years things have, for example, changed drastically in Eastern Europe. FEBC recently reported an agreement with the Russian government giving the organization access to a country-wide net of local radio stations.[10]

So, in practice, we often find that the possibilities for use of radio are limited. In order to reach the majority in a community, local stations would be the first choice, but they are often controlled by government agencies. If local stations cannot be used, the church leaders will need to carefully consider if powerful stations outside the country should be used, or perhaps use a satellite in order to broadcast into a given country. Even where local air-time is available, the question of Christian stations versus Christian programs on secular stations needs to be carefully evaluated.

Christian radio stations have seemingly relatively few non-Christian listeners, but most Christian stations do not carry out basic research on listenership so estimates of audience size are unreliable.[11]

7.4. CHRISTIAN-OWNED RADIO STATIONS

Powerful international shortwave stations "cover the world," and the giants in the field are Far East Broadcasting Company and their FEBA Associates, Trans World Radio with numerous broadcasting facilities around the world, HCJB in Quito, and a few others. They all broadcast in numerous languages and they use primarily shortwave stations. Such stations reach far, but reception of shortwave programs is more difficult, and it does require that people have such receivers.

There are a few powerful medium-wave international stations used by Christian organizations, such as Trans World Radio broadcasting from Monte Carlo in Southern Europe and from Sri Lanka in South Asia. The Sri Lankan station reaches a good part of India. Another medium wave station covers a large section of China.

In recent research carried out by the BBC, extreme differences were found between countries as to listenership to radio stations from outside the country. In Japan hardly anyone is listening to a foreign radio station, while in Tanzania they found that one in four listened to programs from abroad.[12]

Local stations broadcast on FM or medium wave but with a more limited reach. Political complications as well as technological advances during the last few years are not in favor of "big" stations for most countries. The development in Scandinavia and in other parts of Europe of the proliferation of small community stations is a good illustration of such changes. These countries, used to powerful broadcasting monopolies, have opened up for extensive use of small stations. Many of these are operated by churches and Christian organizations. This situation has inspired new magazines, books and consultations on the subject of Christian radio.[13]

7.5. CHRISTIAN RADIO PROGRAMS

Compared to the number of station operators, there are far more program producers. The international stations have made a serious attempt at getting production facilities located among the people they are trying to reach by radio, and we find in most countries several radio studios. Many missionary agencies also operate such facilities.

We need not only stations and good studios but also good programming. The best message demands the best programs. There do not seem to be too many problems involved in getting an audience, or getting non-

Christians to listen. The issue is, rather, how to help listeners believe and follow Christ. Radio will need to link up with other ministries so that the unique contributions of radio can help to bring this about.

A look at the broadcasting schedule for most Christian stations reveals very similar program titles. We find the worldwide program-producing agencies with programs that are produced in numerous languages by local producers as well as the English broadcast. We also find small ministries producing regular programs from makeshift studios.

7.6. RADIO BROADCASTING AND THE DEMANDS OF CHRISTIAN COMMUNICATION

The evangelization of our World demands communication, the communication of the Good News to people of all tribes and tongues so that they will see Jesus as relevant and meaningful to them and respond to him in faith. In chapter five we summarized some of the key demands an acceptable Christian communication theory places on media utilization by churches and Christian organizations. These principles are true for all media, but in the following we shall try to see radio in the light of such demands:

7.6.1. A Commission to Communicate, Reflecting a Dependence on the Holy Spirit.

All Christian communication, including the use of radio in church and mission, must find its mandate and spiritual foundation in Scriptures. Radio must not be an end in itself but must be done on the basis of a clear understanding and dedication to the commission given by Christ to make disciples of all nations. The moment we lose such a perspective our motives may be questioned and we will seek praise for our programs rather than getting the listeners to praise God.

The end results of all our Christian radio will depend on the work of the Holy Spirit. It is Christ who will open the doors to broadcast, call people to himself, and guide us to those he has chosen for the productions. On the basis of such a perspective, prayer will be an integrated function in our work, and a dependence on the power of Christ will permeate all phases of the work. With expectancy and trust in God, plans will be developed in the face of seeming impossibilities.

Many believe that radio has been given to us for times like these, so that in our attempt to reach the unreached with the gospel of Jesus Christ, radio may play an increasingly important role. The so-called people group approach is basically the same as a target audience approach, only sounding nicer and implying a dedication to an audience-orientation rather than one-way communication. When we look at the present situation for Christian radio, we find that the most deserving people groups and the most challenging languages are being overlooked. The statistics mentioned earlier as to the number of hours devoted to various languages by international broadcasting agencies should cause great concern. Major languages are by and large neglected and focus is placed on the English language programs. In other words, where radio could potentially make the greatest contribution for missions, it is used the least. We need to discover such situations where radio could potentially make a significant contribution towards the establishment of God's kingdom. Indeed, in some instances, radio may be the only tool at our disposal due to various political and religious barriers. Through radio, literate listeners in hostile environments may be contacted through correspondence and strengthened through Bible study courses.

7.6.2.   A Person-Centered Approach to Radio.

There are two sides to this demand. The broadcaster must be communicated as a person and the listeners must be treated as individuals and not as an ill-defined "mass." The incarnation of God in Jesus Christ is the ideal or perfect model for us to follow. Even though we cannot in full imitate what he did, we can follow his example where the message and the medium became one. The life and lifestyle of the broadcaster will be observed and the credibility of the message will be judged accordingly. Thus the communicator of Christianity is a more essential part of the message communicated than a communicator of non-relational kinds of information.[14]

Special attention must be given to safeguarding this person-centered approach in radio communication. The tone of voice, the speed of delivery, and the use of words all say something about the speaker and his or her attitude to the audience. The voice has to be good and so appropriate that the listener will actually forget the voice and listen to the content. The use of personal testimonies, whether given through a monologue, in an interview, or through a song, may be the best approach to this.

The person-centered approach may seem like a paradox, as we on the one hand will have to be true persons, but on the other hand be transparent and almost anonymous. An example of such an approach can be taken from another medium, the recording industry. Maranatha! Music has been able to get people around the world to sing praise songs, buy praise albums, cassettes, CDs and videos without highlighting the performers. The performers are almost anonymous, yet they have succeeded in getting people to sing their songs and to praise and worship God. Even record covers symbolize the desired effects of peace and worship, rather than pictures of the singers. This is in contrast to the highlighting of individual names in many program titles, and the development of "stars" or personalities that draw more attention to themselves than to the message. It may be that Western individualism has influenced such developments.

7.6.3.   A Focus on the Needs of the Audience in Radio Programs

Radio people are often called communicators, but we have to confess that not all radio speakers are good communicators, and often we get the feeling that relevancy and the creation of true meaning is not the primary concern of the producers. Consequently, the listeners are not helped and communication has not taken place.

A receptor or audience orientation is a must for Christian communication. If we do not know our audience and the needs of our audience, we really have no right to be on the air. Such a perspective does, of course, seriously challenge the wide use of "canned" programs on Christian radio stations around the world, it may even challenge more the local preacher who seemingly has never asked such questions and may not even accept that they are important.

Jesus carefully started with the needs and context of his audience. He met Nicodemus at night and he spoke to the Samaritan woman. He dealt with their problems and their concerns. He did not just give them a sermon or a theoretical answer. Likewise, the apostle Paul became all things to all that he might win some for Christ.

In a communication process we send messages with the intention of engaging the minds of the listeners in an information processing activity. The big question then is, *Did my listener understand?* Unfortunately, we often do not know the answer to such a question but take understanding for granted. The listeners will understand in their way and within their context. But that understanding may not be the same as that of the broadcaster, in fact, for a Hindu or a Buddhist it may be the direct opposite. The challenge to radio broadcasters is to get to know their audience so well that they know the answers to such questions.

A receptor orientation begins with the development of trust and a concern for the other person. It will take time and work to constantly study the audience and discover their needs and concerns, but as Charles Kraft reminds us, "to love communicationally is to be oriented so that one's primary concern is for the receptors at whatever cost to oneself as source."[15] This was God's way and must be our way.

7.6.4. A Church-Based Radio Ministry.

Attention is increasingly being given to the development of strategies where radio is incorporated into other evangelism initiatives as part of an integrated whole. Many Christian broadcasters are finding that cooperation in mission is the only way ahead and that integration of efforts must be focused on the ministries of local churches. This concern has been expressed by many, in particular Phill Butler.[16] While individual witness has an essential role in God's plan of redemption, there is a special role for community witness. Engel argues strongly for the church as God's primary medium of communication and that the starting point in all our communication strategies must be the local church.[17]

Frank Gray has also called for community, community among radio producers and community-creation among the listeners.[18] For this to happen we will have to develop effective integrated strategies that take their start in community, in particular with local churches in the country. Even if there are only a few Christians, they are the nucleus community with whom new Christians must unite.

So the concern for radio as facilitator of community and our concern for the listeners, in particular the non-literate, provide us with a number of challenges to which we must find true and workable answers. It will obviously lead us into strategic planning, so that "follow-up" can start long before the program is on the air. There must be a system in place prior to broadcasting so that it will function before, during and after the radio programs. Most follow-up programs are still non-community. The task is carried out from a desk in a far-away office building, and the approach does not relate to community, or it brings in community far too late in the process. When basing follow-up on decentralized local churches rather than on media (letters), we will give the majority of our listeners a chance of being followed-up. Part of the solution will be a willingness on behalf of broadcasters to commit significant funds to this activity and a willingness to develop decentralized follow up systems.

7.6.5. A Process-Oriented Approach to Radio.

The spiritual decision process was treated extensively in chapter three, and it was illustrated how people live through stages of cognitive and attitudinal changes. In the decision process, knowledge is needed all through the various steps of the process but in particular at the initial stages of evangelism. Experience shows that this is the area where radio is at its best. By focusing attention on certain subjects, radio also multiplies the effect of that process by getting people talking about it.

It would probably help in developing effective use of radio in mission if we cease to use the term pre-evangelism. The connotation of the term is that decision-making is evangelism, but that other activities are inferior to that. We need to let the initial stages of the evangelization process, where radio is strong, be given top priority. Like Jesus, we teach little by little so that understanding will be achieved and true communication will be the result. Radio can be programmed as a series, but the listeners will not all start at the same time. Each program will then have to stand on its own but at the same time be a part of a whole.

But the primary concern is the use of radio in an integrated process or strategy where the start is the community of God and the result is community. Radio will then be an extension of the ministry of the church, well integrated and used.

In a survey conducted in 1975 at Voice of Peace in Thailand,[19] it was found that radio had started the "process." There was a 12% difference in the cognitive responses between those who had been listening and those with no exposure to radio, and "on the ground" ministries experienced new interest and openness. Others have seen similar effects when radio has been used prior to or at the initial stages of an evangelistic crusade. An exclusive or isolated use of radio will usually have much less results.

7.6.6. Information and Research Used in Christian Radio.

Research is the activity involved in the gathering of useful information for management decision making. By having good information we can make realistic decisions related to our use of radio. Unfortunately research has not always been well acceptable to Christian leaders, and if we should judge the interest by the amount of research being done, the interest of radio people is very low indeed. There has been very little research into the Christian use of the medium. This is fortunately changing and we must give the documentation of the effectiveness of radio in mission high priority.[20] A special consultative group under the leadership of Frank Gray is planning to collect data on radio and seek to identify specific unreached people groups, attempt to understand them in the context of their particular set of cultural, geographical, religious, socioeconomic and linguistic parameters, and so design a radio strategy that will move this people group toward Christ and into the fellowship of his Church.

In a study, "Educational Media in Retrospect" by the World Bank, and reviewed by Ross James, it was found that projects which succeed were characterized by a thorough survey of the general sociopolitical conditions of the audience and also by systematic feedback and data collection procedures that identify trends related to audience profiles, interests and needs. This is carried out by a continuing analysis of listeners' letters, questionnaires completed by listeners, general surveys, and the pre-testing of pilot programs with representatives of the intended audience.[21] This same approach could be applied to Christian communication, and we will probably see the same results.

Gray suggests that the radio medium precludes head counts of converts, and that many of those who work in radio prefer it that way. The reason is that they tend to see themselves as more of an influence for the kingdom of God, moving people toward and into a relationship with the Lord Jesus Christ.[22] But some counting of results must and can be done to verify the effects of radio.

The general way of counting by many radio groups is to count letters. This is extremely inaccurate and can be directly misleading. Research in one country showed that letter-writers were between ten and twenty-two years old and more likely between twelve and seventeen years old. Without such research we may be tempted to just make programs for young people, the letter-writers. The same research showed that at a time when only two hundred letters were received in a month, between six and eight million were listening regularly.

Resources need to be provided for research, both for accountability and for good planning. Radio broadcasters must find ways to greatly improve their research capabilities. In particular, programmers need to learn pretesting and program research among the audience. Active listening to the audience, including the non-literate, is the most superior program preparation method we have. Listen to them that they may listen to you.

7.6.7. Radio Governed by an Intercultural Perspective.

Human beings are totally immersed in their cultures. Within different cultural contexts the communication signals have different meanings. An understanding of a specific culture and our appreciation of that culture will challenge us to further study and use those tunes and sounds that members of the culture will appreciate.

If at all possible, the programmers should come from within the culture and language being used. But as we look at Christian radio, we find programs produced in Germany and broadcasted in Indonesia, programs produced in London and sent to India, and programs produced in Chicago on the air in the Philippines. This is the easy way out; it puts serious questions to the credibility of the programs, and listeners will probably have a rather dim view of the speaker and the singers.

The challenge to Western producers is to allocate resources so that the gospel can be clothed in the local cultural communication patterns and then penetrate that culture with the true life of Christ. But the challenge must also be faced by those local broadcasters who just imitate foreign program formats and produce a radio broadcast with only a sermon and a translated Western hymn or two. Training in intercultural radio production seems to be a real need in most countries.

SUMMARY

Radio has been used extensively in Christian work. The medium has a number of strengths which makes it well suited for use in evangelism. It is sound only, so people can listen everywhere, even when doing something else. It also has wide coverage and it is available at a reasonable cost.

There are numerous Christian radio stations, some local, others large international stations. When looking at the programs available, we find that there is a predominance of English-language broadcasts, closely followed by Spanish.

This chapter looked at radio in relation to the principles stated in chapter five. These principles included a dependence on the Holy Spirit, a person-centered approach, and a focus on the audience in a receptor-oriented communication strategy. We also looked at radio from the perspective of the church, and how radio needs to work on the basis of a process orientation. Information gathered through research and testing is extremely important to good radio, so that it can truly be a medium that functions in an intercultural situation.

QUESTIONS FOR DISCUSSION AND PLANNING: WHAT POSSIBILITIES DO YOU HAVE FOR USE OF RADIO IN YOUR MISSION OR CHURCH?

1. Is Radio a Viable Option for You?

The first question to ask here concerns the availability of radio facilities. *Will the local station be available for your church?* If yes, what kind of program restrictions would they impose? *Can you use a national radio station?* If yes, who would you need to cooperate with to do this? *Is the use of an international shortwave station a possibility?*

The second question relates to *cost*. Radio does not require cost-demanding visual treatment as television does, but the total cost will include air time, and there is also a budget for script writing, production of programs, rent of studios, tapes, salaries, and follow-up materials.

In some countries a certain amount of time is made available free of charge on national networks for religious broadcasting. On commercial stations time must be purchased, ranging in price from very little to exorbitant rates. Most religious stations also require payment for the time, again ranging from a few dollars for a program to several hundred dollars, all depending on size and power of the station.

Will you be able to raise the necessary funds, or would you opt for the use of other media instead?

2. What Would be Your Objectives?

Radio can be used for many things and for many different kinds of audiences. *Who would you like to be in the audience?* Old or young, rich or poor, urban or rural, educated or non-literate?

There is great potential for radio among *non-literates*, whom the churches have overlooked or disregarded with their print-based training materials. The poverty of non-literates may preclude a few from having radios, but the cost of transistor radios makes it possible for most people to buy one. Would the non-literate population be your main concern?

Another example of a potential audience is the *scattered Christian population in a country that is rather hostile to the church*, like the Village Bible School with full curriculum which different organizations jointly sponsor and broadcast to China over the facilities of FEBC. Would a teaching ministry be your main concern?

Or, would you aim at communicating *Scriptures*. Scriptures must be made available to all people, and radio offers possibilities for reaching numerous audiences, such as the majority audiences in countries where the Christian population is very small; people living in countries with authoritarian governments that do not allow the printing and distribution of the Bible; and the many sub-groups in all societies such as the blind. Would audio Scriptures be your primary purpose?

Maybe you want to aim at *evangelism and church planting?* Historically, radio has not been seen as a church-planting medium, but the development of fellowship groups could be encouraged and taught by radio. Experiences from China point to that possibility. Is church planting your primary objective?

Radio can be used effectively by *local churches* who want to be open to the community and *serve its neighbors*. It can be an extension of a present ministry of the church, or it can be a special service to the community. The church can also through local radio serve its members who are isolated in retirement homes or lying on hospital beds. What is your purpose?

3. What Will be your Strategy?

After serious discussion of the questions above, a strategy will need to be worked out. How will your strategy be developed? Who should be involved in this? What would be the role of the local church(es) in the area of reception? How would the community of believers be involved? How can effective follow-up be handled? How will your programs be supported by or integrated with other media and methods?

4. How Can Programs be Produced?

Who should be responsible for the production? Who can write scripts and produce? Where can production take place? Who need to be trained? What topics do you need training in? Where can you get consultancy?

Go forth then and use radio effectively in the proclamation of the Good News to all people.

FOOTNOTES

1 Frank Gray, *Radio in Church-Planting Evangelism (RICE)*. Unpublished manuscript. Manila: Far East Broadcasting Co. 1983:3.

2 Wilbur Schramm, *Mass Media and National Development. The Role of Information in the Developing Countries*. Stanford: Stanford University Press. 1964. C. V. Rajasundaram, *Development Communication, Manual of Development Communication* (with special reference to broadcasting). Singapore: Asian Mass Communication Research and Information Centre. 1981.

3 Paul Hartmann, B. R. Patil, et al., *The Mass Media and Village Life. An Indian Study*. Leicester: University of Leicester, Centre for Mass Communication Research. 1983.

4 *Insight Magazine,* April 24, 1989, "Shortwave Signals a Competitive Era" by Daniel Kagan.

5 Jeffrey K. Hadden and Charles E. Swann, *Prime Time Preachers*. Reading, MA: Addison-Wesley Publishing Company, Inc. 1981:8–9.

6 Ben Armstrong, "Let's Turn Up the Volume on Christian Television," *Religious Broadcasting*, vol. 9, April/May 1977, pp. 33–35.

7 Ben Armstrong, *The Electric Church*. New York: Thomas Nelson Pub. 1979:44.

8 Frank Gray and Jonathan Marsden, computer database, Broadcast Data System. 1990. Far East Broadcasting Company, Manila, Philippines.

9 "Radio Program Research Study" by Voice of Peace, Chiangmai, Thailand, April–May 1975, pp. 33–35.

10 *Action,* WACC Newsletter, number 160, April/May 1992.

11 James F. Engel, *Contemporary Christian Communication, Theory and Practice*. Nashville: Thomas Nelson. 1979:153.

12 Graham Mytton, "Lessons from Audience Research" in *Ricefields Journal*, vol. II, no. 1, February 1989.

13 A good example is Nevland and Jørgensen's book on radio programming in Norwegian, 1982.

14 Charles H. Kraft, *Communication Theory for Christian Witness*, rev. ed. Maryknoll, NY: Orbis Books, 1991:18.

15 Ibid., p. 15.

16 Phill Butler, "Radio and the Local Church" in *Ricefields Journal*, vol. II, no. 1, February 1989.

17 James F. Engel, *Contemporary Christian Communications*. Nashville: Thomas Nelson. 1979:291.

18 Frank Gray, Lausanne Occasional Paper on Radio in Evangelism.

19 Søgaard, "Radio Program Research Study" by Voice of Peace, Chiangmai, Thailand, April/May 1975.

20 Gray, Frank. *Radio in Church-Planting Evangelism (RICE)*. Unpublished manuscript. Manila: Far East Broadcasting Co. 1983:3.

21 Ross James, "Reviewing Project Effectiveness" in *Ricefields Journal*, Vol. II No. 1, February 1989.

22 Frank Gray, Lausanne Occasional Paper on Radio in Evangelism, p. 2.

CHAPTER 8

Video

"It is Impact"

Video is a comparatively new invention but with an enormous impact on society. Changes caused by the widespread distribution of video during the last few years are influencing entertainment patterns and family life. Major changes are impacting classroom instruction and educational methods. Viewed superficially, video resembles ordinary television, but it is a very different medium. With an audience of only one person at a time, it becomes a "personal" medium, controlled by those who use it. It is also a group medium, requiring new types of programs tailored not only for the new medium but also for specific purposes.

8.1. A WORLD REVOLUTION

Video is a communications revolution, not just an evolution of technology. It is both audio and visual, movements and moods. It is real people, it is very close, and it is infinitely varied. Video communication is an event, something that can be shared by many at the same time. Alone in developing countries, it is estimated that the import of video materials amounts to about $400,000,000 per year, and that does not include material copied in violation of international copyright laws, which may be in the range of a billion dollars or more a year.[1] Before the Gulf War 90% of all households in Kuwait were reported to have video players, and a quick trip into any video rental outlet in a Western country on a Friday night is sufficient evidence to show the situation. Long lines of people are waiting at the register with selections of videos for their weekend viewing.

The development of video resulted from the need of the television industry to keep copies of broadcasted programs when the use of color film became too costly for this purpose. Video uses magnetic tape, just like an audio cassette. The enormous advantage over film is that it can be played back immediately without processing, and it can also be erased and re-recorded.

8.2. VIDEO FORMATS

A number of different video formats are on the market. After a rather intense struggle in the market arena, VHS has won the battle over VCR, Video 2000, and Betamax, as far as the home video market is concerned. Sony's U-matic, introduced in the early 70s, is still the standard in the area of more semi-professional uses, and the high-band U-matic is used by many smaller television stations. With the advent of such systems as HI-8 and Super VHS, these standards are also getting into the television stations, primarily due to the much lower weight of equipment. It can all be housed in a light-weight camera, the camcorder, and is therefore in great demand by newspeople. A rather irritating technical issue is the use of more than one standard. The United States and a few other countries use the NTSC standard. Europe and much of the rest of the world use PAL. A French system, Secam, is also in use. The different standards are not compatible but programs can be converted from one standard to another.

8.3. VIDEO USE

For many video viewers, the use of video is largely limited to viewing rented films and music videos; for others, it is primarily time-shifting, that is, recording a television program for later viewing. In areas like the Middle East where movie theaters rarely exist, video fills the void and people can view Western-produced films as well as Egyptian-produced dance shows.[2]

Radio and television were greeted with much more enthusiasm by governments in different countries, as these were media they could control. There is much less enthusiasm about video, which is decentralized. Video provides control of both production and use to decentralized groups of people. Video can be made for a very small group of people, and the technical quality demanded will depend solely on the needs of that group, rather than on the demands of professional production entities.[3]

But even though video returns at least some of the control of the television program to the viewer, who is no longer bound by the selections offered by the television station, the viewers seem to misuse rather than use this new freedom. The irony is that while video technology presents numerous possibilities for alternative usage, such as strengthening family life, improving education, serving minorities, and strengthening neighborhood groups,[4] the statistics of video use and types of programs watched are very disappointing. Horror and war films, crime, erotic and soft-core pornography are at the top, and only a few percentages are for educational programs.

There are serious cultural implications of the proliferation of video, as hardly any governmental or social bodies have set standards of quality and use. Most programs, the "software," originate in America, and consequently are of questionable relevance to the rest of the world apart from serving entertainment purposes. Among the more exotic uses of video have been the education of soldiers in guerrilla warfare in El Salvador,[5] fulfilling the need for home-theaters in the Arab world,[6] video clubs in India,[7] raising community spirit and involvement in government affairs among Australia's aborigines,[8] and Jane Fonda's Aerobics Workout videos.

How big an influence video played in the downfall of authoritarian regimes in Eastern Europe and elsewhere has still to be researched, but the fact of wide distribution of Western video programs, including *Animal Farm*, will have had its influence in breaking down respect for the leaders. Presently video is big business in former communist countries. In Poland ownership of VCRs increased from 0.03% in 1981 to 7.90% of all homes in 1988,[9] and is now increasing rapidly.

8.4. VIDEO IN INDIA

If there ever has been a communication revolution in developing countries, video is it. In many countries video has brought significant changes to the lives of ordinary people. Take India, for example. Video is used by salespeople in training salesmen, and by art schools in training dancers. There are videos in hotels, video restaurants, video clubs, video halls, and even video coaches.[10] It is used primarily as an alternative to cinema, so it is largely for entertainment, and video viewing is becoming synonymous with film viewing.[11] Only recently has video rental been challenged by satellite television.

The penetration of video stretches to the smallest towns and is enhanced by electronic shops, video libraries, and video parlors. This development has primarily taken place during the last ten years, that is, after Indian television turned to full color. Video ownership is still restricted to certain classes, but viewership is much broader due to video parlors, etc. Even homes show videos for a small fee. There is, of course, status associated with the ownership of a video.

With no effective government control, pirated films are used everywhere. The bulk of programs are of Indian origin, and the Indian video-producing industry is increasing rapidly.

But it has far-reaching social implications. The family of a bridegroom will demand a video recorder (VCR) as part of the dowry, and the wedding ceremony is videotaped. No social function is complete without a video, substituting the traditional Indian dances and music, and servants will ask if they can watch films on video as part of their payment.

India has also seen other uses. Political parties are using video, mixing political messages, popular songs, and shows by popular cinema actresses and actors. At the last election when the government-controlled television, Doordarshan, put restrictions on the use of television by the opposition, creative politicians turned to video. Converted mini-vans carried 100-inch screens on the back and in this way brought the messages to small town and village squares. Several dozen vans covered thousands of villages, but how big a part they played in the toppling of the government is not known at this time.[12]

8.5.   EDUCATION

Video provides a tool for distance education, as copies of programs can be sent to individuals and groups spread all over the country. UNICEF and other development organizations have seen these possibilities and are sponsoring video developments in various Third World countries. In Turkey, for example, workers can get videos on rehydration therapy, immunization, breast feeding, water and sanitation, etc. Many of the programs are distributed by UNICEF in a variety of languages. Similarly, the World Health Organization in Geneva produced an AIDS education tape that has been translated into Arabic and sent throughout the Middle East.[13] Since the *intifada*, the Palestinian women's groups have been using video for political education, primarily serving as a catalyst for discussion. Israel has prohibited all news of the *intifada* on television. And in London, Indian families maintain a sense of Indian culture by watching Indian videos.

8.6.   CHOICES

Video offers ordinary people more choices and freedom in use than any other medium does, and the potential uses are almost limitless. During the last few years the video equipment has fallen in price, making the possibilities much greater. Video can be used even by non-literates. They soon learn the text on the equipment as symbols they can recognize. Anyone who is a good communicator seems to be able to use it, even if the program is made on just one camera and recorder without editing. Through the video, people can exchange views horizontally among themselves and not just top-down as we experience on the centrally-controlled mass media. Locally-produced videos do not aim at millions of viewers as television does, so the content can be limited to the interests and needs of a small group. It can truly become a community medium, and this can be extended through cable systems to a whole town or city. And the user often owns the program, the video tape. In a real sense, ready access to the media has become a reality.

8.7. MUSIC VIDEOS

It is also interesting to look at the use of music on video. Jazz never seemed to have the impact that rock has, and this is probably due to the fact that it did not have television and videos to promote it. Certain kinds of music seem also more appropriate for video and television than other kinds. Experiments with "art videos" have not proven commercially viable, while music videos with popular music are big business. Classical music, on the other hand, fits perfectly with radio, records, CDs, and audio cassettes.

Music videos will have their unique effect. We know that popular music can change society by promoting off-beat lifestyles and by bringing together groups seeking an identity. Music can express anger and frustration as well as joy and devotion. Such effects of popular music on society are cumulative. Therefore, it is not surprising that political and religious leaders have at times looked upon music as an evil influence, and, like Hitler and Khrushchev, they have attempted to control its use. In 1979 Ayatollah Khomeini banned music on Iranian radio stations, saying that music "stupefies persons listening to it and makes their brains inactive and frivolous."[14] Obviously these men did not understand music or how to use music, and for this we can probably be grateful as they might have used it for their evil agendas. Video is there and at least some kinds of music seem fitted for this medium, and enough is produced to feed MTV with constant music videos, day and night. Production is getting more and more sophisticated and some music videos are reported to have cost five million dollars to produce.

8.8. POSSIBILITIES OF VIDEO FOR THE CHURCH

Video has encountered much "theological" opposition, but at the same time it has attracted enormous attention by Christian groups. Covenant Video was one of the first in the United States.[15] Other churches have started video ministries, which primarily focus on video recording of special services which can be sold to or borrowed by the congregation. They will usually also have a selection of Christian films dubbed onto video for the same purposes.

Technically speaking, the video cassette does have the capabilities of becoming a powerful tool in Christian communication. Production and equipment are expensive, but all that is needed by the receptor is a video cassette player to plug into his or her television set and some programs. Most Christian film distributors have followed Hollywood and just dubbed their films onto video, but good programs are becoming increasingly available. The potentials of video seem best for use in group studies, rather than personal use. The main reason for this conclusion is the problem of effective marketing and distribution networks, especially when videos are intended for evangelism.

8.8.1. Video combines many signal systems.

A video uses both sound and visuals, movement and emotions. The combination of such factors makes video a medium with almost limitless possibilities. Video is impact, but without a darkened theater, the emotional impact on the viewer will be less than with film. Few will permit tears to flow when watching a film on video, while they may do so in a theater. The context of the home is influenced by the social pressure of others in the room, and an attempt to control personal emotions will be the result.

Moody Video and *Maranatha! Music* have shown that they can master the medium and utilize its possibilities in Christian communication. The inspirational video series produced by the two organizations with titles such as *Perfect Peace* and *This is the Day* use beautiful nature scenes that are blended perfectly with a specially written music track. On this background, or on that "stage," a well-chosen voice recites relevant Scripture passages. Wherever you want to communicate peace and beauty, prepare for a time of worship, or just want a time of personal quietness with God, these videos will be of great assistance.

8.8.2. Video provides alternate times for viewing television and adds possibilities of repetition.

This facility, called time-shifting, is used widely by families who want to watch a television program at a more convenient time. It is also used by teachers who want to bring a program into the classroom at the appropriate time in a teaching sequence. Similarly, it could be used by Sunday School teachers. In one country churches had problems finding times for committee meetings, etc., due to favorite television programs. A video could provide a help to solve such a situation.

Video is not like television where we may miss a point or turn on the program a little too late. Video returns the control of the time and viewing to the viewer who will decide the time of viewing and the repetition necessary. The same tape can be played in different locations. It makes it well suited for video libraries as operated by churches and missions.

8.8.3. Video provides access to groups that are otherwise closed by political or social barriers.

Access to communication media is presently changing in many societies, in particular in Eastern Europe, and this is influencing the use of video. A group of churches in the former Yugoslavia has placed video cassettes in all their churches so that people can borrow them or even purchase copies. It is estimated that there are five million video cassette recorders in the country.[16] The Roman Catholic Church in Poland is producing its own religious films on video, such as *Road to Bethlehem*, but most of their videos are translated films and they are primarily used as part of religious education.[17]

Video provides access in many other countries, particularly Islamic states, where the doors are closed as far as public or mass media are concerned. The groups we need to communicate with may also be too small to warrant mass media approaches. We could take a group like Chinese women in Malaysia. Due to the heavyhanded policies of the Moslem-dominated government, the large Chinese minority has sought to protect their Chinese culture and values. Many of the women are poor readers or non-literate, and they speak a variety of Chinese dialects, making communication even more difficult. Traditionally, it has been the women who have taken care of the teaching of Chinese religions to their children, and women who have given their life to Jesus have been a strong witness in the homes. The Malaysian government restricts religious media programs to Islam, and there are absolutely no opportunities in the mass media for Christians in the country. But video can be used freely after the programs have been approved by the censors. Chinese women are already avid viewers of Hong Kong films and videos, which they share with friends and neighbors. Video would seem to be an ideal medium for reaching the Chinese women and then teaching them the basics of the Christian faith. They could also be helped with general education programs such as nutrition and child care.[18]

In many countries Christians do not have access to good educational programs for leadership training. Video could be used in Bible schools in countries like Brazil. The increasing number of Christians demand training of large numbers of Christian leaders and pastors, and often there are not enough teachers and good material available. At least some of the subjects could be made available on video and distributed to Bible schools and various institutes. Bible schools could also show videos with films like the

Campus Crusade-produced *Jesus film*, then discuss its use with the students so that they can use it effectively in their ministry and churches.

8.8.4. Video is viewed in a lighted room.

Video does not require a dark room as a movie does. This may create some distractions, but it makes it much easier for the teacher who wants to show a film during a daytime class. It also provides possibilities for people in places such as a hospital waiting room to view a video. Some of the first experiments with video in Christian ministry were done in Thailand at Christian hospitals.[19] Recently a Baptist hospital in Thailand reported good response to video in the hospital outpatient waiting room, and the hospital chaplain is available to those seeking additional information or counseling. The primary need is to get new programs in the Thai language, and the long-range goal is to provide a balanced video program of health programs and spiritual messages during the waiting period. Later video monitors are to be extended to patient wards.[20] On the secular video market in Thailand, you have primarily American *action* films and Hong Kong *Kung Fu* films. The video market in Thailand is a booming industry.

8.8.5. Video programs presently available are primarily for passive viewing.

Video provides satisfaction through impact, which is addressed to feelings and should stimulate feeling-responses, but there are very few good programs available that will inspire active participation by the viewers. Yet, the possibilities are there for building in action and response. Most follow the film format, primarily due to the fact that most of the programs available were first in film form.

Video messages tend to focus on personality and, at least in comparison to print, are rather weak with conceptualization. The video message is often a simplification, but this may be due to poor programming rather than to the possibilities inherent in the medium. Video favors specificity while print can deal more comfortably with the "whole picture."[21]

Video can also be effectively used in fund-raising campaigns. A group such as the Christian Communications Institute in Chiangmai can show their Thai dances and music in original settings, providing sponsors with a view of the programs they provide funds for. Through video they can follow the team "on location" in a remote Thai village.

8.8.6. Video is primarily a group medium.

Video is limited to the smaller group and is not suited for the wide audience of television, unless numerous copies are made. Much more than television, video lends itself to being viewed by a group engaged in a particular study activity.

The British-produced, video-based evangelism training program *Person-To-Person* is an excellent example of good production made for the small group.[22] The program is a ten-lesson course in personal evangelism, but it is taught and executed in a group setting. The video carries both information for the leader and actual programs and lessons for the group. There are workbooks to supplement the video and quite extensive practical exercises in evangelism to be carried out by the group. The program addresses one of the most pressing problems for Christians: How to speak effectively and relevantly about faith on an individual level? It has been followed by thousands of Christians in a wide variety of church denominations and is aimed at motivating, equipping, and mobilizing people in the churches for effective evangelism in today's world. The ten lessons begin with a recognition of God's power, then go through the steps on how to tell "your story," praying with people, and caring for new Christians.

8.8.7. Video can be easily integrated with other media.

The "user" is present, so video can easily be incorporated into a much wider strategy. It can be a part of a teaching course, an introduction to a group discussion, or a special feature. It can also be used to extend a special campaign, as was done during the 1984 Billy Graham *Mission England* Campaign. The crusade meetings were recorded on video and sent to remote areas where they were shown in town halls on large-size screens, or on normal-size television sets. A total of 210,000 people attended these showings, at 208 locations. Enquirers numbered 3.8% of those attending. This can be compared to 9.4% among those attending the main event at the arena where Graham spoke.[23] Video is no substitute for personal presentation, but it can be used effectively in such situations if well-trained assistants are present to provide introduction, context, and follow-up. At the Spring 93 crusade in Germany, video recordings were made available in numerous European languages.

8.8.8. Video and Music.

On the secular market, music videos have been extremely popular. They are primarily based on hard rock, and the effect on the viewer seems to be almost the opposite of the inspirational videos mentioned above. But there are obviously unique possibilities for Christian music videos, and experimentation is needed to make them in a way that will be suitable for Christian communication. A number of Christian artists have produced their own videos. The American Bible Society is following the music video format in their new Bible videos produced for American young people.

The music video format has been used quite effectively by *Maranatha! Music* with their *Kid's Praise* Videos, some of which are musicals, others "Sunday School sing-alongs." There is obviously an extensive market for such programs in the United States where they will provide Christian parents with programs of highest technical quality, giving children hours of positive "television." Children will play the videos over and over again.

A special sing-along video produced by the same organization aims at teaching children Sunday School choruses. Christian Communications Limited in Hong Kong has been experimenting with a Japanese karaoke format with color-coded rhythm for people to sing along with the video-tape. They aim at teaching new hymns this way.

8.8.9. Video equipment is portable and provides instant play-back.

Video recording equipment is quite easy to transport, and playback equipment can also be moved from location to location. Video, however, does require the availability of electrical currents. The recording equipment is well suited for missionary reporting. Unlike super-8 film, slides, or other traditional media used for such purposes, the video can be shot and mailed within hours. Humanitarian organizations have used this effectively when a natural disaster has struck in a certain country.

Video provides instant playback, a facility that is important in education. A speech class, for example, can evaluate a "performance" immediately. This is used extensively in all kinds of training and education, and it will fit well into the training of pastors and preachers. Proper evaluation can take place after the speaker has seen the presentation on the video screen.

8.8.10. Video allows for immediate feedback.

If the program is used as part of a teaching program or as a part of an evangelistic approach, immediate feedback can be provided by the viewers to the "user," but not to the producers of the program. Often a program will be produced in such a way that it will call for follow-up discussion in the group viewing.

The program *Messages from the Memory Banks*, produced by the Bible Society in Swindon, England, is a good illustration of such an approach. Together with the video, teachers are provided with questions for group interaction and discussion immediately following the program. The tape itself actually includes the instructions for the leader so that he or she can be prepared for the interaction and follow up.

Recent developments with multi-media where video is joined with computer technology and CD-ROM make it possible to interact with the program material through a computer keyboard and mouse. Such programs have great possibilities for educational programs.

8.9. THE FUTURE CHALLENGES

On the secular market, video has more than any other media been used to carry programs that are extremely distasteful to the Christian communicator and often seem to be in direct confrontation with the Christian values of beauty, peace, love, and respect for the other person. The challenge to use such a medium for the communication of Scripture must be faced by church leaders.

Future expansion of video use in Christian work will probably be in the area of teaching Christians, but it may also become an important evangelistic tool if relevant programs can be produced. In more technically advanced societies, the video cassette may become a very effective tool when used to reinforce one's own testimony while sharing Christ with a friend. The possibility of replay gives added scope, but in this as well as in all other areas of Christian use of video, we need extensive research and experimentation.

Amazingly, people seem to be able to get a video player in spite of the cost. But for most people in the world it is still beyond their reach, so the cost factor will need to be carefully considered in the light of other possible media that could be used. A positive factor is that video tapes are reusable. When a program has been watched or is no longer needed, the tape can be erased and a new program recorded.

The use of video by missions in the Third World will be limited by the high cost of hardware, and the lack of culturally relevant programs. All the hardware in the world is useless without a really first-class script and culturally relevant and good programs.[24] The present use of video in the Third World raises many critical question. As with other resources, the programs are usually produced in countries with greater financial capabilities and therefore questions of relevancy come up. How does the Western-produced program apply to the traditional systems of economics, the social and political contexts, and social interaction patterns of another people? Will we continue, through video, to extend the Western use of media to also dominate the training programs used in other countries? Will video programs also "program" the way people act as a result of the video? For example, if the British-produced evangelism training video were to be shown in Bangladesh, how relevant would the practical exercises and applications be? That which makes a program strong in one society may make it useless in another.

As Christians we should carefully evaluate the use of such a powerful tool as the video cassette. We need more experimentation on which to base our strategies and planning. There are obvious possibilities for use of video in education, and many talk of using video in evangelism, but few are showing us how to use it or developing the necessary programs. We may dream of showing Christian videos in video parlors in India, but the programs people pay for there are drastically different from what Christians will want to produce. There is still a long way to go and much pioneering to do. It is encouraging to note, though, that some Christian producers in India are experimenting with low-cost video productions for use in evangelism in India.

SUMMARY

Video has during its short lifetime caused a communication revolution. It is a medium that changes the way we think and process information. Video works on impact, emotions, and impressions.

The distribution of video is expanding at an enormous rate, and the medium is being used for all kinds of purposes. Video rental is constantly increasing, and statistics indicate that programs with horror and war, crime, erotic and pornographic topics are at the top. There are some good uses also, particularly in the area of education where video has proved to be an excellent medium for classroom instruction.

There should be plenty of opportunities for using video in the church and in mission, but relevant programs are still difficult to find. Again, in the area of education we have seen the best productions, but there are also good videos produced for personal devotion and meditation. Many children's videos are on the market, including some sing-along programs. Christian performers have also entered the field of music video.

The future challenge is to experiment with video and learn to harness it for use in church and mission. There are many unanswered questions, but due to its powerful influence and wide distribution, we need to learn how to use it for the good of humanity. Video is expensive to produce, so the future will also call for new partnerships to be developed for video production.

FOOTNOTES

1 Douglas A. Boyd, Joseph D. Straubhaar, Joh A. Lent, *Video-cassette Recorders in the Third World*. Longman, Inc. 1989. See also, Manuel Alvarado, ed., *Video World-wide*, UNESCO. 1988.

2 Editorial, "The Video Revolution," *Media Development* (World Association of Christian Communication journal) 1/1985:1.

3 Christine Ogan, "Video's Great Advantage—Decentralized Control of Technology" in *Media Development*, 4/1989, pp. 2-4.

4 Ibid., p. 1.

5 Christine Ogan, "Cultural Imperialism by Invitation," *Media Development*, 1/1985, Vol. XXXII, 2-4.

6 Douglas A. Boyd, "VCRs in Developing Countries: An Arab Case Today," *Media Development*, 1/1985, 5-7.

7 Binod C. Agrawal, "Video—A New Diversion for India's Rich," *Media Development*, 1/1985, Vol. XXXII, 14-15.

8 Eric Michaels, "How Video Has Helped a Group of Aborigines in Australia," *Media Development*, 1/1985, Vol. XXXII, 16-18.

9 Jerzy Mikulowski Pomorski, "Alternative Video in Poland," *Media Development*, 4/1989, Vol. XXXVI, 20-21.

10 Usha Vyasulu Reddi, "No limits to Imagination: Video Use in India," *Media Development*, 4/1989, Vol. XXXVI, 15-17. See also, *Communication Revolution: A Study of Video Penetration in India* by Binod C. Agrawal, et.al., 1989.

11 Ibid., p.16.

12 "Bangladesh Observer," Dhaka 7 Nov. 1989.

13 Ibid., p. 3.

14 John L. Hulteng, and Roy Paul Nelson, *The Fourth Estate. An Informal Appraisal of the News and Opinion Media*. New York: Harper and Row. 1983:307.

15 Ericson, "Covenant Video," 1980:21. Author's files.

16 *ICMC Newsletter*, Volume 4, Number 1, 1990, p.12.

17 Pomorski, ibid., p.21.

18 Vicky Li, "The Possible Use of Video in Ministering to Chinese Women in Malaysia". Paper submitted to class on Communication with Non-Literates, Fuller School of World Mission. 1989.

19 David Anthony Huntley, "Video and Mission." Th.M. thesis, Fuller Theological Seminary, Pasadena, 1981.

20 *Asia Baptist Communicator*, May 1989, newsletter of the Southern Baptist Foreign Mission Board.

21 Richard R. Smyth, "In Addition to Print ...," unpublished article, author's files.

22 "Person-to-Person" is produced jointly by the Bible Society, Scripture Union, and Campus Crusade in England. The production has won a major award in the area of multi-media productions.

23 Report published by Mission England.

24 David Anthony Huntley, "Video and Mission." Th.M. thesis, Fuller Theological Seminary, Pasadena, 1981:2.

CHAPTER 9

Audio Cassettes

"I Like to Listen"

They are everywhere, in cities and in villages. They are playing through hi-fi stereo equipment in an urban home, on simple hand-cranked players in tribal villages, over car and bus radio-cassettes, and through the earphones of a walkman. The fantastic audio cassette has impacted civilization more than anyone could have imagined. Its primary use has been for music, where cassettes share the market with records and CDs, but cassettes have many other unique uses not matched by other communication tools. Cassettes were used to repeat the messages of Khomeini across Iran when the shah was still in control, and cassettes have assisted literacy training and basic education in scores of other countries across the world.

Sound recording is not new. The basic developments happened more than a century ago in 1877 when Charles Cross in France and Thomas Edison in the United States developed the theory and a "talking machine." At first, cylinders were used for sound storage, but a decade later the first gramophone record was produced. Developments continued, and by 1921, a hundred million records had been sold.[1]

Electromagnetic recordings were developed during the same period as the phonograph, and as early as 1889 a Danish engineer produced a recording on steel wire. In July 1945 an American serviceman came across a sophisticated magnetic tape recorder in a radio studio in Frankfurt. The machine and tapes were brought back to the States where they were soon improved and the production of tape became a reality. Tape recording revolutionized the record business, and within a couple of years studios were using "noise-free" tape recordings for their masters. All during the 50s the reel-to-reel tapes were used extensively and their capability for editing was used to the fullest. In the 50s, the cartridge systems were introduced for playback, and then in the mid 60s, the cassette revolution began. Initially, there were several different formats and standards, but eventually the Philips cassette became the world standard for audio cassettes.

A number of Christian organizations have been involved in the recording of messages for many years. Among these is Gospel Recordings,

Los Angeles, which has been involved in the recording and production of records for several decades and is presently also producing audio cassettes. Most organizations are national, but among other US based organizations serving international needs we can mention Portable Recording Ministries of Holland, Michigan, and Hosanna in Albuquerque, New Mexico. Hosanna alone produces up to 30,000 Scripture cassettes a day.

9.1. THE AUDIO CASSETTE IS A UNIQUE MEDIUM AND OF SPECIAL INTEREST FOR CHRISTIAN COMMUNICATION

The audio cassette has proved to be an outstanding medium. There is no tape to thread, no records to turn, and no sensitive needles to replace. Much of the equipment is portable, and simplicity of operation, low cost, and availability make it extremely versatile. Music groups, not "big enough" to invest in the production of records, can produce cassette recordings and just make copies according to market demand. The following pages give a number of uses of cassettes, and the medium is compared to some other media, in particular radio which is also a sound medium. Radio and cassettes have much in common as far as production is concerned, but they are very different when it comes to the actual communication situation and possible uses.

Even though the cassette is a humble medium without the romance and excitement of film and television, and without the challenging (potential) audience of millions, which radio promises, its potential for the mission of the church should be obvious. Probably no other new tool used in Christian communication has enjoyed such an immediate acceptance as the audio cassette. The first players were distributed by the Voice of Peace in Thailand in June, 1969, and initial plans called for the use of twelve cassette players in a testing program covering six to twelve months, but within six months ninety cassette players were already in use.[2] A recent example of the potential for cassettes among people from the Western world was the *Desert Storm* cassette produced by *Maranatha! Music* for the American soldiers in the Arabian desert; 100,000 copies were distributed.

The audio cassette has many unique features that make it appropriate foruse in church and mission.

a. Audio: As the name "audio cassette" indicates, the medium is one that uses sound only. You need only to listen. Though the literate person may often prefer reading to listening, reading is too difficult for the semi-literate and it is impossible for the non-literate. As the cassette simply requires the person to listen, it is for everybody. If reading is difficult in the first place, it takes a lot of energy and time to reread, and reading requires total concentration. The cassette, however, can be played and listened to while one is engaged in other activities.

b. User controlled: It is the listener who decides how, when and where to use the cassette. He or she is in full control of the communication situation. In a rural village a church leader may, for example, want to play the teaching cassettes late at night when other members of the family are sleeping, so that he can pay full attention to the content and prepare himself for the coming Sunday worship service.

c. Available: Cassettes are now available almost everywhere and cassette players and recorders can be purchased at all kinds of prices. Tapes are available in a wide variety of quality and length, and cassette recorders range from battery-operated models to expensive stereo equipment. For good use of cassettes in Christian ministry, it is important, though, that relevant distribution systems are set up and managed so that the right programs are made available to the intended audience at the right time and place.

d. Economical: The cassette requires a financial obligation on behalf of the listener, but prices are so low that in many situations the cassette would be the cheapest medium to use. At the outset the cost involved in starting a cassette ministry may seem high, but if all costs are considered, it may be one of the least expensive media. We can, for example, compare the many hours of playing time of each cassette with the cost of a pastor's time, a radio program, or a book. The hourly cost then becomes minimal. Where people cannot afford to buy players or cassettes, loan systems can be set up at churches or mission centers.

e. Compact: The cassette is small in size, and it does not require the same amount of attention and care as an open reel tape demands. Many hours of programs can be carried in a pocket, and a whole Bible school curriculum can be stored on a shelf. The length of a cassette will depend on the tape loaded into it, and it can range from a few minutes to two hours. The longer the tape, the thinner it has to be, and, consequently, the more likely to give problems on cheaper equipment. A standard C-60 that plays a total of one hour is usually the best approach.

f. Simple to operate: In spite of the sophisticated technology involved, cassette players are extremely simple to operate and no training is needed. In this way it is extremely user-friendly, and an illiterate person, or even a small child, can use it. A few simple instructions concerning care, upkeep, and cleansing of playback heads will keep the player running for a very long time.

g. Anywhere: Cassettes can be used almost anywhere. Cassette players usually work on batteries, so electricity is not needed. Of course, where electricity is available, it cuts down the cost for batteries. You can even operate it on a solar panel or use a hand-cranked machine. Cassette teams in

Bangladesh use rechargeable motorcycle batteries to provide hours of playing at very low cost. Cassette players are portable and light. For the person who drives to work, he or she will often spend up to two hours a day in the car. For many, this time has become productive as they listen to cassettes with messages, Bible reading, or good music.

h. Anytime: The cassette can be listened to whenever it is convenient for the user, whether early morning, late at night or in the middle of the day. In this way cassettes compare favorably to radio broadcasting. Radio requires listening at a specific time while an audio cassette can be used at the listener's convenience. A radio program is usually designed for a large, varied audience while a cassette can be tailored to a specific, limited audience segment.

i. The right sequence: Often programs are produced in a series, and the cassette makes it possible to start a series at any point in time. For radio, sequencing is a problem as not all listeners will start listening to the programs at the same time. Each radio program will therefore need to be an entity in itself. Cassette programs can just continue from one cassette to the next.

j. Repetition: The cassette can be listened to as many times as needed. Repetition is an important aspect of learning and in this regard cassettes are far superior to radio which cannot repeat the program. Many are able to learn because the cassette provides this capacity of repetition as many times as needed or desired. A non-literate person will be able to learn the message by heart after a few listenings.

k. Less personal energy: The person who does not read regularly often finds it difficult and exhausting to read. He can relax while listening to radio or cassettes. That is, the programming has to be done in such a way that a person can enjoy the program, find it worth his or her time to listen, interact with the message, and decide to follow the suggestions for action. As direct personal response is usually not possible, the audio program should be produced in such a way that it produces an intrapersonal response and will lead to a behavioral response. Such an effect has been achieved when applying the principles developed for programmed instruction to audio programs.[3]

l. Privacy: The cassette helps to overcome the barriers of embarrassment in interpersonal contacts. A person can listen in the privacy of his or her home. Often a person living in hostile environments will want to learn the basic teachings of the Bible, and cassettes provide the possibilities for this without creating opposition or persecution. It may also be a person in a hospital bed. Cassettes can be listened to through earphones without disturbing the person in the next bed. During years of extensive use and experimentation with cassettes in Thailand, Bangladesh, India, and many other countries, it has become obvious that cassettes can achieve outstanding results when they are produced for such specific and defined purposes. Through personal friendship you reach within a person's latitude of acceptance/rejection. As you loan a cassette tape to that person it meets the needs of that person, expands the latitude of acceptance, and possibly starts a spiritual process towards Christ.

m. Audience segmentation: Cassette tapes can be tailor-made to specific audiences. They do not need to be programmed for a wide inclusive audience like radio. Cassettes programs can therefore be very specific. In a country with a low literacy rate, cassettes can make the difference. Many have heard new Christians comment that they had heard about Christ before and read tracts, but it was the cassette that gave them understanding. In societies used to oral communication and rote learning, cassettes fit beautifully, but it should be emphasized that good production and service facilities are needed in order to have a lasting, effective ministry.

n. Local color: Cassettes can be made to include local color through the use of local music and sound effects. This will make the programs relevant and acceptable to the listener. In the same way as Jesus used the living examples of his immediate environment to illustrate parables, we can use local situations, anecdotes, stories, and ways of expression. For a people like the Marwari in Sind Province of Pakistan, poetry plays an important role, and they love to compose and listen to poetry. Cassette programming can capture such local color to make the message interesting and relevant to the listeners.

o. Local dialects: A cassette can speak the language of the people, as recording can take place locally. In a project in South India, we found that dialects would change slightly even with a distance of only twelve miles. To facilitate the acceptance of the cassettes in a community, we found that it was important that the first couple of cassettes were produced in the exact dialect of the people we were trying to communicate with. Later, it was possible to introduce cassettes produced at other locations with slightly different dialects.

p. Teach music: The audio cassette is increasingly seen and used as a music and song medium, and in many places it is difficult to change that image. Christian movements among some tribal people have been attributed to the use of local music. In Thailand, cassettes and radio programs helped Thai Christians to appreciate and learn hymns written in the Thai pentatonic scale. New Christians who would otherwise need months to learn to sing hymns based on Western seven-tone scales could learn twenty new hymns in a week by just following a cassette. And a visit to any Western Christian bookstore will show a wealth of music cassettes. Christian music is playing and inspiring people through cassettes all over the world. Music can also be used to teach theology and doctrine. As an example, we could mention the worship music cassette series, based on theological or biblical topics, produced by Maranatha! Music in the United States. Titles include "Abba" where all songs are dealing with the topic of God as Father.

q. Need-oriented: Audio cassettes can be made to fulfill a specific need among a specific group of people and have been used for a great variety of such purposes. In Tanzania, for example, cassettes have been used not only for music, messages, sermons, drama, Christian teaching, and Bible school courses, but also for special subjects of interest to women, such as nutrition, childcare, and female circumcision.[4] Other countries have developed similar, specific uses for cassettes. In Indonesia a cassette has been produced for helping Christian families to reach their non-Christian house help. An integrated use of cassettes is the most effective use. This requires both adequate research and active involvement of the local church. Unfortunately most users, or producers, of cassettes have taken the easy way and are producing "packaged" products that do not seem to consider the listeners' needs.

r. Education: The cassette has exciting possibilities for both formal and non-formal education. There exists a high sense of motivation in the listening situation. Educational cassettes will need to be programmed in a different way than those designed for radio broadcasting. The essential difference between radio and cassettes is that you only listen once to radio but many times to a cassette. The cassette will therefore need to be designed in such a way that repetition will be both natural and enjoyable. A long story or joke may be interesting on radio, but boring on cassette after the first time of listening. Educational cassettes are for learning, and anything that does not fulfill that purpose is a distraction, but this does not imply that we should not utilize entertainment formats for education or that education cannot be entertaining. An entertaining program will cause greater appreciation among the listeners.

s. A variety of formats: Cassettes lend themselves to a great variety of formats. The basic ingredients in all programs are speech, sound effects, and music, but these can be combined in a great variety of formats. There can be monologue, dialogue, group discussions, and dramatic presentations. There can be testimonies, questions and answers, features, and singing. Within each of these areas, a variety of presentations can be developed, only limited by the creativity of the producer.

t. Uniform message: Often a message or a story is told with variations introduced by the speaker. Cassettes make uniform communication possible. This facility is desirable when a group of churches or a group of villages need to be instructed in certain skills or in the planning of projects. In many countries where missionaries have worked we also find a great variety of hymns translated from Western tunes. Often the same hymn has been translated by different people. By recording such hymns on cassette, it is possible to teach the same words to all the churches and eventually arrive at the same version of the hymn.

u. Entertainment: Music cassettes are widely used for entertainment purposes. On airline sound systems you may have a variety of both music and "speaking" entertainment cassettes, and in some bookstores, books on cassettes are among the best-selling items. Entertainment is something to which we are prepared to give some of our leisure time, so it has to be enjoyable but not necessarily without interesting content or helpful teaching.

v. Sound tracks: Cassettes can also provide exciting sound tracks for posters, pictures, and slides. This may be with the intent of teaching a local believer how to use posters in personal evangelism. The sound track will be memorized as they listen, and after a few times they can use the poster without the tape. We may also use a cassette sound track together with puppets in a children's program, or as a music track for traditional puppet shows such as the wayang leather puppets in Java. The use of cassettes with slides is also an inexpensive way of adding new dimensions to your communication. A slide-cassette presentation can be produced for a few dollars as compared to the thousands needed for a film or video. And the equipment needed is much less sophisticated and much less expensive.

9.2   EXAMPLES OF WHOLISTIC AUDIO CASSETTES IN CHURCH AND MISSION

The concept of wholistic audio cassettes derives from a desire to integrate communication as a central facilitating element in development projects. Significant experiments in Bangladesh and India, under the auspices of World Vision International, illustrate this concept. The project in Bangladesh was the first but the experiments in India, building on lessons learned in Bangladesh, are much more comprehensive and also more promising.

a. The Garo Grain Bank: The Garos of Bangladesh and Northeast India are descendants of earlier migrants from Tibet who settled in the Garo Hills. Originally these tribal people were animists, but during the period of British rule missionaries came to the Garo area with the Bible; today 60% are Catholics, 35% are Baptists.

Traditionally they are farmers and by courage and hard labor they have turned forest into agricultural land. But, due to frequent wars, natural disasters, and political suppression, the present economic condition of the Garo is poor, and most are landless. Their educational level is too low for them to gain jobs elsewhere in Bangladesh and the government has a plan to evict all forest dwellers, most of whom are Garos.

A new source of help was provided by a revolving village-based credit system, called a *grain bank*. The Garo Grain Bank sought to address the famine situation and help the Garo community avoid mortgaging their land for loans and at the same time witness to our Lord Jesus Christ and to build up the local church.

The project was administered through the nine administrative circuits of the Garo Baptist Union. Originally, two leaders were invited from each of these nine circuits to a brief orientation program where they were instructed in how to organize small village committees. The members of such village committees would then visit all Garo villages in the nearby area and prepare a list of loan beneficiaries, distribute the loans to poor Garo families, and keep a bank account and financial records.

The project immediately ran into serious snags, as each representative returned home and told slightly different versions of how the grain bank would function. It became clear that if the project was to achieve its objectives, uniform information was necessary at all levels. It was important that all village committees function on the same principles and that all World Vision project staff give the same instructions. An integrated communication system was necessary. A print-based communication was not feasible as most village people in Bangladesh are illiterate, and radio was not available. The audio cassette was, therefore, chosen as the major medium of communication to solve the problems and facilitate the start of the project.

It was believed that a well-produced cassette tape, containing one hour of programming, would be able to solve the major problems and also achieve the established objectives among all groups concerned. The largest audience for the program would be village committees, but it should also be used as information for the staff and leaders involved. A drama format was chosen for the program.

After a period of six months, the project staff and others involved met for a seminar and consultation to discuss and evaluate the initial effects of the tape and other aspects of the grain bank. There was an overall feeling that the tape had been extremely effective, and without it, the grain bank could not have been established. A number of problems were identified, and it was decided to produce a second cassette to deal with such problems and to make necessary mid-course corrections.

Later, a researcher traveled extensively to evaluate the cassette use, interviewing some people and distributing questionnaires to others. The findings were presented at a second evaluation session one year after the start of the program. Statistics of repayment were obtained for each circuit and the 352 villages involved. According to the findings, only one out of ten had listened to the cassette, but this varied significantly from circuit to circuit. In some places almost everyone had listened, in others hardly any. Twenty-five percent of the total loans had been recovered, and this was seen as a positive sign of success. A closer look at the statistics revealed that the rate of repayment varied significantly from circuit to circuit, from a high of 76% to a low of only 4%. Further investigation revealed that there was a direct correlation between the number of people listening to the tapes and the rate of repayment. Where the cassettes had been used widely, the rate of return was high, and where only a few people had listened to the cassettes, the rate of return was very low.

The integrated communication developed for the grain bank was based on good communication theory, and that theory was used to select a medium that was relevant for use among the Garo. It was also a research-based strategy. Extensive research and evaluation took place ahead of time and was carried out at intervals all during the project.

It was obvious to everybody concerned with the project that the communication system helped to make it work. Without the cassettes, the project would have failed and large sums of money would have been wasted. There were also some results for the church, as a higher view of the church was communicated, but as far as actual spiritual effects are concerned, we have to see beyond the grain bank and how the new communication system helped to open the door for other ministries among the Garo. Lessons from this particular project were used to develop an even more integrated project in India.

b. Evangelism enhancement in India: Due to a concern for wholistic effects through its involvement in hundreds of projects, World Vision of India proposed a project titled *Evangelism Enhancement Project*. The goal was to ensure effective witness integrated into community projects. The audio-cassette medium was chosen as the approach by which this could be achieved.

Later the proposal was given a thorough review on the basis of principles of integrated ministry communication, and it was decided to start with only two experimental areas where appropriate systems for India would be developed. One project was in Tamil Nadu in South India and the other among the Kui tribe in Orissa state.

Extensive research was carried out to define needs, both those felt by the communities involved and those defined by project staffs on the basis of experience with community development in India. The lifestyle of the people, language, cultural patterns, interests, opinions, and many other points were studied in preparation for the production of cassette tapes and the development of distribution systems. Planning sessions included the development of critical success factors, and a facilitating communications strategy.

Tapes were produced on the basis of a priority list, and topics included a variety of issues relevant to the villages. There were a few specific Christian topics, but it was primarily a case of wholistic, integrated approaches. There were programs on water, aimed at getting village people to drink water from the well rather than from the local, dirty pond, which the people said tasted better. There were tapes on unity and cooperation, and a somewhat hidden dimension of such tapes aimed at breaking down caste-barriers in the towns and villages. Other programs addressed social evils like excessive drinking. One tape is built on questions and answers concerning the organization itself and the purpose of Christian development agencies. The list goes on, but basic to the project was a receptor-oriented communication theory and a dedication to participatory development, including the writing of scripts and production of programs.

The Tamil Nadu project was subjected to an intensive evaluation less than one year after the first tapes had been distributed. The findings were dramatic and they confirmed the viability of the applied principles. The project started as evangelism enhancement, but the data revealed that a key to effective development communication had been discovered. It was concluded that wholistic ministry is both a valid concept and a practical methodology which produces concrete change in people's lives and in their communities. So, in this project, effective, integrated communication helped to achieve the best of development and the best of Christian witness. It confirmed the perspective of those planning the projects that we should not focus on evangelistic activities as such, but focus on evangelistic effects caused by the whole project.

Among the specific findings we can mention two villages where community projects had been undertaken by newly-formed associations, inspired by the cassettes. In another community, a low-caste person had been elected village president rather than the high-caste incumbent after the villagers listened to the tapes. The tape on diarrhea had challenged people to drink clean well water, and the occurrence of diarrhea had dropped dramatically, as had that of some other diseases. The tape "One God One Community" had caused greater respect among different castes, and they even sat together at evening classes. There were many reports of healings as people prayed in the name of Jesus, and in one Hindu village where there was no church, a group of forty to fifty people met for prayer and Bible study.

The tapes had also produced significant changes in the lives of the project staff. They expressed more interest and motivation, and they felt greatly helped by the tapes which broke the ice of resistance in villages. Some staff members had moved out to live in the villages to be available to the people during evening times, answering questions raised in response to the tapes.

This particular project affirms and proves that applied ministry communication is practical and viable, and that it can drastically change the effects of a development project. We are following the principles of good communication, including lessons from general development communication, and we are finding that when the Christian communication dimension is added, we have a "system" that is far superior to any other approach. The audio cassette is an appropriate and effective medium in the Indian situation when it is treated seriously. But so are all media of communication in specific situations. We may be lucky sometimes, but sustained effectiveness is only achieved when communication principles are applied to both media selection and media use, and when such applications take place within a well planned and research-based strategy. The experiments in India prove these principles.

9.3   AUDIO SCRIPTURES.

Cassettes have provided the Bible societies and the church with a new medium of Scripture distribution. Traditionally, the Bible has been "a written book," and Scriptures have been distributed as whole Bibles, testaments, or portions. Today, the Bible societies are faced with the challenge of making the Word of God available to all people in a world where an increasing number of people cannot read, and many more of those who can read, do not read. Of the millions of school children learning to read and write, it is estimated that about half of them will probably stop the learning process before any measure of reading skill has been achieved. Persons with no more than four years in school will probably become functionally illiterate, as their reading skills will deteriorate for lack of use. We have a tendency to neglect this large group of people, but we must remember that for thousands of years before printing made mass literacy possible, God was at work, and he is not limited to one single medium of communication.[5]

It is interesting to think of the situation in the churches during the New Testament times when the church spread rapidly throughout Palestine, Asia Minor, and on to Europe. They did not have a written New Testament, and the Old Testament was not readily available. Eventually, the stories were written down, but for decades they existed as oral tradition, being told and retold as the gospel spread. As an example of audio distribution, the Bible Society in Bangladesh has sent cassette teams out to work with local churches. Instead of giving out printed portions to people who do not read, they have played cassettes in the villages and towns.

Jesus communicated with ordinary people through the oral medium. He spoke with authority, and his speech was richly colored by local pictures and illustrations. In the same way audio Scriptures are not just a matter of reading a written text, but the translation of that text into a living sound that will spring into life in the minds of the listeners. The Word becomes incarnated into the life, lifestyle, voice, and imagination of the speaker or reader, and then, in a similar way, in the minds of the listeners.

The audio cassette is providing organizations such as the United Bible Societies with unprecedented opportunities as many of the world's cultures are oral rather than literate cultures. The real impact of the spoken word is not in the words alone, but in giving attention to correct emphasis of words, natural phrasing, and appropriate expression. These qualities, together with change of volume, pace, and pitch combine to reveal the true feeling behind what is spoken, without which the true meaning may be hidden or distorted. Consequently, an adequate understanding of Scriptures is not guaranteed by a good and accurate script alone but by many other factors in sound production as well.

The real challenge is to make an audio translation with the same content as the written text. In the Bible, we have chapter headings, explanatory notes, word explanations, pictures, cross references, etc. We also have maps that illustrate the place where things happened. When translating all of this into audio, we need to translate the maps, the pictures, the footnotes, and all the explanatory notes onto the tape as well. At the time of writing, Bible societies all over the world are working on this issue, trying to develop the necessary skills. The hope is that many Christians, ordinary members as well as church leaders, who have been largely neglected due to their lack of reading capabilities, will now have the Word of God available to them for personal study and leadership development.

Pilot programs have clearly shown that extensive word and concept explanations are often needed if a non-Christian is to understand the written text as read on a cassette. The explanations will need to be provided in a format that is appropriate to both the medium and the listening context. It may be a father reading the stories for his ten-year-old daughter, providing background information and contextual applications as they go through the book. Or it may be a dramatic series of daily readings, presented in the context of a village family, and a narrator who will provide the necessary help with background information so that the listeners can place the text in its geographical and cultural context. In this way the narrator has the same function as footnotes and pictures have in a printed Bible. An appropriate term for this function could be *guide*.

The Bible Society in Bangladesh has produce an Easter cassette. Fourteen Scripture passages were chosen to give a full story of the Easter events. Composers were then asked to put the text to music. The result is a cassette with fourteen Bengali songs communicating the story of Easter.

9.4. CASSETTES AND THE LOCAL CHURCH.

The most effective use of audio cassettes is in the context of the local church. By having cassette libraries and cassette players available for members to borrow, a church can greatly extend its evangelistic and teaching ministry. In the following only a few examples are mentioned, but the possibilities are almost without limit.

9.4.1. Cassettes in Personal Evangelism.

Cassettes can help the individual Christian in his or her personal witness. It can be the giving out of a cassette with a Scripture reading and message as a "tract" as demonstrated by Hosanna in New Mexico. They have found that a cassette is received with a smile and thanks, as compared to a printed tract which is often refused or thrown away. Many others have found that it is often very helpful to let a friend listen to a cassette and then discuss the content at a later meeting.

In Thailand we discovered that when local Christians witnessed to neighbors, they often ran into difficult questions. As unschooled, rural people, they did not know if answers existed to such questions. The result was ridicule, and the believer would be reluctant to engage in personal evangelism again. A number of the common questions were gathered and became the topics for two audio cassettes. The specific goals of the cassettes were to assist the local Christian in answering questions and help him or her in personal evangelism. The content was quickly memorized by the Christians as they played the cassettes for friends and neighbors. Numerous testimonies told of how they helped so-called passive Christians become active in evangelism.

9.4.2. The Extension of a Conference.

At many Christian conferences, the messages or the music are recorded for sale or distribution to participants. In this way the conference messages can be listened to again for closer analysis and better understanding. Similarly, many churches record Sunday services for distribution to those who are in the hospital or at retirement homes, people who are used to going to church but for various reasons cannot attend.

9.4.3. Cassettes for Children.

There are numerous possibilities for children's cassettes. Hosanna has produced a carrying box, *Fun-To-Go,* with Scripture-based stories for children together with coloring books and crayons. Many others have produced cassettes with songs and Bible stories for children. It would also be possible to produce "promotional" material for children's camps that would provide parents with both incentives to let their children attend and at the same time give them good information on the camp and what to expect. This might also provide a good introduction to your church and the programs your church has for children and families.

The Bible Society in Pakistan has produced a series of cassettes for children in the Urdu language. Old Testament stories are used and the material is present in a creative format, including singing, drama, dialogue, and interviews. Children are then asked to color the pictures in the accompanying book.

9.4.4. Cassettes and Music.

This is, of course, the most widely used form of cassettes. Some churches have recorded their choirs and sold the cassettes as an extension of the ministry. The worship cassettes produced by Maranatha! Music have been used the world over and inspired people for worship and renewal. Many Christian leaders will testify that it was such a cassette that introduced them to new dimensions in their worship and singing.

SUMMARY

Throughout this chapter an attempt has been made to place cassettes in relation to the demands of Christian communication theory. We have seen that the audio cassette is a unique communication medium that fits extremely well into many different uses in church and mission. We have seen that (1) cassettes can help us fulfill the task as Christ specified in the Great Commission. We have also seen that (2) cassettes work best in a person-based approach. They are in themselves only tools, but they can be used to extend the ministry of the church, especially when used by a Christian in his or her ministry. (3) Cassettes can be produced for the specific needs of an audience, and they will be even more effective when the audience is involved in the production as a participatory event. (4) A cassette ministry needs to be closely related to the local church, and we have found that cassettes are used much more effectively when the strategy is based on the church. (5) In the total Christian communication process, cassettes can be used at various stages, but they will be primarily used as teaching tools. But teaching, or cognitive input, is also needed at all stages of the spiritual growth process. We have also seen that (6) effective cassette ministries need to be based on good research. In order to be specific in our programming, we need good information. Finally, (7), cassettes can be made to fit perfectly into a given intercultural context. Local color and local dialects can be used in most cassette programs, making them relevant and effective communication tools.

FOOTNOTES

1 See Ray Eldon Hiebert, Donald F. Ungurait, Thomas W. Bohn, *Mass Media IV, An Introduction to Modern Communication,* for an extensive coverage. New York: Longman, 1985:452-490.

2 Viggo Søgaard, *Everything you need to know for a Cassette Ministry,* Minneapolis: Bethany Fellowship Publishers, 1975.

3 For example, the Bible Reading test program developed at Voice of Peace in Thailand for the United Bible Societies in 1975, and subsequent Bible Society pilot programs in Nepal and India.

4 Ong, "Development Communication" in *Development Communication.* Christian Foundation of Asia. 1981:94.

5 Viggo Søgaard, *Audio Scriptures Handbook,* Reading, England: United Bible Societies, 1991.

CHAPTER 10

Print

"Write It Down"

Literacy is a threshold to another world. The hieroglyphics of ancient Egypt communicated ideas to a select few, but today hundreds of millions can communicate with one another through the printed page. The distribution of literature has reached a staggering level. For example, *Reader's Digest* enjoys a circulation of more than thirty million in a total of 163 countries and is published in sixteen languages.[1] The whole Bible has been translated into 329 languages, and testaments or individual books into another 1,680 languages for a total of 2,009 languages,[2] and more than 51 million Bibles and 76 million New Testaments are distributed annually.[3] For many of us, papers and books are filling our shelves and offices, as well as our time. That books are highly regarded and play a dominant role in education is also evidenced by the size of libraries on university campuses. A large part of education is self-study with books and papers.

But, in comparison to other media considered thus far, literature is a medium that makes a big demand of the receptor: he or she must be able to read. In other words, it takes years of study for a person to establish an approach or ability to use this communication medium. We are faced with a mass medium that cannot, like radio and television, reach the masses by its very makeup. It reaches only one segment of the population, a segment that is increasing in some areas of the world and declining in other areas.

Books have a long history. Clay tablets the size of shredded-wheat biscuits were used in Babylon as far back as 2400 B.C.[4] They were used to record legal decisions and financial accounts. An entire library of such tablets existed in Nineveh in 700 B.C. But writing is even older, with papyrus used as writing material in Egypt as early as 4000 B.C. Later parchment became widely used, all up to the ninth century A.D.

The single most important development for book publishing was the invention of the printing press with movable type. The Chinese were the first to develop this and the oldest known printed book is "The Diamond Sutra," printed in China in A.D. 868.[5] It is made of large sheets pasted together to form a 16-foot scroll. But the real development took place in Europe where Johannes Gutenberg produced the printed Vulgate Bible in

1456. This signaled a revolution and print became the popular medium. Within fifty years, more than 30,000 different books were printed. During the subsequent years print has spread across the world and new advances in printing techniques have taken place. Recently, with the help of computers a new era has begun, and an individual with a personal computer, "desktop publishing" software, a laser printer, and a xerox machine can produce "printed" books one by one.

10.1. THE LIMITS OF THE PRINT MEDIUM

As mentioned earlier, print is not for everyone. No matter how fond of reading some of us may be, communicating with people is a matter of reaching out to where they are and accepting them in the way they are. That means, for the church, resisting the temptation to make literacy a requirement for salvation and spiritual development.[6] Unfortunately, this has not always been the case. When the Bible became "print," people were separated into two classes: those who could read and those who could not read, and as time has gone by, the church has put more and more of its information and learning into print.

Recent UNESCO figures estimate that just over one billion people are non-literate, but official literacy rates need to be taken with caution as they can be rather misleading. This is especially true of the term *functionally illiterate*, as it depends on the definition of the term. A four year education has in many places not produced students who are functional literates, that is, able to read and write normal and available publications.

India, with its more than 800 million population, has a national average of less than 40% literacy. Highest is the state of Kerala with approximately 70% literacy. (Incidentally, Kerala is the most "Christian" of India's states with 40% of the country's Christians living there.) The lowest literacy rate is found in Arunachal Pradesh with only 20% official literacy.[7] For Tamil Nadu, the figure is 45% and in Andhra Pradesh only 29%. These are official rates, but in terms of functional literacy, or even readership, the figures will be much lower, giving India a population of up to 600 million non-readers. In Bangladesh only 10%-15% of the population can be reached effectively by print.

Even in countries with a comparatively high literacy rate, the percentage of actual readers will be less than official figures indicate. For every individual who cannot read, many more cannot read at a level that would make persuasive written communication an effective form. Reading is hard work for them and written messages are avoided in favor of oral messages. This is true of the majority of the adult population in Asia, but even in highly developed countries the majority may not be able to read at a level where persuasive communication is possible.

There is a call for the publishing of books for "neo-literates," that is, those who have gone through basic literacy programs. There seems always to be a rather large gap between the level of reading skill of the majority community and of that used by writers of books. In a study of an adult literacy program in Bangladesh, we found that most of those who go through adult literacy classes have nothing to read after they "graduate," that is, nothing at their level. The United Bible Societies have produced a series of materials for New Readers, but that selection is too limited for a person to improve, or even to keep his or her level of reading skills. Other kinds of literature must also be available, based on limited vocabulary.

Reading skills are also declining in the Westernized world, probably due to advances in video and television. A recent study in Denmark, a country that boasts of a 100% literacy rate, revealed that 30% of the population above fifteen years of age do not read books or serious literature, and they never write a letter. Just a few years ago the figure was 20%. The research also identifies a rather sharp distinction between the readers and the non-readers. They could be divided into those who are "intellectuals with a book-based culture," and those who live in the "electronic picture culture."[8] Such a study is revealing, but it is also challenging as the program fare on the electronic visual media does not, generally speaking, appeal to the intellectual side of life. There is a real need to face up to this situation and to devote extensive resources to the development of high-quality material on the electronic visual media of television and video.

But this must in no way reduce our emphasis on teaching people to read and write. This is still a priority that needs our careful attention, and we need to study ways by which this activity can be strengthened and made more effective. The United Nations declared 1990 as International Literacy Year in order to launch a renewed effort and to create public awareness, so that literacy projects could be strengthened and multiplied. In March 1985, the Fourth UNESCO International Conference on Adult Education made a declaration on "The Right to Learn." We can give our full support to this declaration.

The right to learn is:

> *the right to read and write;*
> *the right to question and analyze;*
> *the right to imagine and create;*
> *the right to read one's own world and to write history;*
> *the right to have access to educational resources;*
> *the right to develop individual and collective skills.*

The United Nations "Convention on the Rights of the Child" also includes an article on education. Article 28.a states that all states are obligated to "make primary education compulsory and available free to all."[9] It is estimated that there are presently more than 100 million children who are not receiving primary education.

10.2. ISSUES AND DISTINCTIVES RELATED TO PRINT MEDIA

The influence of print is greater than the number of readers would indicate. Newspaper readers are, for example, much more influential than those who do not read. This is very evident in countries with a low percentage of literates. There is also a certain amount of prestige associated with print, and at a recent consultation with leaders from a rejected tribal group in South Asia, there was a strong call for audio material, but at the same time they requested that all the material also be made available in print. Only a small minority of the tribe are literate, but it was felt that self-esteem and unity within the tribe would be enhanced by the very fact that printed material was available in their own language.

Print significantly alters the communication patterns of the oral message. In oral form the message is influenced by such factors as intonations, sound of words, communal interaction, emotional impact, and personal appeal, as compared to print where sounds have to be guessed by sight during silent reading. In fact, the message itself changes as it is put into a written, linear form instead of the direct, telling form of oral presentation. Ability to use and understand print presupposes formal educational processes beyond just learning to read. Printed communication involves intellectual processes, understanding of subtleties and of figures of speech. Print has so changed and influenced our educational systems that formal education cannot be envisaged without books and papers.

Print does have the capability of interaction between the material and the reader, between source and receiver. A passage can be read, reread, reflected on, and memorized. But the memorization then follows a printed form rather than an oral form. As the sentences are carefully crafted and follow a linear form of argument, the memorization is a mechanical process rather than a living process as with storytelling and drama. Questions can be posed and a thinking process started (which is one of the intentions of this book). Due to the permanency of printed material, the same content can communicate to people that live thousands of miles apart, or are separated by hundreds of years. The Bible is an excellent example of this.

Print reduces the sense of urgency, as no time frame is imposed by a speaker. The response also changes, as the reader is not limited to a response format or response content requested by a speaker. Reading is done privately, and the corresponding intrapersonal responses are seen by no one else. All is done in solitude. The impact will not be from an external event or a context but from the content of the message itself.

The following points summarize some of the ways in which print influences and changes the shape and effects of communication.[10]

a. Print encourages individuality. It confirms an individual's right and ability to make personal choices, to agree or disagree with others, and also to discern the value and relevance of alternatives. On the other hand, results of such individuality have been seen in the rather strong tensions created in societies where the older, respected leaders are not literate. And they have been seen in the church, where the non-literates, in particular men, have been absent due to a focus on reading skills.

b. Print forces logical and linear thinking. This has made print useful to education and to democratic decision-making processes. Oral communication is event-oriented, print is sequential and linear. This is probably the primary reason for calling many educational systems "Western." In a way, they are not Western or Eastern, but as the West has captured the print media and given it such a central place in the educational process, print has been perceived as a "Western" medium.

c. Print forces objectivity. When reading, the individual can distance himself or herself from the text and objectively confront ideas, words, symbols, and meanings. This has made print so important in leadership development. But in a society where the common good is more important than the individual's interests, it has caused much tension between the younger and older generations.

d. Print makes it possible to handle a wide range of abstractions. Print can give word pictures, mathematical calculations, illustrations, etc., that prepare and equip a person to handle abstract ideas, and the material can be reread and studied again and again. On the other hand, if we try to transfer suc illustrations directly to other media, such as film, the person who is not literate will often not be able to grasp the point.

e. Print provides for self-gratification. A person can enjoy reading, and he or she can enjoy the grasping of difficult concepts and ideas, even though the immediate society does not understand or grasp the same ideas. This kind of self-gratification was seen in Europe during the time when literacy was a privilege of the few, "the learned," who in turn received and demanded high respect from the common people.

f. Print encourages self-discipline in learning. The mastering of skills is a process that demands dedicated work, and books inspire such discipline, guiding a person step by step. Such skills enable the person to gain more information and thereby more influence.

g. Print can utilize a wide variety of symbols. It is not limited to words, but pictures, color, illustrations, and headings all enhance the communication through print. This has given rise to a wide variety of publications, ranging from text only to comics.

h. Print provides relaxation. For the person who masters the print medium, reading can provide enjoyment, entertainment, and relaxation. According to a recent study, people are more relaxed, in a better mood, and more able to concentrate after reading a book, while the opposite seems true of television.[11]

10.3. FORMS AND USES OF PRINT IN CHURCH AND MISSION

Print, or literature, is many things: newspapers, magazines, comics, tracts, books, direct-mail, and so on. It is the oldest mass medium, and it has been used in all aspects of Christian work. Some believe literature is the most effective, far-reaching medium we have, and it is difficult to find churches or missions without literature departments, church magazines, or printed promotional material. Literature has therefore been treated extensively in articles, books, and magazines, and numerous instructional materials are available on how to write and how to use literature in church and mission. The David C. Cook Foundation quarterly magazine, *Interlit,*[12] could be mentioned, as well as other journals dealing with Christian communication.

The Bible is by far the world's number one bestseller, and as already mentioned, the first book to be printed by moveable type was the Gutenberg edition of the Vulgate Bible. It was this invention of print that made it possible for the Word of God to be made available to all people and to be kept in their homes.

10.3.1. Books.

According to David Barrett, more than 22,000 new commercial Christian book titles are published each year, and there are more than 23,000 periodicals.[13] By far the most books published by Christians are for Christians, and only a minuscule portion are suitable for evangelistic use. Those that are good for such purposes are usually testimonial in nature, such as *The Cross and the Switchblade,* or those written by well-known personalities like Cliff Richard or Billy Graham. Graham's book *Peace with God* has sold around the world.

Unfortunately, most Christian books available in the Third World have been written by foreigners and then translated into that language.

There is a need to encourage the writing of books by nationals of the country and to facilitate the publication of such books. The translation of books will usually be a poor second best.

In a survey, 2,700 "newer" converts in the Philippines were asked to choose which one factor was the single most important influence which convinced them to follow Christ.[14] Of those surveyed, 34.3% identified Bible reading or Bible study as the most important factor. For most, though, it was a combination of factors, and when asked to list all factors which combined to influence their decision, 73% listed Bible reading or Bible study, again the highest percentage. The results were similar for all denominations surveyed. We cannot tell from the available data if this means that new Christians are primarily from reading sectors of the population, or if the respondents do not distinguish between the reading of the printed Bible and the "re-telling" of the Bible message, but it does indicate the importance of reading.

As noted above, print has its limitations and reading skills are declining for many people. In order to assist the reader, different variations of graphics have been used to enhance the written text, such as illustrations, color, headings, and so forth. Illustrations and pictures can greatly enhance the text and can in themselves be integral parts of the message. A similar effect is found in journalism, where a picture is "worth a thousand words."

Some modern translations of the Bible carry extensive background information, maps, and color pictures. The "Colour New Testament," published by the British and Foreign Bible Society, is an excellent example of such attempts at making the Bible more readable and interesting for people who read less and less. During tests we have discovered that people perceive the text to be much more readable, enjoyable, and easier to understand than the same text in a "normal" Bible. It carries word explanations in boxes inserted into the text itself rather than at the back, and key verses are highlighted for emphasis. Maps and colorful illustrations add beauty, excitement, and relevancy to the text.

10.3.2. Newspapers.

Newspapers can be used in two basic ways by Christians: publish your own Christian newspaper or advertise and write in existing newspapers. Let us take the second option first. How can the secular newspapers be utilized for Christian purposes?

a. Use of secular newspapers. We can, of course, buy space for advertising our Sunday worship service, special events, youth programs, and so forth, but the papers can be utilized for much more extensive coverage of church events, and they can be co-opted for special drives and concerns of the community.

With a few notable exceptions, writers and journalists in the secular news media seem to be ignorant of significant religious ferment and developments. The "biggest story" of our time gets the poorest coverage, and certainly no sustained coverage is experienced. Local newspapers may be exceptions to such a statement, but usually the papers only become alive when scandals and confrontations are involved. It is therefore important that church and mission leaders take the initiative.

The potential for using the secular news media is there. It has been said that William Randolph Hearst in 1949 sent out a two-word memo to his nationwide chain of newspapers: "Puff Graham." The young Billy Graham was conducting an evangelistic crusade in Los Angeles, reporters and editors obliged Hearst, and Billy Graham quickly attained national fame.[15]

The use of secular news media by missions has by and large been neglected, but by aiming at equipping church leaders with the necessary skills of reporting and the dissemination of press releases, for example, the mission of the church could be enhanced. We need to learn how to "sell" our story to the papers in such a way that they will communicate it to their readers in an unbiased and factual way. This demands good and constant press relations. Any church will see its ministry enhanced by the cultivation of such press relations by one or more of its members or leaders. By developing relationships with the local media, a church may open up for communication channels that can assist in influencing a whole town. If good relations exists, then a telephone call or a news release is all that is needed when something happens.

A number of Christian organizations have developed press services. Some of these are very local or national in character, others are worldwide in scope. We could mention the German IDEA or the information service offered by the World Evangelical Fellowship.

An organization may also be helped by arranging significant events that will attract the media. If a new mission hospital, for example, is dedicated by a prominent figure, such as a prince, a president, or another highly-placed government official, media coverage will be assured. A sympathetic journalist may also be invited on a trip to observe missionaries in action. His or her articles may be much more valuable than thousands of dollars spent on our own advertising. Churches and Christian organizations should develop a "public relations orientation" to facilitate this. Unfortunately, such words have not always been well accepted by Christian groups, partly due to a misunderstanding of the concept involved. But it is important that we have good relationships and have an acceptable and positive image in the eyes of the world around us. Public relations is devoted to getting others to see the world as we see it. It is a persuasive effort, aimed at winning public acceptance and approval. If we believe in what we are doing, this should be one of our primary goals.

We do, of course, also need to advertise in the newspapers. Careful layout, good copy, and attractive design is needed to draw the attention of busy readers. In some places Christian organizations have placed ads in papers and magazines for evangelistic purposes. Usually, such ads call people to write in to get free literature, engage in a Bible correspondence course, or get answers to personal and spiritual problems. In a number of countries, especially where governments are rather restrictive on the activities of churches and missions, such advertising has seen good results. The distance gives the writer a sense of privacy, as he or she considers the pros and cons of the Christian faith. Careful research as to areas of need, topics of interest, and problems faced by the readers of a given paper will help you design the right communication message.

b. Publish a Christian newspaper. Newspapers need readers to survive, and a major concern of many Christian papers and magazines is to achieve a high enough circulation to pay for expenses and to attract enough advertising at the right price. There are Christian newspapers with a few hundred or a few thousand readers, and there are papers like the one being published by the Full Gospel Church in South Korea with a reported circulation of over a million copies.

Weekly Christian newspapers that aim at informing and inspiring Christians seem to be the most common. Older established papers are often daily papers, and they have usually taken a mainline church approach, while more recent efforts with charismatic influence are published weekly, and they provide information on Christian activities and advertisements to Christians.

Like many other countries, Denmark has one of each. There is a "respectable" daily Christian newspaper, *Kristeligt Dagblad,* with a circulation of some twenty thousand. It prides itself on being the paper most often quoted by politicians and by other papers. Its primary purpose and mission is to provide reliable news coverage of church-related events in the nation and abroad and give special attention to matters of interest to the church at large. But they need regular fund-raising drives to balance their budgets. A weekly challenger is the *Udfordringen* which is written in a popular style and primarily reports on evangelical activities, as well as includes an extensive number of ads. Its primary purpose is information about church and mission, and it obviously has a missionary or evangelistic goal as well. Both of these papers have their place in the life of church and mission. We cannot say that they compete, yet competition will always be there, for good or for worse.

10.3.3. Magazines.

Christian churches have used literature extensively, and most churches have their own newsletters and magazines, so there are numerous magazines for the Christian market.

Of special interest here are the magazines published for evangelistic purposes. We could mention *Breakthrough* in Hong Kong which provided a real breakthrough for Christian evangelistic magazines. The magazine, started by Chinese students and aimed at high school students in Hong Kong, is selling on newsstands in the city. The ministry has later expanded with extensive counseling services and audio visual productions. *Breakthrough* does not carry any advertisements. But advertisements are seen as important to a Middle Eastern magazine, *Magalla*. The publishers see ads contributing to the acceptability of the magazine. The purpose of the magazine is to remove misconceptions about Christianity and to communicate the basics of the gospel to the readers.

Step is a Christian magazine published in Nairobi, Kenya and circulated to most of Africa. The experiences of *Breakthrough* were studied, and extensive field research was conducted before the magazine was launched. *Step* is now the best-selling English-language magazine in Africa, with a circulation of more than a hundred thousand. This outstanding magazine is published by a multi-denominational African staff on a low budget, and with only simple technical tools and facilities.

The initial field research indicated, among many other findings, that there was a need for a youth magazine. Youth were avid readers. They were concerned about education, success, career fulfillment, but they also longed for acceptance and security and a greater knowledge of Jesus Christ. The research also indicated that the magazine must be inexpensive, with flashy and popular topics, entertaining while at the same time focusing on the needs of the young people. The evangelistic thrust of the magazine should therefore seek to provide teaching that would lead to acceptance of Christ, as well as provide articles on Christian growth.

Due to the openness by which *Step* treats topics like money, sex, generational gaps, witchcraft, loneliness, honesty, etc., it is often used by pastors as ice-breakers, and young people use it as a forum for discussion. *Step* provides wholesome counsel and shows practical solutions to problems faced by students and youth, including the problem of unemployment. Christ is presented as the only real solution to the human search for peace, comfort, and direction.[16]

Common for all periodical literature is that it is fairly easy to start a magazine, but very difficult to keep it going. It is also a very difficult transition to turn a magazine started by a missionary agency over to local

Christians. Usually, they do not command the same financial or human resources.

10.3.4. Comic books.

Everybody likes good comics. Our usual perception is that comics are for fun, and even though widely read by adults, they are perceived to be primarily for children. But comic books can be used for serious content and communication, and in Japan, for example, comic books are available on a wide variety of subjects. Ted Hope suggests that we look at examples of the comic medium in three categories: cartoon, cartoon strip, and comic book.[17]

Faced with the problems of semi-literacy, many Christian organizations such as the United Bible Societies have produced comics for children, and only recently have we seen comics aimed at the adult population, even though the primary market still seems to be children. Bible comics, which are special translations of the Bible in comic book format, are now on the market and selling well. The actual text has been translated into pictures as well as written text. A picture may be used to communicate instead of words or together with words. Expression on faces makes textual references to moods unnecessary. In other places, monologue is transformed into dialogue. This special combination of words and pictures therefore constitutes a unique translation of the biblical text. Translation consultants make sure that the true meaning is preserved in the "comic" translation. Nowhere in the comic books is God represented in a form recognizable by the audience. "The overall guiding principle is to express faithfully and effectively the meaning and intention of the Biblical text in a form which fully exploits the genius of the comic medium."[18]

10.3.5. Direct mail

In direct mail, letters are sent to a select group of people on a mailing list. The group will have a measure of homogeneity, and by the use of a computer with a mail-merge program, letters can be mass-produced with a seemingly personal appearance. Direct mail is primarily used for fund-raising. A forerunner of the modern direct mail is the missionary prayer-letter sent to a group of friends and supporters for prayer and financial support.

10.3.6. Newsletters, brochures, and tracts.

Engel has brought a decade of donor research together, and his monograph on the subject provides illuminating insights into the use of print media, both direct mail and organizational magazines. He has found that only one-fourth of all those who receive a publication from a Christian organization read all or most of the typical articles which appear.[19] "The burden of proof is on any organization that continues to use a magazine for its clientele."[20] Today, readership does not always justify the expenditure. The answer is research-based strategic planning and audience segmentation.

Follow-up materials used by Christian writers are usually in the printed form. Tracts have been used for more than a century and have actually given rise to the name of Christian organizations as "tract societies." We have also literature organizations such as *Every Home Crusade* whose aim is to distribute Christian literature to all homes. Such random distribution will have its effects in terms of contacts and it can give an opportunity for meeting those who have been prepared in some way or other. But usually, specific distribution of literature to designated audiences will be more effective. The Great Commission will not be fulfilled by a random distribution of literature, especially if the majority of the people cannot or do not read. The best and most effective way to use literature is when a Christian gives it to a neighbor or friend as a result of a personal conversation.

SUMMARY

The development of print has been described as the most important invention of mankind. Almost every aspect of our lives are today dependent on print. Our school system is totally focused around books, and all our democratic processes are based on written material. The lack of reading and writing skills severely limits a person's capacity to find a job and to function in a Western society. For the church, print is the primary medium, and it is almost impossible for us to envisage evangelism and Christian nurture without the use of printed materials and books. Indeed, we have built our ministries around such material.

On the other hand, we are still faced with a severe and limiting factor regarding print. It is a medium that only reaches part of the population. About one fourth of the population in our world is officially illiterate, and probably more than one half is functionally non-literate or non-readers. The advance of electronic media, in particular video, has developed post-literate societies. Many people who have learned to read are not reading and they are gradually losing their capacities to read. This will provide one of the most formidable challenges to the church and its mission during the coming decade.

Print will continue to be a major medium, though, and the church will need to study and use the medium. As a medium it has many advantages not matched by any other medium. The use of print includes books, newspapers, magazines, comics, tracts, direct mail, newsletters, brochures, and so forth, and all of these will continue to play a central role in our communication strategies. All have their use and all will be used.

FOOTNOTES

1 John L. Hulteng and Roy Paul Nelson. *The Fourth Estate. An Informal Appraisal of the News and Opinion Media.* New York: Harper and Row. 1983:166.

2 United Bible Societies. "1992 Scripture Language Report," December 31, 1992.

3 David Barrett, "Annual Statistical Table on Global Mission: 1990." *International Bulletin of Missionary Research*, Vol. 14:26-27.

4 Ray Eldon Hiebert, Donald F. Ungurait and Thomas W. Bohn. *Mass Media IV: An Introduction to Modern Communication.* New York and London: Longman. First ed. 1974. 1985:270.

5 Ibid., p. 272.

6 Ted Ward, in foreword to Viggo Søgaard, *Everything You Need to Know for a Cassette Ministry.* Minneapolis: Bethany Fellowship Publishers. 1975:5.

7 Malayale Manorame Year Book, 1984. Published by the Malayala Manorama Publishers, Kottayam, Kerala, India.

8 Jyllands Posten 31 marts 1989. Research by Denmarks Biblioteksforening, forskningskonsulent cand. polit. Henrik Christoffersen and AIM Research 1993.

9 WACC *Communication Resource*, December 1989.

10 Some of these points are adapted from Richard Smyth, p. 7ff, unpublished article in author's files.

11 Robert Kubey and Milhaly Csikszentmihalyi, *Television and Quality of Life: How Viewing Shapes Everyday Experience."* Rutgers University, 1990.

12 *Interlit* deals with a wide variety of topics related to the use of print media in Christian communication. It is available from David C. Cook Foundation, Cook Square, Elgin, Illinois.

13 David Barrett, "Annual Statistical Table on Global Mission: 1990." *International Bulletin of Missionary Research*, Vol.14:26-27.

14 A survey conducted by Christ for Greater Manila and World Home Bible League and reported by Kings Times in 1989.

15 Jeffrey K. Hadden and Charles E. Swann, *Prime Time Readers.* Reading, Mass: Addison-Wesley Pub. Company, 1981:20.

16 Bedan Mbugwa, *Case Study on Step Magazine*, presented at the Asia Christian Communication Fellowship Conference, Manila, June 11-15, 1984.

17 Ted Hope, *UBS Triennial Translations Workshop 1978.*

18 Resolution from the Asia Pacific Regional Consultation on Translation (ASPRESCOT), the United Bible Societies, 1983.

19 James Engel, *Averting the Financial Crisis in Christian Organizations: Insights from a Decade of Donor Research.* Orange, CA: Management Development Associates. 1983:23.

20 Ibid., p. 30.

CHAPTER 11

Film

"The Magnificent Screen"

Few media are more persuasive than film. As the viewer relaxes in a darkened theater or room, he or she becomes a participant in the action on the screen and experiences the full range of emotions as the story unfolds. Limited effort is demanded of the viewer. In minutes he or she can travel thousands of miles and span centuries of history. Movies have always exercised great influence on fashion, the Hollywood style, and on even the type of cars people buy. Movies have had a profound influence on attitudes and behavior, creating dissatisfaction with a present situation and awakening desires for change.

Film and audio-visuals are treated together in this chapter, as they are alike in the actual communication situation. Both take place in a darkened room, with all attention paid to the screen and sound track by a comparatively large audience. Video, on the other hand, may be watched in a lighted room, have group interaction and response, and usually be viewed by individuals or very small groups. As potential media for Christian ministry, the possibilities for film and audio-visuals are the same. The scope covers the whole range from a simple setup with one projector and tape recorder, through multi-media setups to movies.

Film-making had its beginning at the end of the last century. Thomas Edison produced one of the first motion pictures in 1896 when he recorded the inauguration of William McKinley.[1] At first, it was silent films and the technical apparatus was, of course, extremely primitive. The pictures were short takes of dances, parades and other events, but within a few years pictures with a plot were produced. Sound movies were introduced in the mid-20s and color a decade later.

After World War I, film-making developed into an amazing industry with Hollywood as its prime center. The move to Southern California, which began as early as 1910, provided year-round sunshine and unlimited scenic backdrops for all types of films, making Hollywood the film capital of the world. With increasing costs of production, other countries have not been able to challenge the American lead. Today, India produces more films but their marketing and use outside of India are minimal.

Films have traditionally been shown in movie theaters, but television and video are challenging this tradition. Fewer and fewer people go to the theater to see a movie. In Denmark, for example, the number of movie theaters has been reduced by 50% during the last twenty years, and the number is still going down.[2] The theaters that do succeed are integrating the "movie experience" with a wider context of entertainment and restaurant visit. As an average, only 1.8 ttickets are sold annually in Denmark for each member of the population. In the U.S.A., the figure is 3.9.

11.1. AUDIO-VISUAL LANGUAGE

Film and other audio visuals utilize a special language that is different from print, that is, the audio-visual language utilizes a combination of several basic media symbols. There is vision, black and white and color, space and depth, movement, and unlimited variations of sound. In an audio-visual presentation of the Bible, for example, the text must be translated into a new "script." On a cassette, you do not have to say "Jesus was angry." He just needs to sound angry. On a film you do not even need to say "Jesus said," if the character speaking has already been identified as Jesus. The picture—whether paintings, drawings, photography, graphic displays, or cartoons—is part of the translation.

During recent years with the rapid development of video, it has been difficult to see how the future would be for the "simple" slide medium, but it seems to have found its place among the other media, providing us with an audio-visual medium that is both flexible and inexpensive, can be produced at a very short notice, and can be changed and adapted with a minimum of work. New slides can easily be inserted into a slide series as new developments take place. Any teacher or speaker can readily bring along his or her slides to almost anywhere in the world and expect to find a projector readily available. Hardly a conference center, meeting room, or educational center is without such facilities. Some are primitive and simple, others sophisticated and expensive. The future for films seems more uncertain, but the development of projection video may give it new life.

Anyone working with audio-visual media must be capable of handling multiple-signal systems. Spoken words are not always the most effective way of making a point. It is interesting to note that Charlie Chaplin continued making silent movies for a long time after others worked with "speaking" films. He contended that "Words will only take away from my movies. They can add nothing."[3] Everyone can understand Chaplin's movies, but each viewer does not necessarily interpret its meaning the same way. Words would confine Chaplin's movies to a specific period of time, but when watching a silent movie, everyone is free to understand the message in his or her own "private" way and context.

In an audio-visual presentation, many pictures flow into one whole. An artist will paint a picture that is complete in itself. A journalist may make the picture a part of the story, and in a multi-media show, individual slides become parts of the whole, as links in a chain or members of a body. This process is complete in the "movie" (i.e. moving pictures). Among the Christian organizations with large multi-media programs we can mention *Paragon Productions* of Campus Crusade and *Twentyonehundred Productions* of InterVarsity Fellowship. Both of these use up to twenty-six slide projectors, movie projectors, and special visual and sound effects. Such productions require a special team for the presentations and as such limit distribution.

As the audio cassette is different from radio, so is film different from television and video. Only one audience is viewing the film at a given time, and the user or controller of the medium is present. This generally limits the audience size but, on the other hand, has the advantage of immediate feedback and follow-up.

Television and, more recently, video have had an influence on the production of movies as the technical capabilities of these media require different approaches. Made-for-television movies put more emphasis on close-ups, because of the small screens on which they are shown. The sets for production are kept simple compared to what they were when movies were made only for large-screen showings. Text on the screen must occupy much larger areas of the screen or they cannot be read on television. So, shorter messages are needed for written captions.

Secondary use of the productions for one medium by another medium has become common practice. So a book is rewritten and made into a full-length movie for theater showing, and soundtracks from films are made available on LP's.[4]

The credibility of film is difficult to assess, since it is influenced by many factors. It will, for example, be judged by the credibility of the person or organization showing the film. Careless production and use will also carry an implicit lack of care for the message communicated. If we want to use film to communicate the truth of the gospel, we need to make sure that the viewers will be able to distinguish between fiction and reality. Since film is always "staged," the viewer may assume that it is only fiction. Film ministry should, therefore, be tied in with other types of ministry.

11.2. STRENGTH AND WEAKNESSES OF THE FILM MEDIUM

Film as a medium is being challenged strongly today by video, and video may win the battle. But film does have some strengths that make it an important medium in Christian ministry.

(1) Film uses multiple signals: visuals, sound, motion, and the whole context of a darkened theater adds dimensions to the effects of film.

(2) Film is popular with people. Alone in the dark, a person can concentrate on the action on the screen, dream with the actors, let emotions flow.

(3) Film can communicate with a large group at one time. Even though there is a tendency to make movie theaters smaller, film can communicate with thousands at a time. Furthermore, it can be copied and shown in many places at the same time.

(4) Film can easily be incorporated into a wider strategy. As the "user" of the medium is present, the film can be used in a multiplicity of situations. There can be introductions before the film and there can be discussions afterwards.

(5) Film makes immediate follow-up possible. There is no need, like for radio and television, to write to a station. The users are present and can meet with people, both the literate and the non-literate.

(6) Film is a ready-made story. This is both good and bad. It takes a long time to produce a movie, and there is no facility for change in the story line. All will get the same message. On the other hand, this makes it possible to prepare printed materials and other events that fit exactly with the film.

(7) Film is inexpensive for the viewer. There may be free showings in a marketplace (or on television), or a small fee is paid for entrance to a movie theater. On the other hand, the producers must have extensive capital for investment into the production of the film, often running into millions of dollars.

We are often presented with "statistics" concerning the effects of a certain medium, like, "We remember 10% of what we read, 20% of what we hear, 30% of what we see and 50% of what we hear and see." Based on such quotes, taken as true statistics, some writers have pointed to film as the most effective means of communication available to the church today. Our answer will have to be that such reasoning is erroneous because it attempts to reduce all variables into a simple one-cause statement. These "statistics" may be good for one subject in one situation but totally erroneous for another subject in another contextual situation. A piece of music, for example, will certainly be remembered more by listening, and the repetition effect of audio cassettes will in many instances provide almost total memorization.

11.3. FILMS IN THE THIRD WORLD

The use of film in cross-cultural situations will always give problems due to perception, interpretation, and the use of pictorial language. Most Christian films are produced in Westernized countries. It has taken almost a century to develop the highly refined and sophisticated pictorial language in which the films are based, and people have learned to understand this language and to interpret it. We call this pictorial literacy. It includes the close-ups, camera angles, flash-backs, etc.

But we have often misunderstood cultural differences and the topic of pictorial literacy, so we have exported films to people who do not know the language and consequently cannot give correct interpretations. This is especially true in a number of so-called developing countries where people have not had the opportunity of learning Western pictorial language on which most films are based.

Fuglesang questions many of the assumptions on which we base our understanding and use of films. For example, Is color film actually superior among non-literates? Non-literates may prefer black and white.[5] Similarly, animation in the form which we know from Westernized cartoons is a doubtful film technique in many other countries. Flowers growing up out of the soil in split seconds, brushes painting men who suddenly become alive are gimmicks that can only appear puzzling to many audiences.

Fuglesang suggests that the only functional technique is to have live action by local people with whom the audience can identify. Live action on a neutral blocked-out background is more functional in the context and will not give distractions. Fuglesang deals with this issue from a development expert's perspective, but we have similar problems with Christian films.

11.4. CHRISTIAN USE OF THE FILM MEDIUM

There has always been an uneasy relationship between church goers and the film industry. In many countries Christians do not go to the local cinema. There are obvious reasons for this, as the film industry has focused on immoral and unethical issues such as violence, drugs, and sex to make their films exciting and attract large audiences. On the other hand, Christians have produced films for education and evangelism, but usually such films have not been shown in public movie theaters but rather in church halls and market places. Today we have some outstanding exceptions with organizations such as International Films leading the way. Their movies are made for the theater. Hollywood has also periodically discovered that there are commercial possibilities in religion and we have the "classics" such as *Ben Hur* and *King of Kings*.

The *Jesus* film produced by Campus Crusade for Christ has been translated into numerous languages. Initially produced on 35-mm for theater presentation, it is the story of Jesus produced on the basis of Luke's Gospel. Huge audiences are reported by the organization.[6] The film is now available on video in all languages spoken by more than one million people.

As mentioned above, the effects of Christian films are to a large extent dependent on how well the use is integrated into other ministries. An interesting case study of effective integration is provided by the mobile film ministry of the Africa Inland Church in Kenya, called Cinema Leo. Each showing is coordinated by local church representatives who are also involved in the follow-up aspects of the ministry.[7] A certain town will be visited by the film team on the same date each month. Prior to that, members of local churches have been trained and equipped for follow-up, and they will give the welcome to the crowd. They will also pray with people and bring them to the church. They "own" the event, and the Cinema Leo team are their servants.

There seems to be an obvious shortage of Christian filmmakers with creative skills. A high standard in technical production as well as artistic quality is needed to make a film acceptable to the movie audience. This also demands heavy capital outlay. Such a problem is especially critical in cultures where the only available films are Western imports. The need for culturally relevant films is expressed all over the world.

There is atill a strong interest in films and an example of this interest can be seen from the fact that *Media Development* devoted a whole issue to film in India.[8] Other Christian journals have also given extensive space to the treatment of film.[9]

11.5. PLANNING THE SLIDE SHOW

As in any other media program, it is important to carefully state the objectives of a program. If such objectives are clearly defined, the producers will know the effects that a certain production needs to achieve. The basic question is, *What do we want the audience to know, feel, and do after they have seen this program?* It is also important to include the necessary audience research so that we know their background and context and how they will interpret the visual images. The more that is known about the audience, the better the program will be.

Some of the questions that need to be asked during the planning phase are:

•What kind of photographic equipment is required and what is available?
•What kind of slides and material is already available?
•What is the ideal length of the program? What would fit best into the situation?
•Where should the pictures be shot? Is the location very important?
•What sound will be needed?
•Has the budget been prepared, and what limitations does the budget impose on production?
•Where will the slide show be presented? What influences does the context have on freedom of expression?

Many other questions could be asked but these will be enough to high-light some of the issues.[10] Eric Miller has suggested a process for the production of slide-tape programs:[11]

•State objective.
•Research and define target audience.
•State proposition.
•Outline content.
•Determine appropriate media.
•Assess resources.
•Assemble script.
•Produce rough soundtrack.
•Produce storyboard or rough visual treatment.
•Revise sound and visuals.
•Produce final soundtrack.
•Produce final visuals.
•Synchronize visuals with soundtrack.
•Deploy your finished product.
•Evaluate effectiveness.

SUMMARY

Many Christians have had an uneasy relationship with films due to the common focus on sex and violence in commercial films. This uneasiness is understandable and it is not getting better. As Billingsby observes, "To be sure, as far as sheer craft is concerned, commercial films are better than ever, and the American product still dominates the world market. In pure technique, certainly, everything is state-of-the-art. But it is surely one of the great ironies of our age that, at the very time when the technology is the finest, the people who command it have so little to say."[12]

Due to its persuasive effect and due to the presence of the "user," film has great potential for use in Christian evangelism. It also carries possibilities for Christian teaching and inspiration.

Both audio-visuals and films can be copied onto video, and indeed this is done extensively. It is obvious that there is a need for such dubbing, but the audio-visual medium is an effective medium in its own right and will often surpass video in its capacity to influence behavioral changes. The use of films and audio-visuals is much more complicated than video with the need for projectors, screen, loudspeakers, etc., than just putting a videotape into the player.

In many Third World countries, film and audio-visuals provide the church with media that are relatively inexpensive to use as opposed to the much more expensive video equipment. By clearly identifying purposes and objectives, having clear goals, and a good knowledge of the audience and viewing situations, audio-visuals can be made very attractive for use by many Christian leaders and teachers.

FOOTNOTES

1 John Hulteng and Roy Paul Nelson. *The Fourth Estate: An Informal Appraisal of the News and Opinion Media*, 2nd edition. New York: Harper and Row, Publishers. 1983:324.

2 "Kampen for Biograferne," *Danair* Magazine 2, 1993.

3 Radio Montage on Radio Denmark, January 3, 1982.

4 John Hulteng and Roy Paul Nelson. *The Fourth Estate: An Informal Appraisal of the News and Opinion Media*, 2nd edition. New York: Harper and Row, Publishers. 1983:328.

5 Andreas Fuglesang, *Applied Communication in Developing Countries*. UNESCO and Dag Hammarskjold Foundation, 1973.

6 Campus Crusade promotional material.

7 Carl Becker, "How to Start a Cinevan Ministry and Keep it Going and Growing." Unpublished manuscript, author's files.

8 *Media Development*, World Association for Christian Communication. 3/1983.

9 For example, *ACCF Journal* Vol. 2, No. 2, 1983.

10 See *Planning and Producing Slide Programs* by Eastman Kodak Company, 1975.

11 Material presented by Eric Miller at the Asian Institute of Christian Communication, AICC-6, in Chiangmai, Thailand, 1989.

12 K. L. Billingsby, *The Seductive Image, A Christian Critique of the World of Film*. Westchester, Illinois, 1989:204.

CHAPTER 12

Music, Painting, and Dance-Drama

"I Can't Sit Still"

Whether you are on the streets of Bombay, Delhi or any other major Indian city, the itinerant street artists will soon gather a crowd. Outstanding tricks and artist performances may be enjoyed for a few rupees collected from the crowd. But for an Indian street performer it is a struggle to survive.[1]

Or, on many a city street all over the world you may meet artists painting pictures based on age-old legends and handicraft skills thousands of years old. In their constant manipulation of light and darkness, symbols and implicit meanings, they speak to people of every generation.

Or, the performance may be a clown on a busy street in a Western city on a hot summer day. The mime, the make-up, and the gestures appeal to the fantasy of young and old. The story may be the horrors of nuclear war or the plight of freedom fighters in a Latin American country.

And everywhere you meet the musicians, the lonely guitar player in a subway passage, or a lively band in a park. In all of these situations, we see how men and women are thrilled, inspired, and agitated by the performing artists.

12.1. ARTS AND FOLK MEDIA

The term "traditional" or folk media applies mainly to the performing arts such as puppetry, shadow plays, folk drama, folk dance, ballads, and storytelling. Many of these had their origin in rituals, cultural events, or religious ceremonies,[2] but this may be true of all performances. They have their roots in the culture of their birthplace. In this chapter we are primarily concerned with the use of such art forms, be they informal folk arts, or formal stage performances, in the service of church and mission.

The significance of folk media in societies varies—some reinforcing a traditional social hierarchy, others expressing a group's collective vision and worship. Sometimes they are used to affirm the status quo or to channel information from a higher to a lower level of a hierarchy; at other times they inspire exchanges in group situations.[3]

Folk media need to be based on folk culture. A folk culture is characterized by its simple form, its availability to all at no cost, owned by none as it is public domain. It is usually anonymous in origin, and it reflects the values shared by the group. There is little differentiation between producers and consumers, and the producers and performers are amateurs. Folk media need to be used by the people of the specific cultural group among whom the traditions started. Outsiders will be criticized for lack of respect. Yet in many church situations we have seen outsiders provide the incentive that will make a group feel free to use their cultural heritage in worship and in proclamation.

There is a fairly widespread belief that indigenous media of communication are relics of the past. Those who live and work in the Third World realize how unfounded this belief is.[4] For the Christian mission, traditional or indigenous media and communication systems provide exciting possibilities. The indigenous communication system is consistent with the oral traditions in many countries, where audience participation is not only common but important. The credibility of the information or messages is transmitted through the channels of the traditional media, which are most effective in promoting changes in beliefs and attitudes. There is also a smaller cost involved with the use of indigenous communication systems as compared with modern technology-based media.

12.1.1. African Traditional Media

At a seminar on folk media and traditional channels of communication in Africa, held in Nigeria in 1974, a list of such media was developed. That the list is African is seen from the omission of dance-drama, which is found in many parts of the world, in particular Asia. The American *musical* seems to be an adaptation of folk media. Among the folk media suggested for Africa were:

(1) **Gongman/Town Crier**. The gongman who usually is a member of the household of the local leader is responsible for delivering messages from the traditional leader orally to local elders and community leaders. He moves about on foot, usually within a five-mile radius. Since he symbolizes the chief's authority, he has become an institution which is respected, even envied; he is thus very authoritative and the local people have implicit confidence in him and the credibility of his messages. The gongman is still extensively used in some parts of West Africa.

(2) **State/Talking Drum**. The drum is essentially a musical instrument. However, the state/talking drums, which are bigger than normal

drums, become the channel of communication for call signals, inter-village communication, official messages.

(3) **The Hornman.** The hornman was in the past the transmitter of social messages and in modern times also of important government messages. Hornmen who use a horn for call signals belong to voluntary associations and are active in a neighborhood. The present use of hornmen is very limited.

(4) **Visual Symbols and Colors.** The use of visual symbols and colors for specific messages is still widespread, particularly in Africa. The Akinkra symbols of Ghana used for decorating textiles, ceramics and murals are a good example. The messages transmitted through this channel are mainly moral and artistic. The impact of this channel is great.

(5) **The Minstrel.** The minstrel communicates through songs often accompanied by local instruments. He seeks his audience in a homogeneous group. The songs generally have a bearing on a particular situation. The messages transmitted are mainly of a social nature.

(6) **Poets and Reciters.** In Africa, as well in many parts of Asia, reciting is widespread. It has been a very popular channel of communication up till modern times. Through this channel are transmitted moral, social and educational messages. It is currently popular in radio transmissions.

(7) **Storytellers.** Storytelling is an ancient medium of communication which still is widely used in both Africa and Asia. The messages are educational, historical or entertaining, and are usually loaded with morals for children and adults.

(8) **Drama, Including Mime and Puppetry.** Drama is still used extensively both in Africa and Asia to convey educational, moral and social messages. It is a convenient vehicle for the integration of a variety of traditional media and is capable of carrying this advantage to all types of modern media.

In general, all these folk media have been channels of communication for a variety of purposes: official, educational, social and economic. Herbert V. Klem suggests that African oral art can be used to meet the churches' urgent need for teaching the Scriptures.[5] Even after more than 100 years of mission effort to teach literacy, up to 90% in some areas cannot read a simple paragraph. The churches find themselves using ineffective means based on literacy, schools, public and private reading, which is seriously hindering effective teaching of the Bible.

African oral art is identified with the non-reading masses and the very soul of the culture. It is ideally suited to communicating spiritual truth in a form with which the people can readily identify. From his study of African oral art, and the systems for communicating it, Klem found that West African structures for oral communication are very similar to those of

Bible times. These are very adequate and powerful systems for communicating religious messages. African oral communication utilizes a wide variety of symbols in a way that is emotionally rich and communicationally powerful.[6]

12.1.2. Folk Media in Asia

One type of traditional media that has been used widely by churches and without apparent opposition is puppetry. But puppetry is usually reserved for work with children. Puppets are used for entertainment, for teaching, and have been used quite effectively in programs on video and television. Puppets, unless you use well-known figures, do not in themselves carry connotations. Indonesian leather puppets are an example of figures taken out of the cultural history of Java and consequently have special meaning to those who are familiar with the story. However, sensitivity and discernment are needed in order to use such figures for the proclamation of the gospel. It has been done and can be done effectively.

Traditional folk media can be extended through the electronic media, but due to the need for audience participation, such extensions may be best handled by an audio cassette in a group situation. A dramatic format on a cassette has proved to be very effective in a number of Asian countries, while video tends to restrict involvement, as the viewers need to keep watching the screen.

Among Christian organizations that have used folk media we should mention Christian Arts and Communications Service, Madras,[7] Christian Communication Institute, Chiangmai,[8] and The Balinese Church, Denpasar.[9] Many others are using traditional media or music extensively. India with its rich cultural heritage is a strong leader,[10] and a number of consultations on the use of dance-drama have taken place there.[11]

12.2. DRAMA

Dramas are performed for a great variety of reasons, including education, entertainment, and celebration. Dramatic forms can serve to make issues and topics vivid to children, drawing upon their emotional as well as intellectual capacities. The staging of dramas with the involvement of children can in itself be an educational experience, teaching preparation, cooperation, and many other qualities.

Drama seems to have been a medium used from the earliest periods of human history. In ancient Egypt the crowning ceremonies were elaborate plays, and the European drama is rooted in ancient Greece. Most of this grew out of the worship of the deities and the many tragedies of life. The

Roman Empire used a rather base form of entertainment with bloody fights between gladiators and wild beasts. Just such a background may have turned the Christian church against drama and theater for centuries.

Today we are also encountering opposition to the use of drama in the church. In many cultures the original use of dance and drama has been related to the temples, but usually the church has taken an extreme position, not willing to recognize the validity in these forms of communication for today. There seems to be a certain amount of fear among Christians for using drama, a medium that has potential as an evangelistic and nurturing tool. The presentation can be tailored to suit each specific audience, and the audience in turn can respond with immediate feedback to the communicators. In a real drama, the actors and the audience are all participants in the presentation. All are pretending to be somebody else, as well as pretending a different situation and different times.

Drama is a way of presenting truth in a vivid and unforgettable way. Jesus often told stories, like that of a man beaten and left to die by robbers, of a priest who passed by, and a Samaritan who stopped to help. The parables are all stories told by the master storyteller to teach spiritual truths. The prophets often acted out their message, like Jeremiah standing in the marketplace with a yoke on his shoulders. The Bible is full of drama.

Drama is not, of itself, Christian or non-Christian, but through the play a story is told and a philosophy of life is presented.[12] For the church, it is important to look at drama as a communication medium to teach the truth as we have it in the Word of God. But this truth must be incarnated into the lives of people so that it can be seen as relevant and important.

Drama has tremendous possibilities for presenting the Christian message in a living and experiential fashion.[13] So much of the Bible message, in particular the stories and parables told by Jesus, can be acted out, dressing them in contemporary clothing and cultural context and language. Jesus used parables to challenge and confront people with spiritual truths that created impact and demanded response. Such messages can probably be communicated no better than through dramatic reenactment.

Actually, much of that which goes on in a Christian church during a worship service could be defined as drama. The whole communion service is a dramatic reenactment of the meaning of the death and resurrection of Jesus Christ. In all Christian festivals we see drama. The birth of Jesus is enacted through dramas at Christmas, ranging from the play by a few children in a small school or church, to the magnificent, Hollywood-style presentation of the "Glory of Christmas" at the Crystal Cathedral in California. In Catholic countries, such as the Philippines, the Easter season provides a unique opportunity for extensive drama and reenactment, including crucifixion.

The use of drama may have its greatest potential in a country such as India. The South Indian dance-drama is a fantastically rich system of communication, where the actors and actresses utilize numerous signal systems: the eyes speak a language, the facial expressions speak another language, the postures have their own language, and the movements are a language. Additionally, the dance-drama is enriched by a musical system of seventy-two music scales, all interpreting and giving meaning. Christians who master such a complex system of communication will also find ways of using it for the proclamation of the gospel.

12.3. MUSIC

Good music is instant evolution; it changes your breathing, the way you focus your eyes at the world; it shifts the rhythm of your thinking, hoping, fearing. It dances your mind into places where its ordinary processes, however subtle, would never take you.[14]

It would be impossible to envision a society without music, and the ministry of the church would be severely handicapped without music and singing. Music is universal, but there are many different kinds of music and an almost infinite variety of musical languages, with their own styles, rhythms, and functions.

There are numerous biblical references to the use of music, from the very beginning of humanity. Singing is mentioned in the second chapter of Genesis, and all through the Old Testament we find Israelites using music and singing in their worship. They sang in celebration after crossing the Red Sea, and at the dedication of the temple they had both choir and orchestra. Music was also used in war: for example, the three hundred men with Gideon blew their trumpets and defeated the Midianites. But David is, of course, the primary source of Old Testament music, and his psalms are still inspiring people around the world, as they would have inspired him and his people three thousand years ago.

In the New Testament we find Jesus using poetic language and singing with his disciples, and the early church followed the music patterns from the temple and synagogues. The apostle Paul encouraged Christians to address one another in psalms, hymns, and spiritual songs, singing and making melody to the Lord with all their heart. As the gospel spread through Asia Minor and Europe, the local cultures influenced the type of music being used.

In the Middle Ages, the church congregations did not sing along at the worship services, but during the Protestant Reformation Luther produced hymns and songs for the church, often using tunes from secular music heard in the streets. His purpose for using popular tunes was to educate the Christians as well as to attract the non-believers. Similar approaches were followed during the great revivals, and indeed in many places today.

Today we are also finding numerous music ministries. There are bands, choirs, and soloists who minister throughout cities, countries, and even the world, like the Eagles Communication in Singapore whose ministry is largely a music-based ministry. They stage concerts not only in Singapore but in cities across Southeast Asia. Choirs of "Continental Singers" perform all over the world, and Christian singers are giving concerts everywhere.

Most churches have choirs as well as musical instruments, in particular organs and pianos, but also guitars and a variety of other instruments. But music has often been a cause for tension in the church, creating distances between Christians rather than building bridges. There has often been a reluctance by the church to accept new music styles, often brought in by young people, so, in spite of the wide use of music for worship, education, fellowship, and witness, the church lives with a paradox of using only some kinds of music, and these are often called old-fashioned by those we are trying to reach.

This problem is universal. Some Christians reject popular tunes, calling them "cinema music" because they are like the music used in films but not usually heard in church. But the experience of local music can be exhilarating. A worship service in an African church, using organ and Western tunes, can feel cold and dull, while the use of African tunes and drums can turn that same place into an exciting and warm experience.

For the black African, the rhythm is more important than the lyrics or the melody as meaning is communicated through the beats chosen. The meanings of words change as beats change. Through music they can express their feelings, their intentions, and their faith. Music can be selected to calm us down, to express our excitement, to guide us in worship, or to express our sorrow. The Africans may do that through the beats chosen; others do it through the melody.

Earlier missionaries were, unfortunately, not well-prepared for cross-cultural work, and they often failed to see the rich beauty in the culture where they brought the gospel. Consequently, they all too frequently exported an alien culture with its songs and music. And local Christians took over a new religion permeated with Western forms of communication. They did not know that God could be praised in their own tunes and through their own traditional instruments.

The same hymns can be heard in churches across the world, and there are probably many such magnificent, worldwide renowned masterpieces, but I have also experienced Thai Christians struggling along for a year trying to learn a Western tune set to a seven-tone scale. The same people could learn a similar song with a Thai tune in the pentatonic scale and immediately sing and be excited. A further complicating factor is that the Thai language is a tonal language. For the literate person with a hymnbook the problem is not too big, but for the person who only hears the words, meaning can be seriously distorted. In Thailand, for example, the word "far" is *klai* with an even tone, and the word "near" is *klai* with a falling tone. There is no confusion in normal speech, but you cannot sing the falling tone in a Western tune. So the words of the hymn, "There is a place of quiet rest, near to the heart of God" sound like, "There is a place of quiet rest, far from the heart of God."

Music is universal, as stated above, but music is not a universal language. It affects us differently and we understand it differently, and in the great mosaic of cultures it serves multiple functions. Music takes on meaning, or creates meaning, within a specific culture according to the rules of music-making that this particular culture has established. So each culture has developed its own peculiar music language. Let us learn to use music wisely in the ministry of church and mission so that it can build bridges rather than create tension. Music has the capacity of influencing people for Jesus Christ, so let us be ready to accept the challenge and use it in a truly receptor-oriented approach.

12.4. PAINTINGS

Painters have always been surrounded by interest. They have fascinated us with their fantastic creativity in the manipulation of colors and lights, the skills of catching moments of peace and stillness, the expressions depicted in the faces of people, and the communication of reality through light and darkness, sunshine and shadow. Or the capture of a group of people enjoying rest and each other's company as the sun sets on a far horizon. We are fascinated as the mosaic of colors on the canvas is brought to life by the artist.

Christians have used art from the very beginning of the church, and all through Europe we find magnificent artistic decorations in churches. It may be icons in an Orthodox church or a cathedral with an extensive series of paintings, illustrating the major events in the Bible from creation to the resurrection. Or it may be a painting from the life of Jesus at the altar.

Elvie Niel, a Christian artist from the Philippines, dreamt of telling fellow students about the Lord Jesus Christ through the canvas. Through years of study of communication, theology and the arts, she finally saw her dream come true in a series of paintings, titled "ANYO: IMAGE ... of God, Man and the World." The exhibit has been at several university campuses in Manila, as well as in other Asian countries and everywhere received highest recommendations. The paintings are professionally done, and in a 5′ x 5′ size. They depict the beauty of creation, the fall of man, the fruits and consequences of sin, both socially and politically, the redemption through the cross, and finally the second coming. The concept of the kingdom of God is clearly explained throughout the paintings, giving a testimony to the new life which can be experienced only through Jesus Christ.

But Elvie Niel has done more than a series of paintings. She has also shown the practical possibilities of a painting exhibition as a medium for evangelism. Prior to the exhibition Christian students at the universities are trained in personal evangelism, taught how to lead people through the exhibition, and be ready to personally follow up. In this way the exhibition becomes an integrated part of the work done by the local chapters of Christian student organizations and their churches. The paintings are "personalized" by the students, and due to their specific Philippine context and themes, they are intercultural and all can immediately identify with the situations portrayed.

12.5. MANAGING THE ARTS IN WORSHIP AND EVANGELISM

It is common knowledge that successful artists, be they singers, musicians, actors, or even public speakers will have good managers. It is important for an artist to provide quality performance, but it is equally important to have a stage on which to perform, or a context in which to function. And this demands good management and leadership.

A worship service is, of course, not a stage performance, but a worship service must have order, be well prepared and conducted in an orderly manner. Just as a business or a business meeting cannot function efficiently without good management and leadership, neither can the use of arts in a worship service. If a leader is not able to plan and lead, he or she not only frustrates others but is also a poor steward of the responsibilities and gifts God has given. Good leadership of a meeting will be experienced by its unobtrusive presence. In a worship service all the elements must flow into a cohesive program where the worshipper will be led into the presence of God.

To lead artists demands special skills. You have to be able to appreciate people with very different skills and talents, people with strong ideas and creative capacities, people who have something to give. Unfortunately, we have tended to place more importance on the rhetoric of the speaker than on the skills of the organist, the choir or the dramatic performer. A direct indication of this is that the only person paid for the "performance" is the speaker, but the other participants may actually have spent more time in preparation. A drama, a mime, a recital, or even a time of silence, may sometimes be worth more than a thousand words. The leader must have a high esteem for the performing arts.

The worship leader is the manager of the service, and it is the responsibility of him or her to see that things move in the right direction. This will usually require a willingness to live in a creative tension of depending on the leading of the Spirit during the service and the following of a predetermined plan which has also been worked out in prayer and dependence on the guidance of the Spirit.

12.6. CARE FOR THE ARTIST

For many, it is harder to take a stand for the gospel when you find yourself in the spotlight. Even worship leaders can identify with this struggle. How can a Christian performer be used to point people to Jesus Christ? The answer seems to lie in this analogy: The star, that is the performer has to be like a clear window of plain glass through which we see Jesus and through which his light reaches us, and not like a stained-glass window which blocks our view and draws attention to itself. Such a perspective will challenge the artist to see his or her work in the perspective of Christ and his concerns. A guide as to how this can be achieved can be taken from the basics of Christian communication as explained in the first section of this book, as in the following points.

(1). *The Great Commission is to be taken personally.* Gifts of music are gifts ideally suited for evangelism, and the Christian performer will have to operate within the context of today's media. To do that, it is important never to forget the commission given by Jesus, and to carry out the service according to his standards for behavior, for excellence, and for success, standards which are often at odds with the world's.

(2). *Seek the guidance of the Spirit.* Efforts to share the Word of God will meet with hostility from the powers of evil. Only with the Holy Spirit can we fight the spiritual battle involved in communicating the gospel in a dark world. As a communicator, you are a witness and a channel, not a power, and your performance must therefore be committed to prayer and to the ability of the Holy Spirit to convict, heal, and bring wholeness to the hearts of broken people.

(3). *Identify with your message.* God's ultimate communication with humanity came in the form of a human being, his Son. The message could not be separated from the person. This kind of identification between the person and the message must be carefully guarded in the media. As you try to offer a true and compelling image of Jesus Christ, you must also be so sensitive and transparent that attention is drawn not to the performance itself, but instead to the new life of Christ communicated through a changed person.

(4). *Continue the relationship with the local church.* Gifts are given to build up the church, the body of Christ. Apart from the body, lone members, however gifted, are ineffective ministers and evangelists. When we are involved in a local church, we can find practical support for ministry as well as pastoral guidance, and the church can provide a context for spiritual growth. Seeking and receiving training in the church, not only in the area of your gifts, but as a Bible study leader, a youth leader, and in personal evangelism, will help to keep you on track.

There are a number of organizations and associations of Christian artists that aim at helping fellow artists to succeed, both as artists and as Christians. For example, the "Arts Centre Group" in London is an association of Christians professionally involved in the world of the arts, the media and entertainment. It aims to help its members work effectively as Christians in their chosen disciplines and so make a distinctive contribution to our culture. It also aims to stimulate a wider interest and concern for the arts and their influence in the world at large. It acts as a network of friendship, a forum for discussion and a showcase for work and performance. The present membership includes those working in architecture, broadcasting, fine art, crafts, design, poetry and writing, theater and dance, film and photography, popular and classical music.

Members are encouraged to meet others in their own area of work and to draw on the challenge and stimulus which comes from contact with Christians in other disciplines. The Arts Centre Group's program is designed to help its members strengthen their faith and explore ways in which their Christian beliefs can be fully integrated with their creative talents. This is done through fellowship, Bible study, discussion, experiment and specialized seminars, lectures, events and social gatherings. Looking at one month's program for the Arts Centre Group, we see topics such as "Christianity and Fashion: Do they mix?"; "Looking at the changing face of beauty ... is glamour relevant to the Christian woman?"; "Pastoral care course"; "Biblethon, a 36-hour reading of the Bible at St. Paul's church."

SUMMARY

There is so much more that could be said about arts and folk media, but the aim of this chapter has been to inspire you, the reader, to take a close look at the possibilities that exist in your area of the world and for your ministry. We should not let radio programs or evangelistic campaigns become dull or suffer from ineffectiveness when music and other forms of art are available to us. Let the God-given creativity in us, in our church members, and team workers blossom and be widely used.

This chapter has dealt with arts and folk media, and a list of such media from the African context was provided. The wider issue of drama and its importance in the ministry of church and mission was discussed. The importance of music was emphasized for all aspects of ministry and for all areas of the world, even though the use of music varies significantly from one continent to another. An illustration of the use of paintings in evangelism was also presented.

Management of the arts and care for the artist is often overlooked in the church as we all want to admire the "stars," but if a performer is to be effective in Christian ministry, his or her performance needs to be seen from a spiritual perspective, and the church and its leadership need to provide personal and spiritual counsel to the artist. They need to feel a part of the Body of Christ.

FOOTNOTES

1 *Scanorama*, In-flight magazine of Scandinavian Airlines, 1984.

2 Wang and Dissanayake, "The Study of Indigenous Communication Systems in Development: Phased Out or Phasing In? In *Media Asia*, Vol. 9, No. 1. Singapore: AMIC. 1982:3.

3 WACC Communication Resource, December 1981.

4 Wang and Dissanayake, "The Study of Indigenous Communication Systems in Development: Phased Out or Phasing In? In *Media Asia*, Vol. 9, No. 1. Singapore: AMIC. 1982:7-8.

5 Herbert V. Klem, *Oral Communication of the Scripture, Insight from African Oral Art.* South Pasadena: William Carey Library. 1982:182.

6 Ibid.

7 Swami Suviseshamuthu, "Christian Arts and Communications Service." Unpublished report, author's files. 1974.

8 Allen Eubank, "The Gospel in Ligay" in *ACCF Journal* Vol. 1, No. 2, 17-18. Singapore, ACCF. 1979.

9 Wayan Mastra, "The Bali Experience." Also in *ACCF Journal* Vol. 1, No. 2, p. 12-17. Singapore, ACCF. 1979.

10 Kathleen D. Nicholls, *Asian Arts and Christian Hope.* New Delhi: Select Books. 1983.

11 Peggy Yeo, "Madras Consultation on Dance Drama." ACCF Journal, Vol. 1, No. 2, 1-5. Singapore, ACCF. 1979.

12 Kathleen D. Nicholls, *The Prodigal Returns, a Christian Approach to Drama.* India: Traci Publications. 1977:6-7.

13 Kraft, Charles H., *Communication Theory for Christian Witness.* Nashville: Abingdon. 1983:156.

14 Jack Kroll, in John L. Hulteng and Roy Paul Nelson, *The Fourth Estate. An Informal Appraisal of the News and Opinion Media.* New York: Harper and Row. 1983:307.

CHAPTER 13

Computers

"Bits and Bytes"

This particular chapter is the last one to be written. The simple reason is that technical and programming changes are coming so fast that a chapter on computers may be outdated even before the publisher can get the text on the bookstore shelves. Each year the technology approximately doubles and the prices decline. But I am attempting it, as we cannot imagine a book on media without some treatment of the medium that has become both an indispensable tool and a potential medium of Christian communication. Its rapid development has affected every one of us for good and for bad, but basically it has helped many of us do our tasks better and do more, and where used wisely it has helped us to have more time for creative work and personal ministry.

The world we live in gets more and more dependent on computers and they play a part in almost every aspect of our lives. But it is much more than tools and possibilities, it is the basis of a social revolution greater than any we have experienced before. As steam and steel gave Britain supremacy at the beginning of the industrial society or age, so the control of microchip technology will give supremacy in the information society. And it is the microchip computers and fiber optics that are the basis of such inventions as high density television (HDTV), which will eventually provide a large picture on a flat screen with a much higher quality and a much more lifelike picture than we know from television sets of today. Together these new technologies will transform business, education, and art.

So, the "electronic office" is not just a dream for the future but a daily reality. Computers control our phone calls, check our credit cards, control manufacturing equipment, and write out supermarket receipts. Executives on the move carry laptop computers that can operate in hotel rooms as well as on airplanes. A computer can handle and store large amounts of information and organize and retrieve such information very quickly.

The computer is best suited to do the tedious work, extensive counting, repeating the same information or activity an endless number of times, tasks where humans would often want to give up. Computers are made by people who by God have been given creative abilities. If the users of computers have bad or evil intentions, the computer will assist them in such activities, just as it will assist those with pure and good interests. As with video, the bad effects of computers are basically due to people with bad influences.

This chapter is, of course, written on a computer, but it will not attempt to teach how to use computers. Without being exhaustive, it will be an attempt at highlighting some of the issues related to the use of computers and point to some areas where they can be used profitably in Christian ministry. We cannot envision a world without computers, and the question is therefore not of if we should use them, but how, and how can we as Christians help people control rather than being controlled by the computer and by the people who programmed the computer.

Computers demand computer-literacy and that in turn demands literacy, so we have a medium that again is primarily usable by the literate and reading half of the population of our world. On the other hand, the computer and in particular the advent of CD-ROM and similar data storage facilities give scope for a vast expansion of education through decentralized extension programs. It just may be the tool that can make mass literacy and education a little more achievable. This will, though, demand a genuine desire for this to happen by both government and institutional leaders.

Areas of Christian ministry where computers have been first accepted are areas where the work more closely parallels the activity of a secular business. This may be due to the availability of programs, software, for such administrative and financial activities. It can be rather frightening or intimidating to have to learn new technologies and new skills, especially for those who are not so young anymore, but with the speed by which developments take place today, no one is too old to learn how to handle a computer, and those who refuse will be left behind. Actually, today's "user-friendly" computers and easy-to-learn programs can have some people started in a matter of minutes. The development of so-called "windows" and menus now calls for simple recognition and selection by entering a "yes" or clicking a mouse.

13.1 HARDWARE AND SOFTWARE

Hardware are the things you can see: computers, screens, printers, disks, cables, disk-drives, and so on. *Software*, on the other hand, is invisible. These are the programs and the data that are stored in some kind of memory, a disk or a chip. All computer language is written in one basic system, digital language, which consist of "+" and "-" signals, or of just "0" and "1" and an endless combination of these *bytes*. The figure 8, for example, be written as "– – – –" in computer language. The data is stored in digital form so it can be manipulated, stored, and reproduced without deterioration.

Any computer will need its operating language, and the best known today is MS-DOS (Microsoft Disk Operating System) in its various developments. For example, this present computer uses MS-DOS 6.0. Earlier CP/M was widely used, and new standards are the IBM-produced OS/2 and the UNIX. A computer is also called a *processor*, and that is a fitting name. The basis is the microchip which was first invented in 1958. The chip itself is made of sand in the form of crystalline silicon which in microelectronics is sliced into tiny slivers about a quarter-inch square. On each is imprinted a maze of microscopic switches and wires. These are the transistors and the connecting wires. With millions of such tiny devices in a single microchip, computers can handle information processing at enormous speeds.[1] Today some twenty million transistors can be put onto a single sliver of silicon, but the Japanese have already announced successful tests with up to 200 million transistors.

The central processing unit, CPU, is the brain of the computer. Other parts are used to enter or retrieve data, and to store data. The memory is divided into RAM (random access memory) and ROM (read only memory). ROM is permanent and has the basic information needed to keep the computer functioning. RAM is the working memory, but information stored here will be lost when the computer is turned off if you have not saved it on a disk.

Fiber optic cables, made of glass the width of a human hair, can potentially carry billions of characters of information per second. Such cables provide the necessary capacity for extensive computer networks, high density television, and telecommunications.

Computers come in a wide variety of sizes, from big mainframes, mini computers to the ever-increasing micro-computers, called PCs (personal computers). The latter is getting more and more powerful and through good networking programs, hundreds of them can be interlinked to form huge systems for big companies and be worldwide through telecommunications links as used by the airline booking systems. Several large Christian organizations with a presence in various countries are already linking their offices through such networks. The PCs are the ones of most interest to Christian organizations. *Laptops* or *Notebooks* can be taken almost anywhere. They let you bring your office with you anywhere in the world, and through modems and faxes they can be in contact with other computers wherever there is a telephone plug.

13.1.1. CD-ROM

CD-ROM is the technical name for using a compact disk as storage for computer-generated data. The advantages are large storage capabilities that will make it possible to incorporate video into computer programs. Video demands extensive memory, but it is expected that all personal computers will eventually also be video-processing machines. This will be interactive television. The use of video has special interest to educational programs, and computer-based video will cut out the need for expensive and time-consuming traditional video editing.

Today there is a constant demand for smaller and smaller products. Sony Corporation of Japan has introduced its *Data Discman*, a palm-sized compact disc player that can hold and display 100,000 pages of text, equal to some 300 books. This tiny three-inch CD weighs a mere 550 grams and has a capacity of 200 megabytes of information. This information can include encyclopedias, dictionaries, and other books that one needs to take along on the road. The small built-in screen can show only ten lines, but the unit can also be plugged into a regular TV set and use its large screen.[2] The same unit, the Data Discman, can also play music, using three-inch audio CDs. They can also hold actual video, but present units have a capacity for only five minutes. Most likely, this will be greatly extended within the next year or two.

Presently, a CD can only be written on once and is then permanent, but new versions are around the corner where actual write and read functions are possible. To record on the disc, a small laser beam will heat the spot and apply a magnetic field. As soon as the disk cools, the data cannot be changed.

In the near future we will probably see CDs with the capacity to hold a ninety-minute movie and with a quality that equals that of television today. And there may be even more. The electronic companies are employing thousands of scientists in the labs on basic research and many more thousands in their applied research programs and new product development.

There are a few Christian organizations involved in the development of computer-based multimedia programs. CD-WORD is a CD-ROM-based program developed in Texas. It includes four different translations of the Bible as well as Bible dictionaries. The user can check different translations of a verse or word on the screen, and commentaries can be brought up at the point of the cursor. The American Bible Society is producing New Testament stories in both video and interactive, computer-based multimedia programs. This will eventually be all on CD-ROM.

13.2. WORD PROCESSING

Word processing is basically using the computer for tasks you used to use a typewriter for: writing letters and preparing articles, reports, and papers. But with the use of a computer word-processing program, such tasks can be done much more efficiently, nicer, and often much quicker.

13.2.1. Letters

For those who write many letters the computer has given the possibilities of editing and "re-writing" with very limited extra time. The whole letter does not need to be retyped. The computer will take care of a new printout. And with the use of macros, it can actually type large sections of letters with standard headings, paragraphs and the like by the touch of a few code keys. For many, this has given the necessary capacity and they bypass the use of a secretary. It is almost as quick to type it as to dictate.

In one Christian radio organization that recently "computerized" it was found that a person answering listeners' letters could now write several letters in the same time she used to write one letter since extensive use of form letters and paragraphs could be employed. Individual paragraphs could easily be added. That same organization was able to cut down time for the follow-up department by half, freeing the staff to spend the time on creative activities and programming.

13.2.2. Direct Mail

Most Christian organizations are involved in fundraising which in turn often involves direct mail. The missionary newsletter was a forerunner to direct mail letters. By using such programs as mail-merge, a computer can insert names and addresses from a mailing list into a letter and by so doing create what looks like personal letters. Personal paragraphs can also be inserted as needed. This approach has been used extensively by advertising companies and may be an annoyance to many people but nevertheless is widely used also by Christian agencies and humanitarian groups. Certain groups using lotteries on a regular basis as a support system will "target" the regular supporters or buyers of lottery tickets this way.

13.2.3. Reports

Term papers, dissertations, magazine articles, and field reports will typically have to be rewritten several times. By the use of a word-processing program, sections can be moved, headings added or deleted, sentences and words inserted, footnotes added at the right places, graphics produced or scanned and inserted, all tasks that used to take enormous time but can now be done relatively quickly by an experienced computer operator. There is no need to retype each new draft or edition. The printer can take care of this, and the results will be clean copies. The more recent availability of economically-priced laser printers has made this even more interesting.

Once a document is entered on the computer, it can be changed as needed: one or two columns, be justified, change margins, select numerous different fonts and sizes of letters. Furthermore, you can automatically add page numbers, page headings, and get a ready-made table of content.

13.3. ELECTRONIC MAIL

Computers can be linked directly through a communications program using cables, but we can also use a device called a modem for transmitting data over phone lines. Such telecommunications, the mar-riage of computers and telephone, is getting more and more common.

Electronic mail uses such systems. You can subscribe to companies like MCI, and you are given a "box" number. When a letter or message needs to be sent to another subscriber, you simply direct it to his or her MCI number. When convenient, you just call up MCI on your computer to check if there is any mail for you, and if affirmative then the message or messages will be transmitted to your computer in a matter of seconds. Organizations are also increasingly using such programs internally, so that you do not need to go down the corridor to the other person's office or call by phone. Just leave the message on the computer and you will get a response in due time. If a hard copy, that is, a printed copy, is needed, all you need to do is give your computer the necessary instructions.

Electronic mail has special interest for people on the move. Wherever there is a phone, they can check their "mail-box." We could also envision a denomination using such a system for their churches and pastors, or an international mission agency can use it to distribute information and messages quickly and economically to their offices around the world. Databases could also be set up for individual members to draw on for answers to specific needs or questions. A church will reap good results if the computer is used in its general administration and financial management, but if it is coupled with information management there will be significantly greater results and return on the investment.

A computer bulletin board is also a possibility. We see such applications on television teletext. Information on coming events, books and material available, news items from mission fields, etc., can be posted.

13.4. DATABASES

Databases are programs that store information, and they have a wide variety of uses for the Christian leader and organizations. Address lists can be kept up-to-date for a church's youth program, including phones and addresses of parents.

Databases are already available on a vast variety of subjects. One of the main advantages is that data only need to be entered once and can then be sorted in numerous different ways, depending on the need for a given report or letter. Several Christian organizations have developed data bases which are shared with other organizations, and various international organizations like Amnesty International are making their databases available through electronic mail.

13.4.1. Mailing Lists

Most churches and organizations keep extensive mailing lists for information and support purposes. In a database, certain kinds of information can be added to the individual name, and the computer can then print out lists or labels on the basis of such selections. For example, if the age of the person is included, the computer can be instructed to select just a certain age range. And for funding, the computer can keep track of donors, large and small, regular and occasional. The extensive follow-up departments of evangelistic and media organizations can be helped by good databases.

13.4.2. Records and Information

All organizations need to keep good records of activities, results, and information, so information processing and management is an activity of utmost importance in this information age. There is far too much information available for anyone to cope without good helps.

A pastor can have several different versions of the Bible on the computer and check the translations. Reference books are also available on disks.

Huge central databases have been developed but such systems are becoming bottlenecks rather than gateways to information. In the long run, they will suffer as decentralized banks, possibly based on CD-ROM, take over the market.[3]

13.4.3. Bibles

Hi-tech Bibles are becoming increasingly available from Bible societies. Both the British and American societies have produced software packages with the Bible, and the British Bibliotec, based on the Good News Bible, allows quite extensive searching for words, combinations of words, and sentences. Other countries are following as Bible translation becomes fully computer-based. In Japan, the Bible is already available on CD-ROM.

13.5. ACCOUNTS

The computer's capacity to count has reduced significantly the work of bookkeeping and at the same time made up-to-date information available to decision makers. Also, many pastors and Christian workers find financial management difficult and time consuming and often they have not had any instruction or training in financial administration. A simple computer program can assist the person so that only simple entries need to be made and the computer will do the rest, for example, keep track of all incomes, budget control, and general bookkeeping.

Actually, the whole area of finance lends itself to the use of computers. A computer can handle all aspects of financial records such as statements, receipts, reports, giving, pledges, payroll, mission support, etc. A treasurer for a denomination told me recently that he can now complete a monthly report in ten minutes while he used to spend a whole day on the same task. And he can even do more. Statistics are now readily available, making decisions easier and better, and budget control becomes an almost automatic activity.

13.6. PUBLISHING

No other area has been more influenced by the computer than the publishing business. A wide range of positions, in particular in the graphics industry, have become obsolete. Layout is now done directly on the computer and typesetting is not needed.

13.6.1. Books

The great advantage for Christian organizations and publishers is that we can envision a very small number of books in any one printing. Theoretically, each book can be printed directly. Revisions become fairly easy to handle, and new printouts can be made.

One U.S. publishing company is advertising a system that allows professors to create customized textbooks. Based on large data storage, the system lets a person choose the information for a given textbook—specific chapters, work sheets, journal articles, and original material. The new computer and printing techniques allow the company to search the database for the exact information needed in a customized text, organize it, paginate it, reproduce it, bind it, and deliver it to students in less than a week, and often for less than the cost of a conventional textbook.[4] We can truly say that this represents a revolution in the way books are produced and, in turn, how they will be marketed and sold. And it will help publishers compete with photocopying of material and articles.

13.6.2. Manuals

Through the use of good desktop publishing programs, camera ready pages can be produced directly on the computer and printed on a laser printer, avoiding typesetting, stick-letters, pasting, etc. Such possibilities are of great interest to those who produce manuals for ministry, Bible studies, or Sunday school materials.

13.7. EDUCATION

The potential of the computer for educational purposes has hardly been touched, but the possibilities are almost endless and wide-ranging. Most Western-developed educational systems are far too expensive for most people in the world, and indeed for many countries. Through the use of computers, especially with CD-ROM storage, a system exists that can make education available almost anywhere and at a fraction of the cost of many present educational institutions. It will be education brought to people rather than people brought hundreds or thousands of miles to the educational center.

Several countries such as Germany and the United Kingdom have extensive experience in extension teaching through Open Universities. Students are studying at home, following lectures on television or radio, by audio and video cassettes, and extensive programmed materials. These are then reinforced by regular seminars at central locations. Such systems can be greatly extended by the use of computer technology where questions can be given to teachers at any time. This will, of course, demand new training of teachers, and the organization of such programs needs to be developed on their own needs and merits and not as an appendix to residential courses and universities where they will usually be given second priority.

The computer can assist in upgrading the quality of distributed materials. It can be used to prepare and store lesson plans and handout materials, keep bibliographies up-to-date, and provide case studies and other instructional material ready for use at any time. Lecture notes can be updated constantly and new printouts made just before delivery of the material, insuring that the content is relevant to the given situation. Similarly, pastors can keep sermon notes and Bible study lessons. The possibilities are almost endless. One can create a school in the home, gain access to the best teachers, and get copies of needed text and material.

Many schools have utilized computers for education assistance, and at higher levels of education there is a significant increase in their use. There are even periodicals available for specific areas, e.g., *Academic Computing*[5] which covers computer use in higher education. When computers are used as assistance, a lesson can be repeated as many times as necessary without delaying other students, or if the material is not new it can be scanned quickly and the student can move on to the next lesson. A well-produced educational program will guide the student step by step through the lesson, asking for answers at the right time. This will be superior to other forms of programmed learning as an answer will have to be given before the true answer is revealed.

Research on how technology affects young children in learning situations seems to be positively in favor of using computers. Children seem to increase their thinking, reasoning, and problem-solving skills, develop their language skills and use, and are facilitated in concept development as well as increased social interaction and cooperative learning. Other improvements are in the area of self-esteem.[6]

With the aim of educating school children towards a better understanding of the Bible, the National Bible Society of Scotland has established an education center that uses computer technology. Through interactive computers children can learn about Bible themes and characters, test themselves on Bible knowledge, or just play a game of Bible trivia.

Games can be used extensively in education, not just games for fun but for education and simulation. Numerous organizations, in particular in the United States, have already produced computer games with Bible content. The aim is to teach children Bible stories.

The airlines cannot train pilots to function in critical situations in a real airplane as this would probably be tantamount to a crash, so they use simulators where turbulence and other serious situations can be tested. Similarly, Christian leaders need to learn to function in turbulent times, times of serious financial cuts, staff problems, government restrictions, persecution, etc. Through the development of interactive computer games and simulations, crisis management skills can be developed.

Multimedia programming, including sound, music, video, animation and graphics, as well as text, is made possible by hypermedia programs such as HyperCard. This is an interactive multimedia program, incorporating text, sound, and video, and as such gives tremendous potential to educational purposes. Until a new device is developed, the storage of such programs will probably be on CD-ROM due to the need for large memory.

13.8. CHALLENGES

Computer technology effectively works towards decentralization and segmented markets. In the area of video and entertainment, this means providing the users with a range of choices rather than letting the broadcaster decide. As a result, there will be an increasing demand for good programs and presentations in all fields, and it should be obvious for Christians that the future is not so much a question of controlling the distribution channels (like radio and television transmitters) as a question of producing good software. But we do need to develop relevant distribution channels and distribution systems. As is so often the case, the technology is far more advanced than the programs, and even Christians often seem to get more interested in the technology than in creating new and good ways to use it. Hopefully, the computer will inspire competition among different systems of education and entertainment programs and bring out millions of creative products. They have to be smart enough to stand competition and the intelligence of the user. We are not speaking of top-down decisions as experienced with television but a bottoms-up interactive computer network. Programs have to be good and smart enough to stand competition and be selected by the users. It is going to be an age of individualism and personal choices unprecedented in human history. Let us make good choices available. Microchip technology makes good quality possible, software makes it usable, and people with a message make it valuable.

13.9. SUMMARY

Computer technology is advancing extremely fast, and it is difficult to keep up-to-date with developments. The computer is making inroads into all aspects of Christian ministry, helping us do our tasks more efficiently. This chapter has dealt with questions concerning hardware, and it has discussed some of the more traditional ways of using the computer in word processing, electronic mail, databases, accounts, and so forth.

The development of large storage capacities, based on CD-ROM, gives new and exciting possibilities, and it makes it possible for us to mix video, audio, and "print" on the computer. The result is interactive programs where a student can interact directly with material stored on the disk, including video and audio material. The possibilities for using such programs in education are enormous, and it will be possible to have whole libraries available in countries around the world at a fraction of present costs. One disk may contain up to three hundred books.

FOOTNOTES

1 George Gilder, *Life After Television*, Whittle Direct Books. 1990:23.

2 "Tracking Hi-Tech" in *World Executive Digest*, August 1990 edition.

3 George Gilder, *Life After Television*, Whittle Direct Books. 1990:40–41.

4 *The Chronicle of Higher Education*, November 15, 1989, page A19.

5 "Academic Computing," *Covering Computer Use in Higher Education*. Academic Computing Publications, P.O. Box 804, McKinney, TX 75069-4425, USA.

6 Yolanda Jenkins, "Multimedia Technology: Tools for Early Learning," in *Interactive Multimedia: Visions of Multimedia for Software Developers, Educators, and Information Providers*. Redmond, WA 98073-9717: Microsoft Publishers, 1988.

SECTION III:

PRACTICAL GUIDELINES FOR
MEDIA IN CHURCH AND MISSION

Introduction to Section III

Among the posters I have collected through the years is one that reads, *Now that we are organized, what do we do?* Maybe the reader will feel the same way after going through the first two sections of this book. We have studied principles and strategy, media and possible applications, but how do we actually get started? This section is aimed at helping with that question.

Apart from the actual activity of using communication material and products, there are three basic areas of practice regarding applied media communication: planning, making, and evaluating. Or, we could say strategy, programming, and testing. The way we approach these areas may be slightly different from medium to medium, but the basic principles are the same, and therefore they are treated in this way in the coming section.

In chapter three, the principles of strategty were explained. Here we will put them to work. Chapter fourteen provides a series of helpful suggestions as to how you get started, how you select your media, and how you make plans. There are guidelines on the development of critical success factors, as well as a facilitating communication strategy.

For all media, programs need to be produced. Good programs do not come prepackaged, but they are developed in the context of real situations with people with real needs. Chapter fifteen gives you a series of steps that will guide you through the programming process. The process is similar for all media, but the practical work involved in producing programs or products will, of course, be different.

The final chapter deals with evaluation and pretesting. Unfortunately, many Christian media organizations do not take these activities seriously, but it is my conviction that they are imperative for good and effective media programs. The steps illustrated in this chapter are fairly easy to follow, and they deal with both internal evaluation procedures and pretesting among the intended audience.

CHAPTER 14

Strategic Communication Planning

The Leader's Tool Box

The Christian communicator of the nineties is living in what Peter F. Drucker calls Turbulent Times. In turbulent times an enterprise has to be managed both to withstand sudden blows and to avail itself of sudden, unexpected opportunities.[1] Few Christian leaders can avoid turbulence. It may be serious splits in a local church due to charismatic issues, or it may be sudden new opportunities for mission and evangelism as experienced at the collapse of communist regimes in Eastern Europe. It may be the president of a Christian humanitarian organization who suddenly sees drastic reductions of funds. Or it may be issues of communication as new opportunities are available and choices have to be made, such as which medium to choose for Scripture distribution when the intended audiences are no longer reading. Many organizations and churches are also experiencing serious leadership crises as leaders are not available, or a rapid changeover in the leadership team demands both loyalty to old principles and new approaches as opportunities are seized.

When things are more normal, or we could say more predictable, fundamentals tend to be taken for granted. It is important, though, that fundamentals, especially those we defined in chapter one as being foundational to all Christian communications, are constantly kept in mind and managed carefully and conscientiously if we are to achieve effective use of media.

Principles don't change, but the way we apply our principles changes from place to place, from culture to culture, and from goal to goal. Engel suggests that the only way to cope with turbulent times is to affirm the sovereignty of God while we at the same time engage seriously in strategic planning.[2] Strategic planning is a continuous process of making risk-taking decisions. Such strategic planning, coupled with a reliance on the Holy Spirit, will lead to proper stewardship and provide the leader with assurance in the midst of uncertainties. This is the kind of stewardship which has been the primary purpose behind the discussions in the preceding chapters. Our concern is that the "harvesting equipment" will be used to its full potential, so that we avoid ill-conceived assumptions and outdated approaches that often result in ineffective outreach.

14.1. STRATEGIC COMMUNICATION PLANNING TOOLS

In chapter 2 it was concluded that an adequate Christian communication theory can be developed, and chapter 3 demonstrated the availability of the tools of strategy and planning. We have also seen that research can help us with many aspects of the planning process as it provides us with the information on which we can base our decisions and make possible intelligent use of media. Actually, research, with its provision of reliable information, is an indispensable dimension of strategic planning.

We also need a good media understanding. We need to enter the "hardware store" of media with discernment and shop for the tools we need to accomplish the task ahead of us as well as for those we can afford to buy and afford to use. The previous section aimed at giving an introduction to such insights.

Strategic planning puts all of this together in a comprehensive overview or plan. It is not something you do once-in-a-lifetime, but is an ongoing process of reflection and planning. Edward R. Dayton and David A. Fraser have suggested a simple model of THINK-PLAN-ACT-EVALUATE which is an excellent summary of strategic planning.[3] As you think, you will also pray and seek the direction of the Lord, and as you plan you do that as a devotion to him. You act in obedience to his command, and you carefully evaluate if you did the right thing and learned your lessons.

As you go through this cycle again and again, reflecting and planning, it will lead to systematic organization of the various parts of your mission and use of media. Strategic planning is based on a receptor-oriented approach. The goal is to find a need and respond to it, or determine the needs and wants of a specific audience and meet them through an organized response.

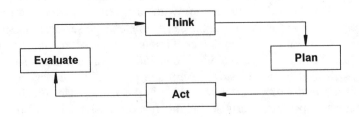

Figure 14.1. Summary of Strategic Planning

Later in this chapter we shall review and apply the steps in detail, as we use the eleven-step planning cycle adapted from Dayton and Fraser.[4] But just to refresh our minds, in chapter 3 it was stated that as a general definition of the term strategy, we can say that it is an overall approach, plan, or way of describing how we will go about reaching our goal or solving our problem. Strategy is a way to reach an objective, a kind of map of the territory to be covered in order to "reach from here to there."

Strategy is, then, a conceptual way of anticipating the future, guiding us in making major decisions concerning alternative approaches and decisive action. It provides us with a sense of direction and cohesiveness, focusing on the central issues of our task and philosophy of ministry.

We could also say that in Christian communication, strategy is the process of planning with an aim to align our plans with God's plans, seeking his will for us and our ministry. Goals become statements of faith. As we go through the steps outlined in this chapter, we do that on the basis of a study of Scriptures, prayer, and relying on the work of the Holy Spirit. First let us look at the Mission Statement and the Critical Success Factors.

14.2. MISSION STATEMENT

"Why am I here?" or, "What is the purpose of our mission or media ministry?" So often this question is answered too vaguely, too broadly, or even too inaccurately by Christian leaders and organizations. The definition of mission purpose or the writing of a mission statement will often prove to be one of the most important aspects of strategic planning. It will also be important for a mission or an agency that has been working for years and seemingly finds itself in an effectiveness crisis. A mission statement will define who you are, what is distinctive about you or your project, and what you are aiming to achieve. It is a statement that gives direction to planning, sets parameters around your ministry, and helps to build on strengths and focus the application of resources.

It may be helpful, as a part of this exercise, to carefully evaluate and discuss the viability of your mission and its use of media. Ask such questions as, Is the mission really necessary in today's context? Are we seeing results that will justify a continuing use of valuable resources? Is our church growing? Just because you were viable and needed ten years ago does not mean that your organization is needed today, or that the direction should not be changed. Is your mission a mission with a mission? Or, as Engel would ask, If your organization didn't exist, would you start it? Or, If your mission stopped tomorrow, what difference would that make to the work of the church?[5] If your programs or publishing programs were discontinued, would anybody notice it or miss your products?

The management team of the British and Foreign Bible Society worked carefully on a definition of the Society's purpose in a changing world. Was the purpose of the Bible Society just to sell Bibles? The answer to that question was, No, we also need to make sure that they are used. Eventually, the purpose was defined as,

> *The British and Foreign Bible Society is people who seek to glorify God in serving all churches by making relevant Scriptures and related service activities available at appropriate prices and qualities so that throughout the world more people own, use, value and share the Bible.*

Such a purpose or mission statement provides a set of characteristics by which both present and future staff can function. It limits the organization to dealing with Scriptures and initiatives that will support such a purpose, but at the same time it is broad enough to take advantage of present and future opportunities and needs. From the statement we can see that the Bible Society is

> God-centered and also people-centered.
> It is audience-driven and utilizes research and information, so that it can make available relevant Scriptures.
> It is concerned with the whole world and serves the whole church.
> It aims at more people having a Bible,
>   more people using the Bible,
>   more people valuing the Bible, and
>   more people sharing the Bible with others.

14.3.   STEPS FOR DEVELOPING MISSION STATEMENT:

The more people involved in actually defining/developing the mission statement, the wider the felt ownership will be on behalf of the staff. The following approach can be suggested:

1. Leaders (and staff) discuss what the mission is all about, what you want to achieve.
2. Write down (on the board) words that identify your ministry.
3. Identify the key words that must be included.
4. Formulate a purpose statement in one sentence on the basis of such key words and concepts.

A purpose or mission statement will often be followed by a set of specific objectives. Such objectives may be time-bound and lead to specific goals. We could say that the purpose statement defines the trunk of the tree, and the objectives will define the branches. Or, that purpose gives direction as to where we are going and why we use media. Objectives clarify how we will get there and which media should be used and for what purpose; goals define when we will get there and in what condition.

Unity in objectives is critical to an effective staff and to a well-run ministry. The time spent on describing the visions for the future of the ministry and arriving at realistic goals is time well spent and will be rewarded by effectiveness. But when an organization has defined its objectives and goals, it is equally important to spend time on the issues or factors that would facilitate such goals or would hinder their implementation. We have chosen to call such factors Critical Success Factors.

14.4. CRITICAL SUCCESS FACTORS

14.4.1. Identifying Potential Barriers and Necessary Bridges for Reaching Our Purpose and Goals

It is exciting to dream of the future, engage in brainstorming and possibility thinking, but such visions remain dreams without planning and action. There will, though, be both internal and external factors that can either hinder successful application of our strategy and plans, or they can function as bridges for even greater success.

The term Critical Success Factors is borrowed from an article on systems evaluation in *Newsweek* in 1984 by Gerrity and Crescenzi. In the article, "Designing Information Systems that Work," they described how an organization can build a cost-efficient information system based on the company's actual needs for information, which in turn is based on critical success factors.

Effectiveness does not, according to the authors, begin by designing an elaborate data-processing system, but by identifying the company's critical success factors, that is, the things managers do that are crucial to achieving their business objectives.

It is my experience that the process of identifying the critical success factors often proves to be as important as the actual end results. Interestingly, even a secular company producing a simple product will often find that four out of five top critical success factors will be in the area of human relations. The manufacturing of quality products is obviously critical, but so is the relationship between managers, the working climate for the staff, the relationship to clients, and other areas of relationships.

14.4.2. Examples of Using the Critical Success Factors

Applying the process to the planning of Christian mission has been attempted by this author a number of times and has proven to be a most helpful activity. The process has proven to be a powerful tool in the planning process. After identifying the factors that will facilitate your reaching the goals, it is a matter of dedicated planning to ensure that barriers are removed and that the supporting factors are activated and enhanced. If the critical success factors are put in order of priority, the management should concentrate on the top four or five factors, and we can be more or less assured that subsequent factors will be solved in the process.

Work on Greenland.

The Danish Covenant Church has been involved in a social-based evangelistic work in the town of Ilulissat on the west coast of Greenland for five years. The missionaries are placed in secular positions in the town, and they use their spare time in the ministry. Short-term youth workers are also helping. The ministry is built around a club for children and youth who are in need of warmth and love due to serious alcohol problems in the town. Good facilities have been built for the work, and a good acceptance has been gained in the town.

Then, five years after establishing the ministry, a process of evaluation and planning took place. Great visions and goals were defined for the next five years. The critical success factors were defined. The result of this process was profound. A tremendous sense of unity was experienced and a new dedication to solve the issues that would hinder an effective ministry was evident. The critical success factors were, in order of priority:

1. The language problem must be solved so that all workers speak the local language.
2. Local co-workers must be recruited.
3. A full-time or part-time worker must be appointed within a year.
4. The work must be expanded to include a ministry to adults.
5. The fellowship among the staff must be strengthened.
6. Prepare material for the inspiration of more prayer.
7. A greater continuity among the staff is mandatory.
8. The necessary economical resources must be provided.
9. The work should be more goal-oriented and directed to a smaller group with greater impact.
10. Expanded P.R. for the ministry, both in Ilulissat and in Denmark.

The first three factors mentioned were seen as the most important factors that would facilitate the following points and the effectiveness of the ministry. Immediate action was taken on number one: language study was planned and the necessary budget was obtained. For number two, a list of potential people was worked out and is the subject of serious planning. For number three an initial approach was made to the Danish Covenant Church board, indicating the desire to have the salary for a full-time worker on the budget. Recruitment should begin immediately to get the person involved in language study as soon as possible.

Evangelism Enhancement Project in India.

A similar process was used for two community projects in India, one in the Madras area, the Sriperumpudur project, and the other a project in the Khond Hills of Orissa state.

The evangelism enhancement project is integrated with general community-based projects of development. Because of illiteracy, it was decided to experiment with audio cassettes. Quite extensive planning sessions were conducted, and a session on critical success factors was included. The factors identified were,

1. The quality of script, subject matter and format.
2. The cooperation of project staff.
3. Good distribution system.
4. Effective monitoring system.
5. Careful handling of equipment.
6. Proper preparations in the villages.
7. Integration of the project and follow-up.
8. Budget available.
9. Participation by local churches.

The above items are not in priority order, but each item was given a value as to its importance and priority. Detailed planning was then carried out to mobilize the necessary resources for relevant training programs and communication strategy that would meet the needs of the critical success factors.

A similar system was used in another project in India, and for a number of projects in the Philippines. In each case the process has helped by focusing attention on the most critical areas and committing the primary resources towards its solution.

14.4.3. Steps for Identifying Critical Success Factors

It is important to gain wide involvement by staff and leaders in the process of identifying critical success factors. The following approach can be suggested,

1. Let all, alone or in groups, write down five points they consider important for the success of the organization or the project.
2. Write all suggestions on the board, or possibly circulate to all involved.
3. Give each person four votes among the suggested points.
4. Put factors in priority order according to number of votes.
5. Concentrate planning on the points receiving highest priority.

14.5. PLANNING A SPECIFIC PROJECT

As mentioned earlier, the eleven-point circular model is a helpful tool in designing and planning a project or an advance.

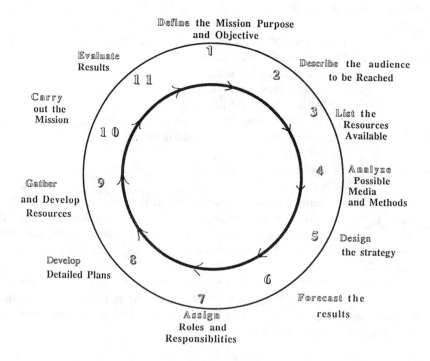

Figure 14.2 Strategy Development Model

Step 1. Define the Mission Purpose and Objectives:

The first stage of actual communications planning is to identify what the cognitive, attitudinal, and behavioral objectives are as far as the project is concerned. Once this has been done, you can plan for the use of all the streams of human communication that would seem relevant and useful and be required in order to move the original set of objectives toward their implementation. The strategy and media mix will vary in every single project.

The development of purpose and objectives can follow a similar approach as the one describe above for the development of mission statement, so there is no need to repeat that at this point. Let us just look at one example. The purpose for a specific cassette program could be as follows:

> The purpose of this program is to provide Scripture
> selections for use by local Christians in their witness
> to neighbors and friends.

Step 2. Describe the Audience to be Reached:

Who is your audience? If we as Christian producers and media organizations are trying to reach everybody, the result will probably be that we reach a very few. This is often true of magazine distribution, radio programs, fundraising, and evangelistic approaches. Four key questions need to be answered: Who is my listener/viewer/reader? Where is my listener/viewer/reader? What are the needs of my listener/viewer/reader? How can I meet the needs of my listener/viewer/reader?

Audience segmentation is not an option but a question of necessity. It is only possible to meet the needs of different audiences one at a time. Some of the information we need to gather in relation to audience segmentation are:

> *Demographic information:*
> What is the age group I am trying to reach?
> What is the educational level?
> Occupation?
> The religion they adhere to?
> The language they speak?
>
> *Environmental information:*
> Do they live in a hostile environment?
> Are they living in a city slum or in suburban houses?

Do they have strong family ties?
What is the lifestyle of their peers?

Knowledge and Attitudes towards the Gospel and the Church:

Are they negative or positive towards Christ?
Do they see the church as a positive entity?
What are the prejudices towards Christians?
How much of the gospel do they understand?
What are the misconceptions concerning Christianity?
How do they understand religious terms?

Media information:

Are they literate? Do they actually read?
Which radio station do they listen to?
What social activities are they involved in?
Do they have access to audio cassette players?
How much television do they watch and which programs?
Is video a favorite pastime?

The collection of such information can, of course, be done through formal research, and we will need to do that at regular intervals, but in our day-to-day work, we can learn much by spending time with members of our audience. Ask questions, spend a few hours conducting in-depth interviews, and constantly observe and study your audience. Listen to them so that they will listen to you. If you understand them, they may be able to understand you and respond to your message.

An organization in Indonesia identified an audience as non-Christian househelps, drivers, and other servants working in the homes of Christians. They were primarily non-literate and coming from poor backgrounds, but they would be curious about the faith of the family they are serving. A program for such a group would be drastically different from a program to the teenage children in the same family, or for the head of the household who may be a church elder.

On the two dimensional model presented in chapter 3, we can identify the location of the target group as follows:

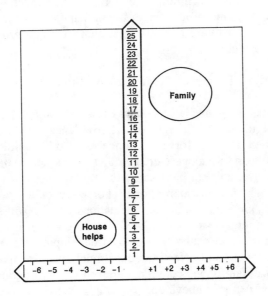

Figure 14.3. Non-Christian Househelps in Christian Homes

Step 3. Describe the Resources Available:

Each mission will need resources, and Christian media work will need a constant flow of finances to keep radio stations on the air and to keep the printing presses running. What is available for our present task? Who are the people we can draw on to help us? Where can we get financial resources? Who are the cooperating organizations that can assist us with necessary skills? Where can we get the necessary media products? It is important to be a "possibility thinker" in this regard. We should never limit our vision to the resources that are immediately available to us.

We need to network resources for the task. It is not necessary for such resources to be under the command of the central leadership or even to have it on one budget. Networking resources will demand good communications, but it will also release resources that would otherwise not be available.

The European Leadership Conference on World Evangelization (ELCOWE) held in Stuttgart in 1988 was a good example of such networking. There was a common purpose and common goals—re-evangelization of Europe—but different churches and organizations provided support. The budget itself was very small, but by having carefully worked out objectives, good internal communication—and building on mutual trust— it was not difficult to decentralize the work and base much of it on individual organizations. One group, for example, handled all the press work as part of their regular interest in this area, another group produced the conference folders, etc.

Step 4. Analyze Possible Media and Methods:

Like professional specialists, many Christian communicators have been trained to see the world through the narrow lenses of their special ministry. It is often difficult for us to conceive of other ministries as being better than ours and to adopt a strategy that places our own ministries in a wider perspective, and not necessarily the central focus. It is not that easy for a spokesman for an international shortwave radio station to advize against using shortwave radio, but in situations with no shortwave listeners or radios in a country, such advice needs to be given. It is also a lot easier to develop single and centrally-produced development programs than to develop appropriate and effective educational software that can be integrated into local family and community development programs.

What has been said above does not imply that we do not need specialized communication units and institutions. As a matter of fact they will be almost indispensable, but their role will be a new one. They will be much more in the responding mode than in the actual catalytic role. They will have to respond with the needed software rather than selling their own message and medium. This question is closely tied to the problem that communication is often equated with electronic mass media. In an integrated project, communications people cannot work in isolation. As supporters of integrated strategies, they will have to work in teams with researchers and others to plan and implement communication. For this they will not only use mass media, but a wide variety of traditional and local media.

So, go through a careful listing of all the possible media that can be used to reach your objectives and goals among a selected group of people. If Chinese women in Malaysia spend all day watching video and never listen to radio, then a radio approach would not be realistic. Similarly, if the people to whom we want to distribute Scripture are not readers, audio Scriptures would be more feasible than printed Scriptures.

Medium	Advantages	Disadvantages
Radio		
Cassette		
Book		
Booklet		
Drama		
Public Speaking		

Figure 14.4. List possible media strength and weaknesses

Step 5. Design the Strategy:

We now need to design the strategy. Which media will we chose and for what purpose? What kind of approach would be appropriate for my local church? We need to decide which media and methods we will not use as well as those that we will use. Most likely it will be a combination of media and methods where international and national programs will have to play a supportive role rather than an authoritative role in regard to local organizations and local churches.

For the househelp serving in the homes of Christians in Indonesia an interesting strategy was needed. It would include the involvement of the Christian family. How would they give the cassette to the person? What would this mean for their personal lives and testimony? How could they prepare answers for the questions that would come up after listening? Was a training course needed for the family? The cassette was only one part of a multi-step approach or media mix. We may illustrate the strategy as follows:

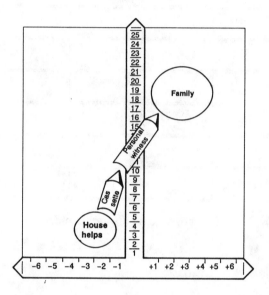

Figure 14.5. Strategy for Reaching Househelps

Step 6. Forecast Results:

Here we ask the tough question: If I follow this strategy, what can I realistically expect as results? If these are not satisfactory in relation to my objectives, I need to go back to step number one and work through the process once again in order to arrive at a strategy that I expect will give the desired results. I also need to consider the next steps. For example, if a new church has been formed, who will be the shepherd?

For large multimedia projects we need to carefully analyze and test the results of each unit in the strategy. For the househelp the desired result may be to get the servant to ask questions of the family.

For the local pastor it would be helpful if the goal for a sermon could be worked out as one sentence, stated in behavioral terms. What would be the desired effect after a person listens to this sermon? What would be the behavioral response? Or stated plainly, what do you want them to do?

Step 7. Assign Roles and Responsibilities:

This is critical in Christian communication. How much are we depending on ourselves and how much do we depend on others? Our own skills and resources are limited. A careful listing of roles and responsibilities will not only help us in planning but will also safeguard us from running into serious complications in management and cooperation later on.

In churches and organizations we should not be so concerned about doing "my thing," but also be responsible for how our task links in with what went before and what will come after.

	Person Responsible
Define the need	
Write objectives	
Describe the audiences	
Develop strategy	
Media possibilities	
Prepare format	
Write script	
Select actors	
Recording	
Testing	
Decision on price	
Prepare publicity	
Distribution	
Evaluation	

Figure 14.6. Assign roles and responsibilities for production of a program or other media product.

Step 8. Develop Detailed Plans:

During planning we need to consider a wide variety of topics. For example, it is important for a development project that the community will be sensitized and mobilized, but it is equally important that the planners be sensitized to the community and to the needs of the area. How do we achieve that? Communication support needs to be planned to bridge the gap.

The role of communication in integrated strategies demands new types of training for communication specialists as well as for pastors and church leaders. It is not enough to just study one medium. Media people need to be specialists in a wide variety of subjects including sociology and research, interpersonal relationships and communication, the role of change agents, and the integration of interpersonal and mass media communication.

Step 9. Gather and Develop Resources:

Instead of the term "gather" we may more appropriately speak of "lining up" resources. Careful negotiations between organizations and churches will often be necessary if resources are to be made available for mutual benefits or for a common purpose. Developing resources is not just fundraising. It can also be a training program for a church so that its members can play their roles in a special project. We could mention the training of counselors for an evangelistic crusade. It may take more patience, but it is a lot cheaper to train and "line up" the resources of a church than to establish our own group.

For Christian radio organizations the challenge will be to develop local, decentralized follow-up systems/centers. The tradition has been to use a central system, based on mail response, but this cuts out all those who cannot write letters. And it does not function well. It may be a big task to train local churches or to make packages of training kits available, but the results would probably be much higher.

Cinema Leo, a film and tape ministry in Kenya, has learned this principle. They have successfully decentralized the follow-up work to their film ministry in marketplaces. A team will help train the local church in follow-up and personal evangelism. The movie van then becomes a servant to the church, a true arm of the church.

Step 10. Carry out the Mission:

The primary concern here is faithfulness to purpose and objectives. We sometimes find that churches and denominations have set church growth goals but have not prepared themselves and their churches for what is involved, and action will be delayed and eventually cancelled.

Another important concern is faithfulness to your communication principles, in particular the concern for a receptor-oriented approach that seeks to safeguard the rights of the other person, seeking his or her free response rather than a manipulative approach that forces decisions. Who you are and the way in which you communicate may send stronger messages to the listener than the words you speak.

Step 11. Evaluate Results:

After the careful preparation of a cassette for a development project in Bangladesh, the leadership and project workers met for two days of evaluation. What were the issues? What was good about the tape and what was bad? What was missing and what was misunderstood?

Each point was carefully evaluated and graded as to importance. A five-point scale was used, going from insignificant to serious. Work was then concentrated on the problems, in particular the serious problems. As a result, a new cassette was produced to make up for the weaknesses of the first one. In this way, a project was strengthened and saved from collapse.

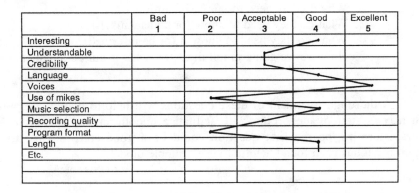

	Bad 1	Poor 2	Acceptable 3	Good 4	Excellent 5
Interesting					
Understandable					
Credibility					
Language					
Voices					
Use of mikes					
Music selection					
Recording quality					
Program format					
Length					
Etc.					

Figure 14.7. Sample Graph for Program Evaluation

14.6. PLANNING THE FACILITATING INFORMATION/ COMMUNICATION STRATEGY: WHO NEEDS TO KNOW?

The planning and management of an integrated information or communication system is the process whereby the objectives, plans, methodology, coordination, and other factors of a project will be properly communicated to all concerned, in order to ensure an effective ministry or project. We can also call this development support communication.

14.6.1. How to Develop Good Public Relations and Press Contacts

The primary purpose of public relations (P.R.) is to facilitate a smooth running operation. It is a matter of establishing and safeguarding the right relationships. P.R. will include press relations and the use of the news media for development purposes, and a primary purpose will be that of Romans 12:28. "If possible, so far as it depends on you, be at peace with all men."

We have seen that evangelistic campaigns have run into serious problems due to the lack of P.R.—courtesy—on behalf of the campaigners. By overlooking the need for good relations with local church leaders and government officials, they have seen their campaigns fail or have meager long-term effects. It is a matter of neglecting simple communication principles. A helpful way to approach the subject is to ask the simple questions:

1. Who needs to know (be informed)?
2. Why do they need to know (be informed)?
3. What do they need to know (or understand)?
4. When do they need to know it (or be informed)?
5. How are we going to tell them (or, what is our communication strategy)?

A thorough treatment of these questions will help to plan a comprehensive system of support that will facilitate a smooth-running operation. A brainstorming on the first question could be a good start and for this purpose it has been found helpful to use a simple model:

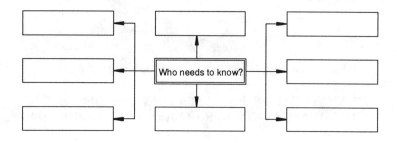

Figure 14.8. Planning Model for Defining Audiences for Publicity and Information Program

The filled out model may look like this:

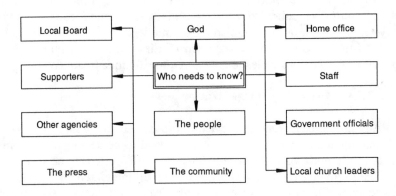

Figure 14.9. Example of Filled out Model of Definition of Audiences

The rationale and objectives for communication with each of the defined audiences would then need extensive work, so that clear guidelines can be worked out. It may be helpful to produce an overview or total plan, based on the results of the above exercise:

Who needs to know? *Audience*	Why do they need to know? *Purpose*	What do they need to know? *Content*	When do they need to know? *Timing*	How can you tell them? *Strategy*
Home office				
Supporters				
Local church				
The people				
The staff				

Figure 14.10. Overview of Plan for Communication Strategy

It is our experience that such a detailed picture of all aspects of the communication task will greatly influence how the strategy, and in particular media use, will be planned. Actually, groups need to be broken down into smaller sub-groups, e.g., local church leadership may consist of (1) the

bishop, (2) the pastor, (3) the local board, (4) members, and (5) seconded
project workers. All of these may need to be contacted individually.

All the groups mentioned above can be categorized into four broadly-
defined groups, or rather, four different kinds of communication: (1) Publicity Communication, (2) Ministry Communication, (3) Public Relation,
and (4) Internal Communication. Each of these kinds of communication
builds on the same principles, but each requires unique treatment.

14.6.2. A Missionary Organization

Any missionary organization needs to communicate with its supporters
and funding agencies, and new supporters need to be developed. The relationship to funding agencies or individual supporters needs to be sustained.

The following figure indicates how such an integrated strategy can be
viewed from the perspective of a major Danish missionary society. We
should note that as the "circles" get smaller, the more intense and personal
does the communication get. Each "circle" within a "circle" is also covered
by the communication to the surrounding circle, i.e., the center circle also
receives the communication directed to all the surrounding circles.

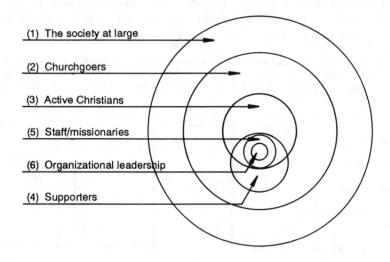

(1) The society at large

(2) Churchgoers

(3) Active Christians

(5) Staff/missionaries

(6) Organizational leadership

(4) Supporters

Figure 14.11. Overview of Suggested Publicity Strategy for a Danish
Missionary Society

The purpose of communication to group (1) is to create a positive climate for missions. The primary media should be mass media: radio, television, major newspapers, educational material for schools.

Group (2) is for the most part passive as far as foreign missions is concerned. The primary purpose of communication to this group is to attract new supporters, but secondly it is to increase the interest in and understanding of missions. To achieve this, there may be a need to start by encouraging active Christian involvement. The media used may be exibitions in churches, programs in churches, local church magazines, and the general Christian press.

Communication to groups (3) and (4) is aimed at increasing and sustaining support to the society. The media selected may include personal/prayer letters, participation in support groups, mission magazines, and conferences, and possibly also miscellaneous audio-visuals.

Group (5) will need to be thoroughly informed of organizational developments, new strategies and areas of ministry. Much of the communication will be in the form of education. (This will be treated further under internal communication.)

Finally, group (6) needs to be in constant communication. They will use letters, reports, phone calls, meetings, and personal conversation.

14.7. INTERNAL COMMUNICATION

People do not usually regard training as a communication problem, nor do they regard it as a process which requires technical communication support. On a number of occasions we have found that sophisticated development projects use only the most rudimentary training methods such as chalk, blackboard, and stencil materials. Thus, the effort here is to apply the principles of program planning or instruction to every possible stage of training. In its widest dimension, this would include all types of training, including that of key project administrators and extension workers.

Internal communication is also called corporate communication. In some organizations that functions pretty well between head office and field offices, but often very poorly between field, branch and local offices and project staff. From field office to branch office the communication is primarily by mail (print media) which is rarely read. As a result, the local project staff is ill-informed and personnel are poor communicators of the image of the organization.

All groups must understand the same principles but not the same amount of information. This will necessitate an ongoing integrated, in-service training and information system, based on relevant and effective media.

It is also important that all who represent the organization tell the same story and communicate the same message. This we call uniform information. Each person carrying the name or "uniform" of the organization must communicate, through word and deed, the ethos of the organization he or she represents.

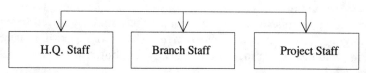

Figure 14.12. Uniform Information is Needed at all Levels

14.8. SUMMARY

Strategic planning is an approach to managing our mission and development projects in times of turbulence and challenge. In this book we are focusing on media, and the question is how do we successfully put the modern media of social communication at the service of mission and development. Furthermore, we do that on the basis of a receptor-oriented communication theory that implies respect for the human person, respect for his or her intelligence and his or her right to self-determination.

In this chapter, a number of models have been presented, models that are tools for the strategist. But prior to all Christian communication and the development of strategies must be a process of listening to people's feelings and aspirations before it is a process of talking to them.

In Christian communication and media use there should be no pure academicians or pure practitioners. Each must take on some of the attributes and preoccupations of the other. Likewise, there should not be those who are only concerned with one medium. All of us will be better listeners, writers, speakers, editors, artists and broadcasters if we fully understand what takes place when people communicate with one another. Theory must be grounded in practical applications, but by the same token, the practitioner must constantly ground practice in sound and progressive theory.

This does not imply that we do not need specialized communications units and institutions. As a matter of fact they will be almost indispensable, but their role will be a new one. They will be much more in the responding mode than in the actual catalytic mode. They will have to respond with the needed software rather than sell their own message.

This chapter has also dealt with "facilitating communication." Much Christian work and development has often been a matter of action or "how to." For example, a Swedish mission group decided to drill 2,000 wells in

India. Wells are badly needed to provide clean drinking water, but often the "why" has not been answered. Why should we drink water from a well when the water from the local pond tastes better? Consequently, we find wells not used and people getting sick from drinking dirty pond-water. Or, in order to avoid wasting precious water, a person will take a bath on top of the well, letting the dirty water run down into the well again. For such a situation we have learned that integrated communication is indispensable to effective development.

PRACTICAL EXERCISE:

1. Define a group of people you want to reach or a task you need to perform. Then develop a purpose statement for you communication.
2. Identify the critical success factors for the success of the activity listed above.
3. Develop a strategy that will help you reach your objectives.

FOOTNOTES

1   Peter F. Drucker, *Managing in Turbulent Times*. London: Pan Books Ltd. 1980:13.

2   James Engel, *Averting Financial Crisis in Christian Organizations*. Orange, CA: Management Development Associates. 1983:3.

3   Edward R. Dayton and David A. Fraser, *Planning Strategies for World Evangelization*. Monrovia, CA: MARC. 1990 (2nd ed.).

4   Ibid.

5   James F. Engel, *Averting Financial Crisis in Christian Organizations*. Orange, CA: Management Development Associates. 1983.

CHAPTER 15

Program Production Process

The production process is where communication theory and principles will stand their test as they are applied to actual program and product development. The different conceptual models can be reviewed as to their applicability and relevance in a given situation or for our present need. Here we will just look at one model, the comprehensive communication theory model presented in chapter 2. The model was built on an eleven-step process going through the various stages of the communication process.

The order of the steps was:
1. Identify source
2. Define receiver
3. Describe context of receiver
4. Obtain necessary information
5. Identify content that meet the needs
6. Select most appropriate medium/channel
7. Describe context of reception
8. Prepare message/program
9. Monitor and evaluate
10. Study response
11. Take constant notice of potential noise factors.

Even though our primary concern in this chapter is the production of programs—point 8 above—we cannot do that without paying careful attention to the other points. All of them are important for an effective media program. The general procedures for making programs—audio cassettes, video, printed matters, sermons, radio—follow the same steps. By following such a sequence of steps, the producer will be able to organize and put together relevant and effective programs.

4 Research
3 Context
1 Sender
5 Content
8 Message
6 Channel
7 Reception
2 Receiver
9 Monitor and Evaluation
10 Response/Research

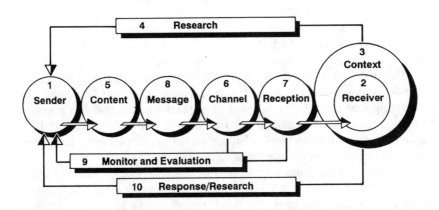

Figure 15.1. Comprehensive Model of Applied Communication Process

We could follow the general communication model, but we can also look at this process as a ladder with a number of steps. The one shown in the following figure is aimed at the production of audio cassettes.

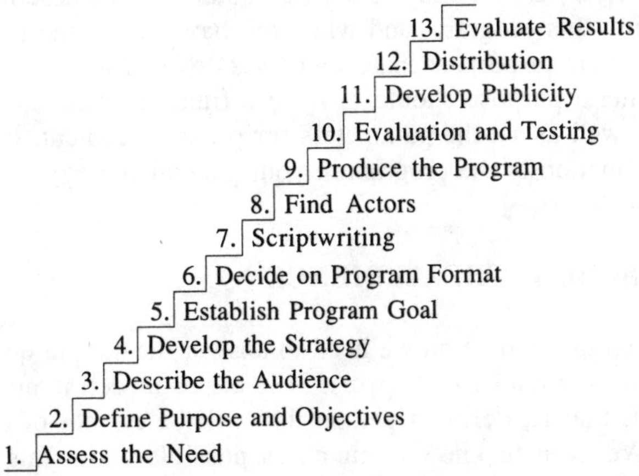

13. Evaluate Results
12. Distribution
11. Develop Publicity
10. Evaluation and Testing
9. Produce the Program
8. Find Actors
7. Scriptwriting
6. Decide on Program Format
5. Establish Program Goal
4. Develop the Strategy
3. Describe the Audience
2. Define Purpose and Objectives
1. Assess the Need

Figure 15.2. Steps for Program Production and Distribution (Illustration from Audio Cassettes)

Most of the points on the "ladder" above have been discussed in other chapters, but let us underscore the importance of carefully working on each step, and then focus on some selected practical hints.

15.1. ASSESS THE NEED:

The first step in any decision process concerning the use of media will be to determine if there is a need, and secondly, what are the possibilities of meeting that need. Often we will have research data that has given information on a specific need, at other times it is years of experience. If the guidelines from the previous chapter on strategic planning have been followed, then most of the questions have been treated.

A good starting point might be to let the imagination run and list all possible uses of media in a given situation and among a specific group of people. In many countries the local broadcasting is monopolized or centrally controlled by governments that do not favor Christian teaching. We might still get on the air with Bible reading programs or programs that feature developmental or social issues.

15.2. DEFINE PURPOSE AND OBJECTIVES:

The general *purpose* may be a broad statement that describes why you are producing this program, and what you have set as the general goals. The development of purpose statements was covered in the previous chapter. The general purpose should provide a frame of reference for review sessions, as well as set the parameters for program content. It should also clarify the function of the program in your general strategy.

15.3. DESCRIBE THE AUDIENCE:

For program production we need to answer the simple question, Who is my listener (or reader or viewer)? It is easier to define an audience in the singular, that is, define a person that will be typical of the intended audience. We need to know as much as possible about this person, for example, his or her age, education, occupation, religion, and language. We also need to understand the environment in which the listener lives and will be during the communication event. Try to describe the social and cultural environment of your listener.

We will also like to know the person's attitude towards Christ and towards Christians. Is he or she positive and open or negative and hostile?

What is the level of knowledge concerning the topic of our program and concerning Christian topics in general? We would also like to find out the person's media exposure. Does my listener watch television? Which programs? Does he or she read a daily newspaper? For each individual program we may want to do some specific investigation concerning the level of knowledge for this particular area or topic.

15.4. DEVELOP THE STRATEGY:

A review of the general strategic framework is helpful when planning a program. In this way you will be reminded of the context and how the program will fit into other dimensions of the overall strategy of your church or mission.

Throughout this book a church base is advocated for media use, and it is helpful to identify the use of media in the context of the following illustration:

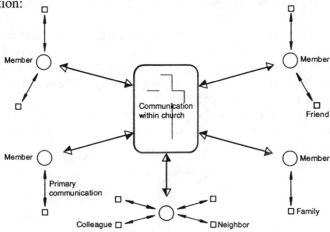

Figure 15.3. Illustration of Primary and Secondary Communication
Situations in a Local Church Context

Obviously, the strategy selected will also need to identify and establish the relevant distribution channels. For cassettes, there has been a tendency to distribute them like books, selling them in Christian bookstores. This may be acceptable for an audience who can afford to buy, but most of those who probably need the cassettes will not go into a Christian bookstore and they can probably not afford the price. The strategy will need to explain which distribution channels will be used, etc. For radio it is a question of station selection and follow-up. For video it is a question of getting the intended viewer into a context where the program will be presented.

15.5. ESTABLISH PROGRAM GOAL:

Each program, whether it be a cassette tape or a television show, should have its own specific goal. Often a program is part of a series, and as such both the series and the individual program objectives should be specified in terms of intended audience, the need that it aims at meeting, and the desired results. Goals should be stated in behavioral terms, that is, what do you want the listener to do as a result of your program?

An example would be:

> *"The goal of this program is to provide the Bible on cassette for illiterate church leaders in rural Bangladesh so that they can use the Scriptures in their sermon preparations."*

It could also be, "This cassette will help rural church members to sing the songs in a new selection of hymns and songs." Or it could be, "to help local church leaders answer questions from their non-Christian neighbors." Or it could have the purpose of guiding a group of believers through a time of worship, praise, and prayer.

It is helpful to visualize the goal of a program in its relation to other programs and activities. For this, we can use the two-dimensional model explained in chapter 3:

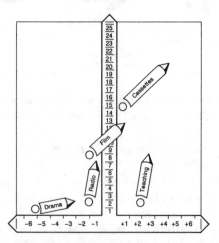

Figure 15.4. Illustration of Media Goals on Two-Dimensional Model

15.6. DECIDE ON PROGRAM FORMAT:

Basically, a program consists of an introduction, the main body of the program, and a conclusion. Parts of the introduction, opening, and conclusion in an audio program serve the same function as the cover of a book. The person listening, especially if he or she is illiterate, does not have the titles, the chapters, headings, etc., so it is important to provide such information to guide the listener through the program. The introduction should seek to relate the selected story to the listener's own life situation and answer the question, "Why is it important that I listen to this program?" If it is a printed book or magazine, the cover and title should provide a similar kind of communication. It is often helpful to let the introduction answer the same questions as a journalist always tries to answer in the opening paragraph when reporting a news story: Who, What, When, Where, Why, and Wherefore.

15.6.1. Speech, Sound Effects, and Music

Variations are always needed in media programs or people will become bored and tired of listening. By using dialogue rather than monologue, we can often overcome this problem. But the actual variety of program formats seems endless, and decisions concerning format will always depend on a number of variables. If we are dealing with the audio media, all programs will consist of just three basic elements: speech, sound effects, and music. We could even say that there are only two elements: speech and sound. Format variations depend on our ability to create different combination and uses of these basic elements, and how the various signal systems discussed in chapter 3 can be utilized. A few such combinations would be:

1. One voice in a monologue or a commentary
2. Two voices in a dialogue or an interview
3. Many voices in a drama or panel discussion
4. Several voices in a quiz or a classroom setting
5. Speech with background sounds
6. Speech with instrumental background
7. A montage of sound effects
8. A person singing with musical accompaniment
9. An orchestra playing a well-known piece of music
10. Musical bridges and effects in a drama

In written texts, we can use pictures and other illustrations, as well as interesting layout and bold headings, to attract attention and make the publication more attractive and understandable. In audio we cannot use "real" pictures, but we can create similar effects by skillful use of sound effects, music, and variations in the use of the human voice, as well as through interesting editorial comments. For example, some people actually prefer to listen to a soccer match on radio rather than watch it on television. The sound helps them create their own mental pictures and associations.

15.6.2. Visualize the Format:

It is easier to "see" fifteen minutes if graphically depicted than when we just write a certain number of minutes and seconds. When we are working with a printed text, it seems normal to make our layout in full size, probably beginning with a sketch; then as we progress in the preparations, the pages will be more and more like the final copy. We need to follow a similar approach in other media. The following illustration is from the development of a fifteen-minute program, where the suggested "model" can function as a blackboard on which the format can be developed:

Each line represents one minute. You can then try to fill it out, giving each segment the correct time. Little by little, as you work with the "layout" of the program, you will see the picture emerge. You can actually "see" the minutes you have allocated to a discussion, or how much space the three-and-a-half-minute song will take in your program. Let me give an example of a simple program format. When just writing it down, it will look like this:

     1 min. Theme music
     2 min. Introduction and comments
     4 min. Song
     5 min. Dialogue
     1 min. Music
     1 min. Editorial comments
    <u>1 min.</u> Theme music
   15 min. Total length of program

A graphic outline helps us visualize this program:

| Theme music |
| Introduction |
| Song |
| Dialogue |
| Music |
| Editorial comments |
| Theme music |

Obviously, you will want to be much more specific about the actual content, the topic of the dialogue, the title of the song, etc. Be prepared to rework your outline several times until it "looks" correct.

15.7. SCRIPTWRITING:

A script should be written for all media products, whether we are using audio, video, or written media. Each one will demand different kinds of writing.

Aural writing: even though we *write* a script for an audio program, it is important that the language is aural. Writing as such is linear, and we can include complicated sentences. For the audio media, sentences must be short and in a conversational style. For the beginner, it is often helpful to try to tell the story without a script, record it, and then write it down exactly as is was recorded, with all the "ahs" and "ohs" and pauses. You can then improve the script, but keep it in the original style.

A Few Tips on Writing for an Audio Medium
1. Write short sentences. It is difficult to follow long and complicated sentences when listening to a tape.
2. Repeat details and important lessons. Repetition may be done by saying the same thing but using different words.
3. Avoid using abbreviations in the script. For example, write "dollars" rather than just "$" to help the reader.
4. Make figures simple. It is easier to read, say and understand "around five thousand" than "4,987."
5. Avoid unnecessary words. Sentences become clearer and more direct when unnecessary words are removed.
6. Don't use clichés, as they are usually vaguely defined and make the program boring.
7. Use living words. Be active and creative, using colorful words and colorful descriptions.
8. Be positive and friendly. A friendly expression may help you win your listener.
9. Think "aurally" as you write. Speak or read aloud as you write, and develop the art of aural writing.
10. Write the script double-spaced and preferably on quite heavy paper. This makes it easier to read and prevents noises from paper-handling getting to the microphone.

15.8. TALENTS AND ACTORS:

Media use requires creative talents. Some people can master the pen so that a thrilling story is put on paper and we can hardly put the book down until the last page. When dealing with television, the looks of a person, his or her dress, movements, and facial expressions will have a strong influence on the communication effects. In the same way, a recording becomes more enjoyable to listen to if we use a pleasant voice and a conversational tone. A bit of humor also helps. A strange and unpleasant voice may, on the other hand, be a distraction in a program. For the reading of a Bible text, we therefore need a speaker with a pleasant and sincere quality of speech. But even more so, the voice must fit the person being portrayed. It is usually best to use a well-trained voice rather than an untrained one, which may be unclear when put on tape. The microphone has a tendency to strengthen the personal idiosyncrasies of a voice.

In the audio media the listener cannot see the person, but the voice will immediately give rise to associations in the mind of the listener, creating a mental picture of the speaker. The voice will probably remind them of someone they know. We will also do well to coach the speakers, even if they are professionals, so that the right emphases can be safeguarded. It is not just what you say, but even more so, how you say it. Feelings in your voice tell the listener if you are happy or sad, angry or cheerful. With the voice you can communicate love, interest, concern, respect, or trust. Christians are all familiar with the pastor's sermon, and often a "preaching" voice is used on radio and cassette. This should be discouraged, as the listener will not be sitting in a church, but more likely in a home. Usually, you don't preach in somebody's home. In the home, you have conversations.

Checklist for Use of Voices
1. Were the right voices chosen for this script?
2. Were the words chosen those my listener understands?
3. Were interesting and colorful words and phrases used?
4. Did the voices sound natural?
5. Was the right mood created in the program?
6. Was listening to the recording a pleasant experience?
7. Was it truly aural language and not written language?
8. Were good sound-pictures created?

15.9. MUSIC

Music is very important to all media use, just as it is important to the services in our churches. Music appeals to our feelings, our emotions, and with music we seek to influence the feelings of others. Music can give us a romantic feeling, or it can make us uneasy and nervous. Most people will remember famous songs and musical masterpieces, and they give us associations. Just think of the *Messiah*, or some of the great musicals like *The Ten Commandments*, or *The Sound of Music*. We see it happen in our minds.

Music can influence people in both a positive and a negative way. Christian radio stations usually receive much more response or reaction to their selection of music than to what is said. People seem to be much less concerned about the spoken message than the kind of music played.

In a program, music is used not just to fill out a pause or to entertain but to be a powerful communication in itself. Music is not neutral, so it has to be used wisely and for a specific purpose and therefore selected with great care. The primary concern is our listener's understanding of the music. How will he or she feel when hearing this particular piece of music? How will they respond to it? Will the music make it easier for them to understand our message?

15.10.   PRODUCTION OF PROGRAM:

Communication principles are also important during production of programs so that all elements will support the program content. This will include microphone distance. By moving in and out from the mike, the program will gain depth, but the speaker will, of course, need to respond with the correct level of voice. Again, visualization is important. Ask questions like, Who am I representing? How close should the listener feel I am? Experiment in the studio so that the correct level can be obtained and accurate messages communicated.

In an interview the interviewer represents or plays the role of the listener, and the listener should therefore feel that the questions being asked are his or her questions. Consequently, the interviewer should be closer to the microphone than the interviewee. The listener will then experience the situation as if the answers come from "out there." This can be illustrated as follows:

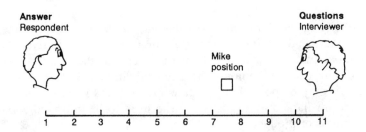

Figure 15.5. Illustration of sound-perspective in microphone placement during interview.

15.11.   CONDUCT EVALUATION AND TESTING:

The following chapter will deal with this topic in much more detail, but we need to remind ourselves at this point that testing and evaluation is not just a task of the researcher. All involved in program production should take part in some forms of pretesting, even though many artists and producers may be reluctant to listen to the people's opinions. If the people are non-literate, for example, some may feel it below their dignity to ask uneducated people whether or not they understood the intended message. Therefore, all involved in a program need to understand the objectives of the program. Not all artists are good communicators, but most can learn to be that, and often the most important lessons are learned during pretesting sessions with the intended audience.

15.12.   DEVELOP PUBLICITY:

Those who need to use the materials, printed as well as audio, need to know the materials are available. Often we find sets of material, produced years ago, but no one else knows of its existence so it is not used. Publicity should aim at making all involved, the potential market, aware of the products, how they can be used, and at what cost. As a guide for the development of your publicity material and promotional strategy, ask the following basic questions:

1)   Who needs to be informed about this new product?
2)   Why do they need to be informed about this product?

3)   What do they need to know about it to fulfill the purpose?
4)   How can I provide them with the needed information?

Publicity material will include catalogue descriptions, brochures, ads in magazines, and exhibition material for conferences. It will also be instructional material that will help the user use the material for the intended purpose and among the selected audience. For some new programs it may be possible to prepare special press releases for circulation to the media and to key persons who need to be informed about the new programs or products.

15.13. DISTRIBUTION:

Distribution of media products depend on many different variables. Each medium is different and demands different distribution systems. In this book we have argued for use of media as an integrated function with other media and ministries. Distribution systems will therefore need to be integrated with other ministries. Media are tools in the hands of the church and mission agencies. The producers need to provide the users and distributors with information that will safeguard an effective use. Cassette covers should, for example, tell the buyer for what purpose the material has been produced. In some cases, it would be helpful to conduct seminars on the use of special programs.

The following illustration shows how audio cassettes could be distributed.

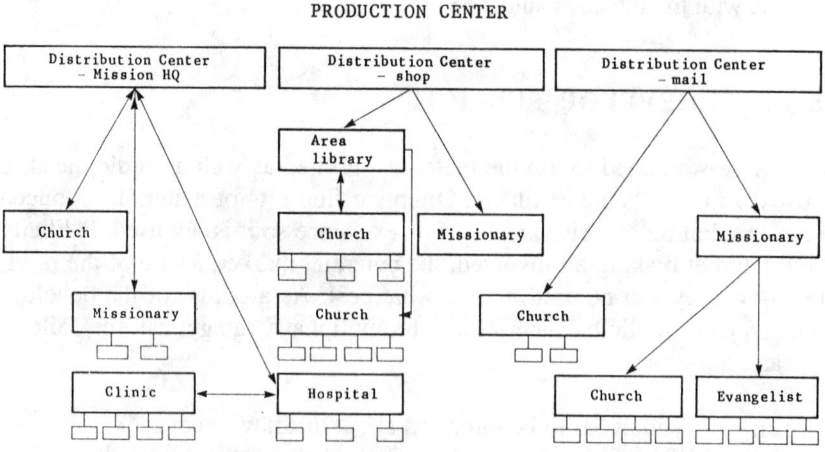

PRODUCTION CENTER

Distribution Center – Mission HQ	Distribution Center – shop	Distribution Center – mail

Area library

| Church | Church | Missionary | Missionary |

| Missionary | Church | Church |

| Clinic | Hospital | Church | Evangelist |

Figure 15.6. Illustration of Cassette Distribution

For the distribution of mass media programs like radio and television, much will depend on the local situation and the possibilities we have. If possible we should select stations and times of broadcast that are most appropriate for our audience.

15.14. EVALUATE RESULTS:

Did we reach the desired goals? No communicator should be content without having at least a partial answer to this question. Is the program making a difference? Or would nobody notice if the program was taken off the market? If we don't ask such questions, we may just be repeating the mistakes of the past and, in turn, cause the media products to be ineffective or useless. Evaluation of results should be based on actual research data, sales figures, and general response, and all involved in the production should participate, if possible. Lessons learned will be applied during the production of the next program or product.

SUMMARY

The production of media programs will call on all the collective creativity God has given us. It may look difficult to the novice, but it is really a simple process if we know our task, understand the media, but even more important that we know our audience and their needs. Throughout this book, four key questions have been suggested as the primary guidelines for program production: (1) Who is my listener? (2) Where is my listener? (3) What are the needs of my listener? (4) How can I meet the needs of my listener? The same questions can be used with print media by just substituting the word *listener* with *reader*. And those who work with performing or video media just ask, Who is my viewer? These questions will force us into a receptor-oriented perspective, and we will be able to imitate the communication approach of our Lord Jesus.

This chapter has provided a series of practical steps for development of programs and products, and it has dealt with issues related to format, talent, recording, and distribution.

PRACTICAL EXERCISE:

1. Prepare a brochure for people in the neighborhood of your church in order to highlight a program of your church. Develop specific objectives for the brochure.
2. Prepare a distribution plan that will achieve maximum effect.

CHAPTER 16

The Process of Evaluation and Pretesting

Someone may say, "I have worked hard on this, I have prayed for God's guidance, I know the message, why then should I 'waste' time and money on testing?" The simple answer is that it is good stewardship and a prerequisite for effective communication. If we do not evaluate and test, we may indeed be wasting time on producing materials that do not reach our intended audience in an effective way.

Programs and various communication materials are usually developed by educated people living in urban areas, and often they do not know, or have forgotten, how rural people live and speak. And as producers are constantly working with their special topics, they tend to forget how other people respond to their messages. In many countries Christians are a minority. They have developed their own subculture and in so doing they have lost effective contact with the population at large. The American televangelist who broadcasts copies of his US-based program in Nairobi or in Manila will not know the audience or have even a faint idea about their felt needs. Careful evaluation and pretesting, even with the time and expenses involved, would in the long run prove to be much more cost-effective for the proclamation of the Kingdom of God.

Evaluation and pretesting are, then, cost-effective ways of reducing error or mistakes in programming, so we should not be content with production of materials that are broadcast or published without such relevant testing. A limited amount of internal evaluation cannot substitute for actual field testing or pretesting with the intended audience.

16.1. WHY SOME PEOPLE AVOID EVALUATION AND PRETESTING

There seem to be a number of problems and reasons that cause Christian organizations to avoid evaluation and pretesting procedures. A primary one is the sheer lack of knowledge and experience in pretesting. After all, few pastors pretest their messages. Another often-quoted excuse is lack of time, as the tyranny of production schedules prevents producers from going into the field and testing their materials. A lot of lip-service will be given to the issue, but rarely do managers provide the time and expenses needed. In the secular world, it would be considered a waste of money and far too high a risk to take if advertising is not well tested before it goes on the air or is published in a magazine.

Another underlying but usually not expressed reason seems to be that people think they know how the audience will understand the material and respond to it. After all, a city person should have education enough to understand the villagers. But we experience again and again that this is not so. Village people are sharp enough to understand this and consequently screen out a radio program that might otherwise have helped them, or they laugh at the life-style of the actors in the video rather than listening to the message.

Another reason is defensiveness on the part of the producers and artists. Unfortunately, they often misunderstand evaluation and pretesting as criticism of "their" work and skills, but we then have to ask whether they are in the ministry for the sake of their art, or if they are there to use such skills to communicate the Gospel clearly to a needy world.

I do believe, though, that Christian leaders want their ministry to be effective, so let us trust that someday Christian managers will take evaluation and pretesting as prerequisites and build in such procedures in production and distribution processes. It can be done so let us work for adequate allocation of time and funds to see it happen.

Evaluation and testing is a multifaceted task. It is a process of constantly monitoring both the production process and the actual communication process, so that we know how a particular program, or series of programs, performs in relation to the objectives. It covers the whole process: scripts should be tested, test-recordings should be made and evaluated, the final product should be tested before release, and finally a field test to see if it really happened as we hoped it would happen.

16.2. SELF-CRITIQUE

The first phase in the evaluation process is your own self-critique. It is necessary to be hard on yourself when writing and producing a program.

The first step is the script itself. A script will usually need to be rewritten. Good writers usually rewrite their scripts several times. Go through the script, possibly using a felt pen, strike out unnecessary words and sentences. If this is a script for an audio medium, read it out loud for yourself to "feel" if it flows naturally and reads easily. If it is a script for a dramatic performance, try to "act" as you read through your script, making changes as needed.

For an audio program, the next step would be to record the message on tape. For the script writer, this can be done on a simple home cassette recorder. Then listen critically to the reading, and try to put yourself in the place of the intended listener. If you are a performer or speaker you will need a fairly good recording for such personal critique. As you listen, there may be several things with which you are not satisfied. Maybe the natural flow of the dialogue needs improvement. Try to ask some critical questions of yourself. Here are a few suggestions:

1. Did the voice sound natural, like talking to a friend?
2. Was it happy enough to make the listener smile a little?
3. Did the program have an interesting beginning?
4. Would the program be interesting to my listener?
5. Was the reading or talk the right length?
6. Did it sound believable and trustworthy?
7. Were the words simple enough for my listener?
8. Did it deal with issues that my listener would find important?

If the program is for a visual medium such as television or video, or even if it is for a personal delivery such as a speech, you may want to have a preliminary video recording to see how you perform and how the message comes together as it is translated through both sound and visuals. You can, of course, also do some practicing in front of a mirror.

By carrying out such a self-critique before going into further evaluation with colleagues you will save time for all concerned and be more ready to listen to the advice from other members of the team.

16.3. INTERNAL EVALUATION

The next phase is the internal evaluation by your own colleagues or staff. For this purpose it is helpful to have an evaluation form which people can fill out as they listen. Usually a five-point scale is adequate for judging the response. The following evaluation form is suggested for the internal evaluation. The actual number of issues on the form can be increased or decreased as needed for your particular program. The following form was developed by a media class for the evaluation of a slide-tape production:

STRATEGY		1 Bad	2 Poor	3 Acceptable	4 Good	5 Excellent
1.	Clarity of strategy					
2.	Clarity of objective					
3.	Definition of audience					
4.	Choice of medium					
PRODUCT						
5.	Content relevant					
6.	Reach objectives					
7.	Program format					
8.	Interesting					
9.	Credibility					
10.	Length of program					
11.	Use of soundeffects					
12.	Use of voices					
13.	Use of music					
14.	Microphone technique					
15.	Quality of recording					
16.	Selection of slides					
17.	Graphics					
18.	Quality of pictures					
19.	Number of pictures					
20.						
21.						
22.						

Figure 16.1. Internal Evaluation Form for a Slide Show

If you were evaluating a sermon, you would include topics such as gestures and facial expressions, eye contact with the congregation, dress, etc.

16.3.1. Conduct Evaluation in Group Setting

It has been found that internal evaluation should, if possible, take place in a group setting. If done individually, people tend to be either too nice, and consequently not helpful in the evaluation, or the comments are received as criticism rather than critique. Criticism is negative and destructive, critique can be both negative and positive and its purpose is to provide help for improvement.

If possible, make evaluation a regular event, maybe a session every week or two. At one radio organization a weekly session was conducted and the producers took turns in presenting a program. Some other members of staff also attended the sessions. They found that such an internal evaluation exercise heightened quality far more than many seminars and workshops. The "agenda" for the evaluation session was:

1. The producer explains intended audience, program goal, and how such effects can be observed or tested.
2. All present are given an evaluation form.
3. Listen to program.
4. All fill out form prior to any discussion.
5. The producer gives his or her comments.
6. Scores given by all present are averaged and put on the board.
7. Discuss the results, highlight weaknesses, and make suggestions for improvement.

16.3.2. Develop your own form

As a staff, develop a form that will fit your particular ministry, a form that reflects your needs for evaluation, and of which you as a staff feel ownership. Then make it a point to have a regular evaluation session, weekly if possible. Regularity is important in order to develop an evaluation thinking and to secure long-term effects. If performance is involved, record the presentation on video and then let the performer see the playback before any discussion takes place. Then, let everybody fill out a form individually prior to group discussion. A form may also be shown on the board, and the speaker or producer should then complete the form on the board first. Then, the average of what others have given will be put on the same form on the board. Finally, discussion will follow, aimed at highlighting both strengths of the talk or program and identifying weaknesses. If possible, some help and suggestions should be given as to how the program can be improved.

Practical Exercise:
Take a radio program which you have produced, or a program someone else has produced.
Construct an evaluation form for internal evaluation. Then,
    a. Listen to the program.
    b. Let each member of the group fill out the form.
    c. Discuss your answers.
    d. Note down the main points that came up.

After successful internal evaluation, the program or product is ready for testing with the intended audience. We call this pretesting, or, as is the case with advertising, copy testing. Some producers will, of course, have been conducting some pretesting of programs or items for programs even before they presented the material for internal evaluation.

16.4. PRETESTING OF MATERIALS WITH MEMBERS OF THE INTENDED AUDIENCE

Before final production, all media programs, whether radio, audio cassettes or printed materials, should be tested thoroughly as to acceptability and understanding by the intended audience. The personal and internal evaluation which has been discussed above is important, but not enough to satisfy the need for well-tested and relevant programs. Many former students and colleagues have told me that pretesting procedures were the most important lessons they learned, and that it completely changed their ministries. And often a person has expressed something like, how could we work on media programs for so many years without ever pretesting our programs?

16.4.1. What is Pretesting?

By pretesting we mean field testing of materials at various stages of production. Pretesting is always done among representatives of the intended audience with the aim of testing understanding and actual communication, so that we can judge if the program is achieving its intended communication effects. Pretesting may also have to be repeated several times in order to see how changes have improved the relevancy of the programs. In the chapter on research, we dealt with this topic under the heading of copy testing, as this is the word used for pretesting advertising.

Some of the questions we seek to answer through pretesting would be:

> Is the program to the likeness of the audience?
> Are words and symbols understood?
> Is the language or dialect correct for this particular audience?
> Will any part of it embarrass the reader/listener/viewer?
> Will what I am saying or the way in which I say it cause offense among my non-Christian audience?

There is no reason for causing offense, even if the teaching is directed to Christians only. A non-Christian may also be listening, and then your program should be made in such a way that what he or she hears will make him or her want to listen again.

16.4.2. Planning the Pretest

The timing of pretesting depends on a number of factors. If it is a new production, say a new type of radio program or a new set of flip charts, pretesting may be carried out at several stages, from the early draft to the finished program. A general suggestion would be to start the pretesting as early as you can in the process. A new radio program, using a magazine format, may, for example, be tested on both individual program segments and on the final, complete program. A book can be tested on its cover, on layout, on pictures, on language, etc.

It is often tempting to test the materials on friends and relatives who can learn the ideas quickly, or to go to those with a higher education. But such an approach is totally unacceptable unless the material is produced for them. We need to test with representatives of the intended or target audience.

Testing can be done with both individuals and groups. If you test with a group, it is best to try to get the responses of individuals before group discussion in order to avoid biases influenced by the most vocal members of the group. The number of people in a pretest will vary, but usually a number of twenty or so will do, and sometimes even testing with just five people will give the necessary information. Ideally, you continue testing until you find a trend in the responses. After getting a fairly good idea of the necessary changes, you go back to the drawing board, rewrite and reproduce, and then test again.

Generally speaking, pretesting is something all can do and many should be involved in: managers, producers, artists, writers, performers and others involved in the production, but the actual pretesting will often be done by a researcher. In any case, it is always advisable to consult a researcher in setting up the test plan if it is to be done by those who are not trained in research. The artist and producer may feel tempted to defend their materials and not be objective in questioning, but it has been found that it is important for such workers to at least observe and listen to pretest interviews.

16.4.3. Guidelines for Actual Pretesting

a. Get cooperation to conduct the test.
Pretesting is a communication situation, and is therefore subject to all the principles of good interpersonal communication. In a community, it is

necessary to obtain the necessary permission from the leaders of the community. In some places, official permits are also required.

Sometimes your pretesting will only be to ask a neighbor to help you look at some material. Often it is a matter of asking an individual directly to assist you in testing, at other times you need to test with a group. Very few people will refuse to help if you approach them nicely and ask them to help you improve a program.

b. Establish rapport with the respondent.

The place of the pretest is often very important. In a village situation, many people may want to listen or look on, but it is important that you establish good rapport with the respondent so that he or she does not feel inhibited by the social setting or context. Spend time talking with the person, especially if he or she is a stranger to you. The respondents need to trust you with their time and insights. Another important point is that you should find a time that is convenient for the respondent so that the test can be carried out in a relaxed atmosphere. The purpose of the pretest should be carefully explained to the respondent and all encouragement should be given for him or her to make corrections or suggestions for change.

If an outside researcher is employed for the research, this person will need to be carefully briefed on the material being tested, its purpose and objectives. He or she will also need to study the audience and their previous experience with such material. Are they able to read and write? Is the topic one that they are familiar with? Would certain illustrations be seen as threatening? Is the language or dialect of special importance?

c. Encourage frank responses.

Through the research you are testing programs and materials, not the people. Therefore, point this out clearly to the respondent and explain that there are no correct answers. All we need are their frank responses. Resist the temptation to teach or preach, even if the answers seem to call for that. If teaching or preaching is mixed with the pretest, you will most likely get a biased evaluation of the material, and your attention will be drawn away from the actual purpose of the session.

d. Ask questions.

In asking questions, select unbiased questions. There may be a temptation to ask leading questions that will obtain a praise of the materials or programs, but such an approach will totally ruin the pretest and in turn waste precious resources on poor productions that are not meeting needs. Questions should be objective, calling for extended responses and not just "yes" or "no." In the pretest you can often use open-ended questions, and you will have to go into depth on certain issues. Be inquisitive, try to find out what the person really understands, how he or she feels about the program, interest in the topic, etc. One way of getting at sensitive issues is to ask: How do you think your neighbors would react to such a program? Usually, the person will respond with his or her own view. When an answer or opinion is expressed, give a positive and friendly response, urging him or her to go on. Don't express any surprise at their answers.

The attitudes and behavior of the interviewers will usually greatly influence the responses. The person who usually gets the best and most useful information is the one who is really interested in the work and is keen on getting the reaction of people to the programs or materials being tested. He or she is concerned about making effective material and will therefore not be defensive. Analyze your attitudes to the people who are being interviewed. A lack of respect will be communicated in many subtle ways, but this will be understood by the respondents and their cooperation will be influenced. It is your attitudes that guide your behavior, your way of asking questions, your dress, your language and your responses. People will sense this and a negative attitude and lack of respect will alienate the respondent.

e. Record the responses.

For the purpose of analyzing the results of the pretest, it is important to have an accurate report of the questions as well as the answers. There should also be plenty of space for reporting observations by the interviewer. The answers may be recorded by either the interviewer or by an assistant.

(1) By the interviewer. If the interviewer has to fill in the answers, it may make the situation rather difficult and destroy a line of thought. One way is to use two people, one asking the questions and the other writing down the responses, but if it is a sensitive issue, the respondent may be more frank if only one person is present. If it is a rather short session, the responses could possibly be written down afterwards. A questionnaire will be able to help so that answers can be checked, but that could also hinder responses in areas not covered by the questionnaire. In some cases, it may be possible to record the session on tape and transcribe the responses at a later time.

(2) Self-administered questionnaires. If the person is literate, he or she can fill out a questionnaire and anonymity can be safeguarded. If the pretest is with an individual, the person is known to the interviewer, and true anonymity cannot be promised. A good alternative is to conduct the test with a group of people, and then let each one fill out a form. In this way the anonymity of the person can be kept to encourage frank responses. Let each person fill out a form before discussion is carried out by the

group, so that responses will not be influenced by the insights of just a few people.

f. Analyze and interpret the responses.

Pretesting is not like large research studies where variables have been clearly defined. It is therefore difficult to use a computer for analysis. The number is also small so the work involved is not sufficient to design special computer programs. Of course, in a wider testing with several groups and self-administered questionnaires, a computer may come in handy to analyze some of the responses, and to identify trends.

Practical Exercise:

Pretest an audio cassette prepared for non Christians:

a. Contact a friend or neighbor, ask if he or she minds helping you. Tell him or her that you are working on this program and that you would like to be sure that it is helpful and does not offend anybody.

b. Bring the cassette to the person. Ask how he or she thinks others in the community would respond to it. Would they like it? Would they be offended? Would they understand? etc. You can be more or less sure that the person will be giving his or her own opinions, and you will be much wiser as a result.

c. Re-produce the segment and if possible ask the same person to listen again.

SUMMARY

This chapter wraps up our discussion on the effective use of media in church and mission. In section I of this book, we discussed the basic, underlying principles on which our media communication must rest. We started with God and his Word, and found that communication is deeply rooted in the nature of God, and that in the Scriptures we can find outstanding principles of effective communication.

The following chapters then went on to discuss communication principles and models, strategy and the importance of understanding the audience so that a true receptor-oriented approach can be achieved. There was also a chapter on the function of research in media communication, and the first section closed with a discussion of seven basic principles or dimensions of effective, Christian communication. It was found that (1) our ministry must reflect a dependence on the Holy Spirit and be guided by God's concern for the world. (2) Our communication must be person-centered as this was the approach God used in communicating with us. (3) A receptor orientation where the needs of the other person is our primary concern, irrespective of the cost to ourselves, must permeate our ministry. (4) The centrality of the local church in media communication must be taken seriously if we are to see long-term effects of our activities, and we must realize (5) that a process is involved. The listener/reader/viewer lives through a spiritual process and we must adapt our programs to that process. (6) Information is important so all Christian communicators must engage in serious audience studies, with one of the goals being to develop programs (7) that are truly based on the cultural context and the prevailing modes of communication.

In section II, a number of media were selected for in-depth discussion. Extra space was given to the more pervasive and immediate media such as television and radio, video and audio cassettes, as well as print media. Chapters were also devoted to film, computers, and art forms such as music, painting, and dance drama. In each chapter the medium was discussed and its strengths and weaknesses assessed, and we tried to look at its present and possible uses in church and mission. It was found that there are many pitfalls and many problems, but there are even more possibilities. Media can be used effectively in church and mission if we work seriously on the basis of the principles developed in section I.

The third section came to grips with practical aspects regarding the use of media. One chapter was devoted to strategic planning, giving insights into the developments of plans and approaches and providing practical steps to follow. The following chapter then led us through practical steps for program or product production.

This final chapter has raised the question, Did we achieve what we set out to do? Evaluation and testing should be integrated parts of our ministry and compulsory activities for all involved in Christian media production and use, but, unfortunately, this is not always the case. The chapter has not only argued for the importance of evaluation and testing, but also given practical guidelines as to how it can be done.

Together these sixteen chapters form an approach to Christian communication and the use of media. The hope of this writer is that they will help and guide Christian communicators around the world, so that the Good News may be truly communicated through us and our activities to all people.

Selected Communication and Media Bibliography

ARBOLEDA, Cora R.
> 1981   *Communication Research.* Manila, Philippines: Communication Foundation for Asia.

ARMSTRONG, Ben.
> 1979   *The Electric Church.* New York: Thomas Nelson Publishers.

BABIN, Pierre.
> 1970   *The Audio-Visual Man.* Dayton, OH: Pflaum Publishers.

BARNLUND, D. C.
> 1968   *Interpersonal Communication: Survey and Studies.* Boston: Houghton Mifflin.

BERLO, David K.
> 1960   *The Process of Communication.* New York: Holt, Rinehart and Winston.

BILLINGSLEY, K. L.
> 1989   *The Seductive Image: A Christian Critique of the World of Film.* Westchester, IL: Crossway Books.

BISHOP, Ann.
> 1984   *Slides, Planning and Producing Slide Programs.* New York: Eastman Kodak Company.

BOX, Harry.
> 1992   *Communicating Christianity to Oral, Event-Oriented People.* Unpublished D.Mis. dissertation. Fuller Theological Seminary, Pasadena, CA.

BRUCE, Steve.
> 1990   *Pray TV, Televangelism in America.* London and New York: Routledge.

CHARTIER, Myron R.
> 1981   *Preaching as Communication.* Nashville: Abingdon.

CLINTON, J. Robert.
  1988   *The Making of a Leader—Recognizing the Lessons and Shapes of Leadership Development*. Altadena, CA: Barnabas Publishers.

CLINTON, J. Robert and Paul Stanley.
  1992   *Connecting—The Mentoring Relationships You Need to Succeed in Life*. Altadena, CA: Barnabas Publishers.

COLLIER, John.
  1967   *Visual Anthropology: Photography as a Research Method*. New York: Holt, Rinehart and Winston, Inc.

COMMUNICATION FOUNDATION FOR ASIA.
  1981   *Communication and Development*. Manila: Communication Foundation for Asia.

CONN, Harvie M.
  1984   *Eternal Word and Changing Worlds*. Grand Rapids: Academic Books.

COOK, Bruce.
  1981   *Understanding Pictures in Papua New Guinea*. Illinois: David Cook.

COOMBS, Philip H., et. al.
       Integrated Rural Development and Communication. Singapore: AMIC.

DAYTON, Edward R. and David A. Fraser.
  1990   *Planning Strategies for World Evangelization*. 2nd ed. Monrovia, CA: MARC.

DEFLEUR, Melvin L.
  1975   *Theories of Mass Communication*. 2nd ed. New York: David McKay Co.

DOUGLAS, J. D. (ed.).
  1975   *Let the Earth Hear His Voice*. Minneapolis: World Wide Publications.

DRUCKER, Peter F.

1977   *An Introductory View of Management.* New York: Harper and Row.

1980   *Managing in Turbulent Times.* London: Pan Books Ltd.

DYE, T. Wayne.
1985   *Bible Translation Strategy: An Analysis of Its Spiritual Impacts.* Dallas: Wycliffe Bible Translators.

ENDRENY, Phyllis.
1978   *Pictorial Communication with Illiterates: An Introductory Investigation of the Issues.* New York: Population Resources Center.

ENGEL, James F.
1977   *How Can I Get Them to Listen.* Grand Rapids: Zondervan.

1979   *Contemporary Christian Communication: Theory and Practice.* Nashville: Thomas Nelson.

1987   *How to Communicate the Gospel Effectively.* Accra, Ghana: Africa Christian Press.

ENGEL, James F. and Roger D. Blackwell.
1983   *Consumer Behavior.* 4th ed. Chicago: The Dryden Press.

ENGEL, James F. and Wilbert H. Norton.
1975   *What's Gone Wrong with the Harvest?* Grand Rapids: Zondervan Publishing House.

FAST, Julius.
1972   *Body Language.* New York: Simon & Schuster, Inc.

FISHBEIN, Martin and Icek Ajzen.
1975   *Belief, Attitude, Intention and Behavior: An Introduction to Theory and Research.* Reading, MA: Addison-Wesley Publishing Company.

FLAVIER, Juan M.
1970   *Doctor to the Barrios.* Quezon: New Day Publishers.

FORE, William F.
  1987   *Television and Religion: The Shaping of Faith, Values, and Culture*. Minneapolis, MN: Augsburg Publishing House.

  1990   *Mythmakers: Gospel, Culture and the Media*. New York: Friendship Press.

FUGLESANG, Andreas.
  1973   *Applied Communications in Developing Countries*. Uppsala, Sweden: Dag Hammarskjold Foundation.

GIBBS, Eddie.
  1985   *The God Who Communicates*. London: Hodder and Stoughton.

GRAY, Francis A.
  1989   *Radio In Mission*. Charlotte, NC: Lausanne Committee for World Evangelization.

GRIFFIN, Em.
  1976   *The Mind Changers*. Wheaton, IL: Tyndale House.

HAALAND, Ane.
  1984   *Pretesting Communication Materials*. Burma: UNICEF.

HADDEN, Jeffrey K. and Charles E. Swann.
  1981   *Prime Time Preachers*. Reading, MA: Addison-Wesley Publishing Company, Inc.

HALL, Edward T.
  1969   *The Hidden Dimension*. New York: Doubleday & Company.

HARTMANN, Paul, B. R. Patil, et al.
  1983   *The Mass Media and Village Life: An Indian Study*. Leicester: University of Leicester, Centre for Mass Communication Research.

HESSELGRAVE, David J.
  1978   *Communicating Christ Cross-Culturally*. Grand Rapids: Zondervan, 1978.

HULTENG, John L. and Roy Paul Nelson.
  1983   *The Fourth Estate: An Informal Appraisal of the News and Opinion Media*. New York: Harper and Row.

HUNTLEY, David Anthony.
    1981   *Video and Mission.* Th.M. Thesis. Fuller Theological Seminary,
            Pasadena.

JORGENSEN, Knud.
    1981   *The Role and Function of the Media in the Mission of the
            Church.* Unpublished Ph.D. dissertation presented to Fuller
            Theological Seminary, School of World Mission, Pasadena.

KENNY, Michael and Raymond Schmitt.
    1981   *Images, Images, Images: The Book of Programmed Multi-
            Image Production.* New York: Eastman Kodak Company.

KINNEAR, Thomas C. and James R. Taylor.
    1983   *Marketing Research: An Applied Approach.* 2nd ed. New York:
            McGraw-Hill Book Company.

KLAPPER, Joseph T.
    1960   *The Effects of Mass Communication.* Glencoe, IL: The Free
            Press.

KLEM, Herbert V.
    1982   *Oral Communication of the Scripture, Insight from African
            Oral Art.* South Pasadena: William Carey Library.

KNAPP, Mark L.
    1972   *Nonverbal Communication in Human Interaction.* New York:
            Holt, Rinehart and Winston, Inc.

KOTLER, Philip.
    1982   *Marketing for Nonprofit Organizations.* 2nd ed. Englewood
            Cliffs, NJ: Prentice-Hall, Inc.

KRAFT, Charles.
    1979   *Christianity in Culture.* Maryknoll, NY: Orbis Books.

    1979   *Communicating the Gospel God's Way.* Ashland: Ashland
            Theological Seminary.

    1991   *Communication Theory for Christian Witness.* Rev. ed.
            Maryknoll, NY: Orbis Books.

LASSWELL, Harold D.
1971   "The Structure and Function of Communication in Society." In
        Wilbur Schramm and Donald F. Roberts, ed., *The Process and
        Effects of Mass Communication*. Urbana, IL: University of
        Illinois Press.

LAUSANNE COMMITTEE FOR WORLD EVANGELIZATION.
1974   "The Lausanne Covenant," prepared at the International
        Conference on World Evangelization in Lausanne 1974.

1978a   *The Pasadena Consultation: Homogeneous Units*. Wheaton:
        LCWE.

1978b   *The Willowbank Report—Gospel and Culture*. Wheaton:
        LCWE.

LINGENFELTER, Sherwood G. and Marvin K. Mayers.
1987   *Ministering Cross-Culturally*. Grand Rapids: Baker Book
        House.

MAGLALANG, Demetrio M.
1976   *From the Village to the Medium*. Manila: Communication
        Foundation for Asia.

MASLOW, A. H.
1970   *Motivation and Human Behavior*. Rev. ed. New York: Harper
        and Row.

MAYERS, Marvin K.
1974   *Christianity Confronts Culture*. Grand Rapids, MI: Zondervan
        Publishing House.

MCLUHAN, Marshall.
1964   *Understanding Media: The Extensions of Man*. New York:
        McGraw-Hill.

1967   *The Medium is the Massage*. New York: Bantam Books.

MORTENSEN, C. David.
1972   *Communication: The Study of Human Interaction*. New York:
        McGraw-Hill.

1973   *Basic Readings in Communication Theory*. New York: Harper and Row.

MILTON, Ralph.
1968   *Radio Programming*. London: Geoffrey Bless.

MUGGERIDGE, Malcolm.
1977   *Christ and the Media*. London: Hodder and Stoughton.

NICHOLLS, Kathleen D.
1977   *The Prodigal Returns, a Christian Approach to Drama*. India: Traci Publications.

1983   *Asian Arts and Christian Hope*. New Delhi: Select Books.

NIDA, Eugene A.
1960   *Message and Mission, The Communication of the Christian Faith*. New York: Harper and Row.

NIDA, Eugene A. and William D. Reyburn.
1981   *Meaning Across Cultures*. Maryknoll, NY: Orbis Books.

OWENS, Virginia Stem.
1980   *The Total Image, or Selling Jesus in the Modern Age*. Grand Rapids, MI: Eerdmans.

PELTO, Pertti J.
1970   *Anthropological Research, The Structure of Inquiry*. 2nd ed. Cambridge: Cambridge University Press.

PETT, Dennis.
1972   *Audio-Visual Communication Handbook*. Oklahoma: Word Neighbors.

PRIMROSE, Robert.
1976   *Discipling Non-Literates: A Study Report*. Nairobi, Kenya: Daystar University College.

RAJASUNDARAM, C.V.
1981   *Development Communication, Manual of Development Communication (With special reference to broadcasting)*. Singapore: Asian Mass Communication Research and Information Centre.

REID, Gavin.
1969   *The Gagging of God*. London: Hodder and Stoughton.

ROBB, John D.
1989   *The Power of People Group Thinking*. Monrovia, CA: MARC.

ROBERTS, W. Rhys and Bewater Ingram (trans.).
1954   *Rhetoric and the Poetics of Artistotle*. New York: Malen
        Library.

ROGERS, Everett M.
1983   *Diffusion of Innovations*. 3rd ed. New York: The Free Press.

SCHRAMM, Robert (ed.).
1971   *The Process and Effects of Mass Communication*. Champaign/
        Urbana: University of Illinois.

SCHRAMM, Wilbur.
1964   *Mass Media and National Development. The Role of
        Information in the Developing Countries*. Stanford: Stanford
        University Press.

1975   *Mass Communications*. Urbana, IL: University of Illinois Press.

SHANNON, Claude E. and Warren Weaver.
1949   *The Mathematical Theory of Communication*. Urbana:
        University of Illinois Press.

SHAW, R. Daniel.
1988   *Transculturation*. Pasadena: William Carey Library Publishers.

SMITH, Donald K.
1979   "Using Communications in the Kingdom of God." Study paper
        for Consultation on World Evangelization. Nairobi: Deyster
        Communications.

1992   *Creating Understanding*. Grand Rapids: Zondervan Publishing
        House.

SØGAARD, Viggo B.
1975a   *Everything You Need to Know for a Cassette Ministry*.
        Minneapolis: Bethany Fellowship Publishers.

1979   *Bangkok All Media Penetration.* Bangkok: Foreign Mission
        Board.

1984   "The Communication Process of Evangelism." In *The Future of
        World Evangelization. Unreached Peoples 1984.* Edward R.
        Dayton and Samuel Wilson, 193-197. Monrovia, CA: MARC.

1986   *Applying Christian Communication.* Doctoral dissertation at
        School of World Mission, Fuller Theological Seminary,
        Pasadena. Ann Arbor, MI: University Microfilms.

1989   "Dimensions of Approach to Contextual Communication." In
        The Word Among Us, ed. by Dean S. Gilliland. Dallas: Word
        Publishing.

1991   *Audio Scriptures Handbook.* Reading, England: United Bible
        Societies.

SOUKUP, Paul A.
    1983   *Communication and Theology.* London: The World Association
            for Christian Communication.
SPRADLEY, James P.
    1980   *Participant Observation.* New York: Holt, Rinehart and
            Winston.

TUNSTALL, Jeremy (ed.).
    1970   *Media Sociology, A Reader.* Urbana, IL: University of Illinois
            Press.

VAN RENSBERG, Patrick.
    1979   *Visual Aids for Nonformal Education.* Amherst, MA:
            University of Massachusetts.

VOELKER, Francis and Ludmila.
    1972   *Mass Media, Forces in our Society.* New York: Harcourt Brace
            Jovanovich.

WEBB, Eugene J., et. al.
    1966   *Unobtrusive Measures: Nonreactive Research in the Social
            Sciences.* Chicago: Rand McNally.

WEBBER, Robert E.
    1980   *God Still Speaks. A Biblical View of Christian Communication.*
            Nashville: Thomas Nelson Publishers.

WILLIAMS, Frederick.
    1984   *The New Communications.* Belmont, California: Wadsworth
            Publishing Company.

JOURNALS AND PERIODICALS

ACTION RESOURCE. World Association of Christian Communication.
        London: WACC.

CATALYST. Magazine of the International Christian Media Commission
        (ICMC). Seattle, Washington.

INTERLIT. Elgin: David C. Cook Foundation.

JOURNAL OF COMMUNICATION. New York: Oxford University Press.

MEDIA ASIA, an Asian Mass Communication Quarterly. Singapore: AMIC.

MEDIA DEVELOPMENT. Journal of the World Association for Christian
        Communication. London: WACC.

THE ACCF JOURNAL. Asian Institute of Christian Communication.
        Singapore: ACCF

THE BIBLE DISTRIBUTOR. United Bible Societies, New York.

Index

285

Research-based: 54-55, 103, 168, 170, 186
Rhythm(s): 156, 201-202
Rituals: 13, 196
Robb, John: 58, 75
Rogers, Everett M.: 101, 106
Romania: 115

S
Samaritan woman: 97
Satellite(s): 111-113, 125, 135, 149
Schramm, Wilbur: 43, 53
Schuller, Robert H.: 75, 100, 123, 129
Script(s): 169, 171, 194, 239, 256-257, 264-265
Secam: 148
Semi-literacy: 185; Semi-literate: 161
Seven-tone: 104, 164, 202
Shalom: 18
Shortwave: 130, 136, 143, 236
Signal(s): 36-39
Sind: 164
Slide(s): 166, 188-190, 193-195, 266
Smith, Donald K.: 36, 53
Smyth, Richard R.: 159
Sriperumpudur: 231
StarTV: 113
Step Magazine: 99, 184
Survey(s): 79-84, 141-142, 181
Swann, Charles E.: 128, 187
Swindon: 156
Symbols: 36-39, 179-181, 189, 196, 268

T
Tamil Nadu: 168-169, 176
Tanzania: 165
Tape(s): 32-33, 160-161
Telecommunication: 210, 213
Telephone(s): 32, 34, 118, 126, 133
Teletext: 112
Televangelism: 120; Televangelist(s): 119, 263
Thailand: xiv, 2, 104, 135, 154, 163, 203
Theater(s): 34, 130, 148, 152, 188-193, 199, 206
Tract(s): 164, 172, 180, 185-186
Transistor(s): 130, 134, 210
Translation(s): 13, 29, 101, 170-171, 185
Tunstall, Jeremy: 93
TV: 111, 118-127
TWR: 134

U
Udfordringen: 183
UHF: 112
UNESCO: 176-177

UNICEF: 150
United States: 80

V
Variable factors: 11-12
VCR: 148-149
VHF: 112
VHS: 150
Video-based: 155; Video-processing: 211; Videos: 35, 113, 138, 147-158
Visual(s): 188-195
Voice of Peace: 135, 141

W
WACC: 187
Wagner, C. Peter: 20, 27
Walkman: 162
Wayang: 166
Webber, Robert E.: 26
Weil, Simone: 121
Word: 187
Word Processing: 212-213
Workbooks: 157
Worship Times: 94

X
Xerox: 176

Y
Yeo, Peggy: 207

Z

DATE DUE

NOV 2 0 2014		

GAYLORD   #3522PI   Printed in USA